Insider's Guide to Finding a Job in Washington

Insider's Guide to Finding a Job in Washington

Contacts and Strategies to Build Your Career in Public Policy

Bruce Maxwell

CQ PRESS

Washington, D.C.

CQ Press
A Division of Congressional Quarterly Inc.
1414 22nd St. N.W.
Washington, D.C. 20037

(202) 822-1475; (800) 638-1710

www.cqpress.com

Printed in the United States of America

03 02 01 00 99   5 4 3 2 1

ISBN: 1-56802-473-8

Cover and interior design: Debra Naylor, Naylor Design Inc.

Library of Congress Cataloging-in-Publication Data
In process

For those who dream of making a difference

Contents

Profiles and Boxes

Preface

It was the evening of January 16, 1991, and my wife and I were at Ford's Theatre in Washington, D.C., to see a performance by political humorist Mark Russell. As we walked toward our seats, we gazed up at the bunting-draped box where President Abraham Lincoln was assassinated in April 1865.

We'd just reached our seats when a buzz went through the theater: a U.S.–led coalition had just launched massive air strikes against Iraq. Some audience members scrambled for the exits, heading back to their offices in the government, the media, and elsewhere. The rest of us stayed for Russell's abbreviated performance, although the pall cast by the beginning of the Persian Gulf War muted our laughter. Then we, too, hurried into the night to flick on our televisions for news from Iraq.

That's what it's like to live in Washington: You head out for a light-hearted night on the town, and in an instant a national or international event—sparked by people sitting in offices only blocks away—transforms everything.

Washington, as the capital of the most powerful nation in the world, is arguably the most important city on the planet. It's a city where momentous decisions are made about war and peace, the social welfare of the nation, and a host of other issues that affect our daily lives. It's a city of history, where political leaders—some great, some venal, some of no particular distinction—have left their marks on the nation. And it's a city where young people throng, yearning to make their own marks on history.

Washington also is a city that gets hold of you and won't let go. I first moved to Washington for an internship at the end of my master's degree program in journalism. The city intrigued me, but as a kid who grew up in a small town in the Midwest I also felt overwhelmed. I made a half-hearted effort to stay in the city when my internship ended but gladly fled when I got a job offer at a newspaper back in the Midwest.

I stayed in the Midwest for five years, doing investigative reporting first for a newspaper and later for a television station. My work required frequent calls to Washington, and I even made two trips to the city to do extensive research for stories. Washington still intrigued me, but I never expected to live there again.

Then my wife was offered an excellent job in Washington. I was less than thrilled by the idea of living in Washington again, but my wife and I figured we could stand a couple of years before moving on as we had before.

That was more than a decade ago, and we're still here. Like most, we stay because of the opportunities that Washington offers, both professional and personal. It's impossible to predict the future, but there seems a decent chance that we'll spend the rest of our professional lives in Washington. I never would have dreamed of such a thing when I moved back to the city.

One of the things that most struck me when I returned to Washington was how many of my old classmates from the internship program I ran into. Some had stayed when the internship ended, and others—like me— had been drawn back to Washington after living elsewhere. We remained or came back because of the kinds of opportunities that draw thousands of young people to Washington each year.

Many of Washington's best and most exciting opportunities are in public policy, an arena that offers thousands of jobs—as congressional aides on Capitol Hill, as organizers in public interest organizations, as lobbyists for trade associations, as researchers in think tanks, as subject specialists at federal agencies and departments, and as journalists covering everyone else. But to many people, getting a public policy job in Washington is a process shrouded in mystery.

The purpose of this book is to cut through the fog and explain the process step by step. It's filled with insider tips to help you navigate the quirks that make applying for a job in Washington different from applying anywhere else. If you're looking for an internship rather than a full-time job, there's a ton of information for you as well—including a lengthy chapter devoted to internships.

Besides providing nitty-gritty details about how to get a job in Washington, the book also explains how to find a place to live, how to get around on Washington's subway system, how to learn about congressional procedure if you want to work on Capitol Hill, and many other details that will make your stay in Washington—no matter how long or how short—a lot easier.

Also scattered throughout the book are profiles of recent college graduates who now work in a variety of Washington public policy jobs. They discuss how they got their jobs, what the jobs are like, where they hope their jobs will take them, and how you can follow in their footsteps.

Perhaps most important, the book provides detailed contact information for hundreds of Washington government offices, interest groups, think tanks, trade associations, labor unions, and news media outlets that offer public policy jobs. This information—which isn't available anywhere else in such detail—includes the names of key contacts, telephone numbers, street addresses, Web site addresses, and brief descriptions of each organization.

I'm indebted to many people who helped produce and publish this book. Four deserve special recognition: Patricia Gallagher for asking me to write the book and then helping make it possible for me to do so, Ann Davies for managing the 1,001 production details involved in a project like this, Debbie Hardin for her thoughtful editing, and Debra Naylor for the beautiful design. I'm also grateful for the contributions of Kristen Beach, Katherine Clad, Mary Dennis, Grace Hill, Judy Plummer, and the crackerjack production staff at CQ Press.

As always, my greatest thanks are reserved for my wife, Barbara, who brought me to Washington more than a decade ago. I would follow her anywhere.

How to Search
for a Washington Job:
Before You Arrive

Washington, D.C., is a town run by young people.

This may seem at odds with what you see on the evening news. Take a typical story about a congressional hearing. The camera pans across a row of old (almost exclusively), white (ditto), male (ditto again) members of Congress discussing some topic of public concern.

What the camera *doesn't* show is the legions of staff members who made that hearing possible. Overwhelmingly, they are young—twenties and thirties are common. In all other characteristics—race, gender, ethnicity, religion, political beliefs—they mirror the broad spectrum of American society.

In all likelihood, congressional staff members chose the hearing's topic, selected the people who were invited to testify, and wrote the statements that members of Congress at the hearing read and the questions that they asked. Other staffers at interest groups, think tanks, and associations researched the hearing's topic and wrote testimony for their organizations' leaders. Yet other staffers at federal agencies and departments researched and wrote testimony for key federal officials who spoke at the hearing. And when the hearing was over, congressional staffers wrote any legislation that resulted.

The big shots—members of Congress, directors of think tanks, heads of trade associations, and top federal officials—may get their faces on TV, but it's the behind-the-scenes people—the staffers—who do the bulk of the actual work in Washington. And although these behind-the-scenes folks don't actually vote on public policy issues, they certainly have a major influence on them.

Why a Career in Public Policy?

If you aren't a born-and-bred policy wonk, you may wonder what all the excitement is about. After all, the phrase *public policy* sounds kind of academic and boring. But hiding behind that drab phrase are the people who make the world go 'round.

They run campaigns for everyone from presidential candidates on down. They draft laws for Congress about everything from abortion to Bosnia policy to gun control. They put into action laws passed by Congress by writing and enforcing rules about issues ranging from protecting wetlands to improving education. They research the important public issues of the day, and then lobby the government to pass laws based on their findings. They advocate on behalf of trade associations or labor unions before Congress and federal agencies. And they write news stories about all the goings-on so the public can learn what the government is up to.

Most people in the public policy arena work there because they want to make the world a better place. Some eventually drift off to corporations or other parts of the private sector, where their public policy background is often highly valued. But they usually come to Washington in the first place because they think they can make a difference.

You don't have to major in political science to pursue a public policy career. Public policy affects every aspect of how we live, so the field needs people with backgrounds in agriculture, aviation, biology, business, computer science, criminal justice, economics, education, engineering, English, environmental studies, finance, fine arts, international relations, journalism, law, management, mathematics, public administration, public health, sociology, and many other areas.

Why Washington?

If you're interested in public policy, Washington is the center of the universe.

Washington is where things happen, where battles are fought and profound decisions are made that affect everyone in this country (and often the world), whether the issue is protecting endangered species, ensuring the long-term solvency of Social Security, or declaring war against a country that threatens the United States or its allies.

But those considerations aside, Washington is a great place to live and work. Consider these facts:

- Washington is the fourth best place to live in the United States or Canada—out of 351 metropolitan areas—according to the 1997 edition of the *Places Rated Almanac.*

- Washington is the eighth best city in the country for work and family, according to a 1996 article in *Fortune* magazine.

- As the twenty-first century dawns, Washington will be in the midst of the greatest job growth of any metropolitan area in the country, according to projections by Woods & Poole Economics.

WEB SITES ABOUT WASHINGTON, D.C.

An excellent way to learn about Washington is to visit some of the Web sites devoted to the city. The sites listed are some of the best. Their offerings vary, but you'll typically find maps, entertainment and recreation guides, information about Washington's neighborhoods, restaurant reviews, shopping guides, links to other Washington-related Web sites, and more.

Web sites operated by Washington's newspapers also offer lots of information about the city. They're listed in the box in this chapter titled "Washington Newspapers Online."

123 Washington D.C. Information Guide
http://www.123washingtondc.com

Capitol Hill—Our Nation's Neighborhood
http://www.capitolhill.org

DC Online
http://www.washdc.org

DCpages.com
http://dcpages.com

Digital City—Washington, D.C.
http://home.digitalcity.com/washington

The District
http://www.thedistrict.com

Excite Travel
http://www.excite.com/travel/countries/united_states/
district_of_columbia/washington

Sidewalk Washington, D.C.
http://washington.sidewalk.com

Washington DC—Official Tourism Website
http://www.washington.org/index.html

Washington D.C. Local Page
http://goldray.com/dclocal.htm

Washingtonian Online
http://www.washingtonian.com

Yahoo!—Washington, D.C.
http://dir.yahoo.com/Regional/U_S__States/Washington__D_C_

- Washington had the tenth highest pay level of all U.S. metropolitan areas in 1996, according to the Bureau of Labor Statistics.

Washington is also a great place to live if you'd like to continue your education while working. It has one of the highest concentrations of colleges and universities of any city in the country. Georgetown University, Catholic University, American University, and George Washington University are just some of the schools that call Washington home.

Expectations Versus Realities of Washington Jobs

Some young people think they'll take Washington by storm. Perhaps at school they were student government presidents, editors of the school newspaper, or captains of the debate team. They expect that on arriving in Washington, potential employers will clamber over one another begging them to take cushy, high-paying jobs. Once they choose the best offer, these misguided souls think, they'll spend their days discussing foreign policy with the president, writing important legislation on Capitol Hill, or single-handedly saving the rainforests.

It won't happen.

At home you may have been a big fish in a little pond. But to stretch the metaphor a bit, in Washington you're a teeny, tiny minnow in a gigantic ocean—an ocean teeming with other minnows who are just as talented and hungry as you. The Washington job market is highly competitive, and you're going to have to work hard and be persistent to land a job.

The entry-level job that you work so hard to get will likely pay you about $20,000 annually—maybe a little more, maybe a little less. Much of your work, at least initially, will probably involve menial tasks such as sorting mail, stuffing envelopes, answering telephones, making photocopies, writing letters, and running errands. And especially in congressional offices, which are notoriously cramped, you may not even have a desk at first.

All of this can be depressing—not to mention ego deflating—if you have false expectations and aren't prepared for Washington's reality. Entry-level policy jobs are a sort of boot camp where you learn the basics of how Washington works, get a wonderful education in government, and get to see whether this is the kind of life you want. Lots of people wash out and return home, wiser for the experience.

Why in the world do people subject themselves to such ordeals? Because Washington is the place to be. And because if you go into an entry-level policy job with your eyes open, it can be the opportunity of a lifetime. Just check your ego at the door and enjoy the ride.

At worst, in a few short months in Washington you'll learn more about how the government actually works than you learned during years of sitting in classrooms—and you'll pick up some interesting stories to tell back home as well.

At best, by combining your talent with enthusiasm and hard work you'll quickly move up the Washington ladder into positions of growing responsibility. Washington has a high job turnover rate because people burn out, go back to school, try other career paths, and so on. This means that if you have talent and drive, you won't be stuffing envelopes for too long.

WASHINGTON NEWSPAPERS ONLINE

One of the best ways to learn about Washington is to read its newspapers. Fortunately, all three major newspapers are available online. Here's what their Web sites offer:

Washington Post
http://www.washingtonpost.com
The Washington Post offers one of the best newspaper Web sites in the country. It has the full text of the newspaper for the previous two weeks (even including its extensive comics section!), top news stories updated twenty-four hours a day, a calendar of entertainment events, online chats with *Post* reporters and columnists, a guide to federal government Internet sites, a guide to the Metro subway system, information about the region's colleges and universities, advice for visitors, classified ads, and lots more. Be sure to check out the CareerPost page **http://www.washingtonpost.com/wp-adv/classifieds/careerpost/front.htm** where you can search job ads from the previous two Sunday editions of the *Post*.

Washington Times
http://www.washtimes.com
The *Washington Times* Web site offers far less than the *Post*. It has a very small collection of stories from the newspaper and a searchable database of classified ads.

Washington City Paper
http://www.washingtoncitypaper.com
Washington City Paper is Washington's alternative weekly newspaper. The Web site has cover stories, some columns, and music, arts, and events listings from the newspaper. It also has the paper's classified ads, and offers a special page for the job ads **http://www.washingtoncitypaper.com/jobsite/helpw_top.html**

How to Prepare Yourself Academically

If you're still in school, one of the keys to landing a great Washington job is to get the most out of your education. People who sleepwalk through school may end up with a degree, but they're unlikely to have a prayer in the highly competitive Washington job market. To stand out enough to get a Washington job you must excel, and there's no better time to start doing that than now.

What types of courses should you take? That doesn't matter as much as doing well in all of them. Taking a few courses about government is always a good idea, but you certainly don't have to major in political science to get a Washington job.

And don't forget those extracurricular activities. Whether you write for your school newspaper, work on a local political campaign, or volunteer at a soup kitchen, your activities will help place you at the top of the heap when you look for a Washington job. And, as added bonuses, they'll enrich your educational experience and your life.

Starting Your Job Search

The first steps in your job search—in fact, many steps in your job search—can take place hundreds or even thousands of miles from Washington. You'll eventually need to travel to Washington for interviewing and other later stages of your search, but in the beginning you can live anywhere.

Many people think the first step in getting a job is writing a resume, but that's putting the cart before the horse. You really should start by taking some time to figure out who you are, your strengths and weaknesses, your priorities and goals, and what types of jobs might best suit your personality.

For example, do you thrive on chaos? If so, you may want to explore working on Capitol Hill or in the Washington press corps. If you prefer a more orderly environment, working in a federal agency, a think tank, a trade association, or a labor union may suit you better.

Is money important to you? If so, you may want to consider a trade association instead of a public interest group. Do you eventually want to go to law school? If so, working on Capitol Hill, for an interest group, or for a federal agency may give you the best preparation.

Don't worry if you can't answer every possible question. Many young people are just finding their way and still determining what's important to them. Lots of young people find that spending some time in Washington helps them determine what they want to do with their lives by giving them valuable exposure to a wide range of experiences. And even those who seem to have their lives all planned out often find things turned upside down by unexpected opportunities or changed circumstances.

Down the road a bit, this self-analysis can help you choose which types of Washington employers to pursue. But for now, its primary purpose is to help prepare you for writing your resume.

How to Write Your Resume

When they advertise public policy job openings, Washington employers typically receive 100 or 200 resumes in response—and sometimes more. And day in and day out, Capitol Hill offices and other popular Washington employers are flooded with resumes. You have to make yours stand out.

This *does not* mean you should print it on purple paper using pink ink. It *does* mean that you need to devote a lot of care and attention to creating the strongest resume possible.

The advice in this chapter applies to resumes written for nearly all Washington jobs. However, there are special resume rules if you're applying for a job in a federal agency or department, which I'll discuss in Chapter 5.

No matter what kind of job you seek, the resume's purpose is to get you an interview. In choosing what to include in your resume, look at which of your skills and experiences would be of most interest—and use—to a Washington employer.

Many books about resume writing say you absolutely, positively must limit your resume to one page. That's good advice, in most cases—especially if you're just joining the workforce and have little job experience. But if you have lots of work experience, don't be shy about using multiple pages. What's more important than length is making sure that every word on your resume counts.

Two basic types of resumes fit most needs: chronological or functional. The most common is the chronological resume, which focuses on jobs you've held. The functional resume focuses on your skills and strengths and deemphasizes your employment history.

Which type should you choose? The answer depends on what works best for you. If you have a long and solid employment record, you'll want to use the chronological resume. But if you're just starting out in the job world, emphasizing your skills and strengths in a functional resume may work better. The bottom line: Choose the type that best showcases your abilities.

Writing the top section of the resume is the easiest part. This is where you put your name, address, telephone number, e-mail address, and Web site address (if you have one and it's relevant to your job search). If you're temporarily living at school when conducting your job search, remember to include a permanent address and telephone number where employers can reach you after the semester ends.

Some authorities claim that you next should include a section describing your "career objective." Don't do it. Listing a career objective limits your opportunities. Employers who see a career objective that doesn't exactly mesh with their job opening will throw your resume away—even if the job would have been perfect for you. Leave any discussion of career objectives to the interview. At that point, you can explain how your objective dovetails with the employer's hiring needs.

No absolute rules exist about how to arrange the remainder of your resume. Be creative—to a degree. The only rule of thumb is to put the various elements in descending order of importance. If your greatest strength is your education, put it right under your personal information. If you have special skills or a long work record, you may want to lead with those instead. Remember that people who screen resumes are busy. As they skim through stacks of paper, your resume needs something near the top that will grab their attention and make them read more.

Only two other sections are essential in your resume. One describes your educational background, in reverse chronological order (most recent first). Be sure to include the name of the school, your major and minor, and the date you graduated. If you had an excellent grade point average—think 3.5 or higher—list it too.

The other essential section describes your job history, again in reverse chronological order. For each job, list the employer, the city where it's located, your job title, and the dates you were employed. But that's not enough. You need to give each job life by explaining what you did. If possible, go beyond just listing your job duties to quantify your achievements. For example: "Managed advertising sales for student newspaper, supervising a staff of eight and boosting revenues by 23 percent." Note the generous use of action verbs, which make your resume more dynamic. For a list of some great action verbs, see the box "Action Verbs Make Your Resume Sparkle."

Don't fret if you lack a lengthy job history. The point of listing your job history is to show that you're responsible, can work with others, and have skills. You can show this through lots of ways other than employment.

For example, have you held a responsible volunteer position in a community group or a campus organization? Did you achieve the rank of Eagle Scout? Do you write for your school newspaper? Do you participate in any sort of team activity—anything from the debate team to the volleyball team? Examine all of your activities to see which highlight your qualities that might appeal to an employer. Listing these activities on your resume can help make up for a brief job history.

That's it for the essential sections of your resume. If you haven't already done so, you also might want to list your volunteer activities. Also consider including any publications, awards, or professional affilia-

ACTION VERBS MAKE YOUR RESUME SPARKLE

Action verbs add life to your resume, especially when describing your work experiences. Here are a few to get you started:

administer	create	operate
analyze	design	organize
arrange	develop	overhaul
assemble	direct	perform
assess	establish	plan
budget	evaluate	project
build	forecast	remodel
calculate	identify	repair
clarify	improve	represent
coach	inspect	research
compile	invent	supervise
coordinate	market	write

tions—and anything else that might grab an employer's eye and help get you an interview.

Here are a few more tips to help you create a superb resume:

- When designing your resume, stick with basic fonts and a clean appearance. Washington is a conservative town, so skip the gimmicks and flashiness. Besides which, many employers are beginning to scan resumes into databases, and plain resumes with sans serif type scan the best.

- Don't bog down your resume with long paragraphs of type. Instead, make it easy to read by using short sentences, bulleted lists, and headings.

- Leave out irrelevant personal information—your age, marital status, religion, ethnic background, and race.

- Don't include any details about your previous salaries. Listing your previous salaries puts you in a bad bargaining position when it comes time to negotiate your new salary.

- Avoid any urge to "embellish" your achievements on the resume. Employers carefully check resumes these days, and will immediately drop you from consideration if there's even a hint that you lied. If you do lie and get hired, don't think you're home free: Some employers now immediately fire anyone who they later learn lied on a resume.

- Don't list your hobbies or personal interests unless they somehow apply to the job you're seeking.

- Don't list your references on the resume. Instead, prepare a separate list of references that you can supply to potential employers on request (and be sure to call your references before listing them to make sure doing so is okay). Also, don't say on your resume: "References available on request." That's obvious.

- Proofread your resume. Proofread it again. Have your friends/significant other/parents/roommates/coworkers or anybody else you can think of proofread your resume. You would be shocked at how many people send out resumes with typographical errors, spelling mistakes, or basic blunders in grammar. Employers who receive resumes with obvious errors put them where they belong: the trash.

- After you get your resume copied or printed, check all the copies to make sure they're clean.

This resume advice only covers the highlights. If you need more help, check the online resources listed in the bibliography and the sample resumes in Appendix A. Other excellent sources of help include your campus career counseling center and resume writing books in the library.

How to Target Your Resumes

You've got a stack of resumes on your desk, all neatly printed and ready to go. But where do they go?

How you answer that question has a lot to do with determining the success of your job search. If you just fling out resumes willy-nilly, your chances of success sink faster than a campaign finance reform bill on Capitol Hill. You need to carefully target your resumes.

Many people think the only way to find resume targets is to prowl newspaper classified ads (either online or in the printed paper), and respond to job ads that look interesting. This is one part of resume targeting—but only one part. Just responding to newspaper ads severely limits your opportunities. This is especially true in Washington, where many, many job openings are never advertised. To broaden your chance for success, you need to identify these "hidden" job openings in addition to those that appear in the newspapers.

How do you do this, especially if you're hundreds or thousands of miles from Washington? By targeting your resume at three audiences:

- Employers who advertise job openings

- Employers who look appealing but do not have any advertised openings

- Networking contacts

Let's look at each of these audiences in turn

Employers with Job Openings

In the old days (that's anything more than a few years ago), if you lived outside Washington and wanted to learn about job openings in the city, you had to hunt down a newsstand in your area that carried out-of-town newspapers.

The Internet has changed everything. Today, Washington's newspapers put all of their job ads online, making them easily accessible to anyone in the world. And lots of Washington public policy employers—ranging from federal agencies to public interest groups—post job openings on their own Web sites. This makes finding out about job vacancies easier than ever before.

This book lists hundreds of Web sites you can check for job openings, ranging from those listing jobs at a single employer to huge megasites that describe jobs available at dozens or hundreds of employers. As you read this book, mark those sites that look particularly appealing. Then make it a habit to check them regularly for new and updated postings.

Employers without Known Job Openings

Lots of Washington employers never advertise job openings. They don't have to because they always have plenty of unsolicited resumes on file to fill any openings. You want your resume to be in that file.

The best way to identify appealing employers is to look through the listings in this book for companies, government agencies, public interest groups, trade associations, and others that look interesting. To learn more about the employer, check out its Web site. Many of the Web sites are quite extensive, and will provide plenty of information to help you decide whether you and the employer would be a good fit.

Networking Contacts

Networking is important in any job search, but it's especially critical when looking for a job in Washington. Washington thrives on personal contacts, relationships, and alliances. More so than in many other cities, in Washington getting a job can depend far more on *who* you know than on *what* you know.

But you don't know anyone in Washington, do you? Sure you do. And even if you don't, you certainly know somebody who knows somebody in Washington. That's almost as good.

Start looking for contacts among your friends and relatives. Does your aunt belong to a trade association with a Washington office? If so, see if she can arrange for you to talk with someone there. Your teachers also can be good sources of Washington contacts, and your college placement or alumni office should be able to hook you up with alumni in Washington.

From there, branch out. Contact the local office of your member of Congress, which may be able to help. Talk to your neighbors, classmates, coworkers, Chamber of Commerce executives, friends of your parents, executives in local companies, and anyone else you can think of.

By networking, you can

- Learn about "hidden" jobs that aren't advertised,

- Learn some of the inside information about an organization,

- Obtain names of other people to contact,

- Make friends.

The goal is subtle. You're not seeking the names of people who can actually offer you a job. Instead, you're looking for people who can help you in your job search by providing advice, giving you an overview of the area in which they work, and providing the names of other people who might be useful.

You may feel a bit awkward about contacting people you don't know and asking for job advice, but it gets easier as you do it. And remember that many people will be happy to help you in your job search, especially if you stroke their egos a little (without overdoing it) by letting them know you value their insights and knowledge.

One of the advantages of networking is that you can do it from anywhere. Although it's better to talk to people face to face if possible, you can do your networking over the telephone if necessary.

For each network contact that you develop, send a resume and a brief cover letter. The cover letter might go something like this:

Dear Mr. Habatashi:

I'll be graduating from Midwest University in a few months with a degree in political science, and Pilar Alvarez in the Alumni Office said you'd be an excellent person to talk to about how to pursue a job in Washington, D.C.

Between my political science background and experience

writing for the school newspaper, I hope that I have skills that might benefit a Washington employer. I'm most interested in working on Capitol Hill, although various public interest groups and trade associations also would be appealing.

I'd greatly appreciate any advice you could offer, because I understand from Ms. Alvarez that you've worked in Washington for years. I'll call you soon and hope that you'll be able to spare five minutes of your time to talk to me.

Sincerely,

The next step is to follow up your letter with a telephone call to the contact. Most people in Washington have secretaries, receptionists, or others who screen their calls. Be unfailingly polite to these people—they can make or break you. Simply state your name, and say that you're calling to follow up on a letter you recently sent Mr. Habatashi. If Mr. Habatashi isn't available, ask when would be a good time to call back. Don't leave a message for Mr. Habatashi to call you, because folks in Washington are notoriously bad about returning telephone calls—especially to people they don't know.

It may take you several tries to get Mr. Habatashi on the line, and in some cases you won't be able to get through at all. Don't be discouraged. When you do get hold of Mr. Habatashi state your name, state the name of anyone who referred you to him, and remind him of the letter you sent a few days earlier.

If you promised in your letter that you'll take no more than five minutes, stick to it. Let Mr. Habatashi volunteer more time if he wishes, but don't count on getting extra time. This means you have to plan your conversation before you call.

Figure out what you need to know from Mr. Habatashi. Here are just a few questions you might ask.

- How did you get started in the field?
- How is hiring usually done in the field? By advertising openings? Through the grapevine?
- What kinds of Washington jobs seem to best fit my background?
- What's the usual career path for someone who pursues your field?

Always save time for two last questions:

- Is there anything else I should know that I haven't asked?
- Is there anyone else I should talk to?

Do not ask if there are currently any job openings at the contact's office. The contact may volunteer such information, but asking for it places him or her in an awkward position.

After your conversation, always follow up with a brief letter thanking your contact for taking the time to talk to you. This is simple politeness and ensures that you leave a good impression.

The Art of the Cover Letter

Always, always, always send a cover letter with your resume. The cover letter is more than just a formality—it's a key tool in selling yourself.

I've already discussed cover letters to networking contacts in the preceding paragraphs, so here I'll focus on cover letters to your two other targets: employers with job openings and employers without known job openings.

If you're responding to a job ad, address the letter as it directs. But in all other cases, take the trouble to address your letter to a real human being, not "personnel director" or "to whom it may concern." You'll find names of hundreds of job contacts in this book, and you can find other names by checking out an organization's Web site, looking in directories in the library, or just calling the organization on the telephone and asking to whom resumes should be addressed. Make sure you get the person's name spelled correctly.

Your letter's body should do four things:

- Explain how your talents will benefit the employer,

- Indicate your familiarity with the employer and its work,

- Express enthusiasm about working for the employer,

- Ask for a job interview.

The first one is most critical: explaining how your talents will benefit the employer. Your resume explains who you are and what you've done in the past—there's no need to rehash that stuff in your cover letter. Instead, focus on what you bring to the employer and how you can meet its needs.

How do you find out the employer's needs? That's easy if you're responding to an ad, because most at least briefly describe what kind of person the employer is seeking. In these cases, link your skills and attributes to the exact requirements listed in the ad.

When you're sending a cold letter to an employer who hasn't advertised any openings, it takes a bit more work to find out the employer's needs. Here, you must do a little research. Check out the employer's Web site, directories in the library that might describe the employer's activities, newspaper and magazine articles about the employer, and other sources. Find out what the employer is involved in and then link your skills to its activities. For example: "I see at your Web site that you're undertaking a major campaign to save the whales. I have a degree in marine biology, and would like to put it to use as a staff member working on that campaign or similar projects."

Your cover letter, like your resume, must make you stand out. The employer may have received dozens or hundreds of resumes besides yours, and many of the other job candidates may have backgrounds similar to yours. That's especially true if you're applying for an entry-level job. So you need to use the cover letter to separate yourself from the crowd and describe your unique qualities and attributes that you'd bring to the job.

Close your letter by asking for a job interview. If it's a cold letter (one sent to an employer without job openings), also say that you'll follow up in a few days with a telephone call.

Here are a few more cover letter tips (and Appendix A also has some sample cover letters to help you):

• Grab the reader (gently) from the beginning. Don't start out: "Please consider this letter an application for the administrative assistant opening in your office." That's borrrrring. Strut your best stuff at the top—especially emphasize how you can help the employer.

• Customize each cover letter to a particular employer. With mail-merge software it's tempting to write a form letter and then make a zillion copies with only the address and salutation changed. Don't do it. You can recycle portions of the letter with various employers, but you must customize the key sections.

• Even if an ad asks you to list your salary expectations in your cover letter, don't do it. Listing how much money you want is a lose–lose proposition. If the number you quote is too low, you'll look desperate or like you don't value yourself. And if the number is too high, you'll sound unrealistic and be immediately eliminated from consideration—even if you would have considered a lower salary under the right circumstances. The right time to talk about money is at the interview.

• Proofread your cover letters just as thoroughly as you did your resume.

Then send them out with your resumes. You can spend days, weeks, or months agonizing over writing the cover letter, trying to get it just right. Unfortunately, there is no such thing as a "perfect" cover letter. Do the best you can, and then send your resume packages on their way.

The Art of the Telephone Call

You've put your resumes in the mail, and you park yourself next to the telephone to answer the calls that will stream in from employers. Here's a hint: Before sitting by the telephone, pack yourself a sandwich—or better yet, a picnic basket full of sandwiches—because you'll probably have a long wait.

Employers in general—and Washington employers specifically—are becoming downright rude in how they handle job applicants. Very few employers acknowledge receipt of your application, even if you sent it in response to a job ad. And many applicants who aren't chosen for interviews receive no notice that the position has been filled. Frequently you'll send out a resume package and hear absolutely nothing back in response. Your chances of being acknowledged are even worse if you send resumes to employers without current job openings or to networking contacts. The reason? They have little incentive to take the trouble of calling you and setting up an appointment.

Don't be discouraged by the lack of response. It's not directed at you personally—it's just how the system works (or doesn't work). How do you turn the tide in your favor? By following up your resumes with telephone calls.

This is a crucial aspect to getting a job—and one that many people ignore to their detriment. Making telephone calls can be discouraging, because in many cases you'll get nowhere. Don't let rejection get you down. Keep calling, because the very next call may lead to your job.

The exact nature of your call depends on which type of target you're calling: employers with job openings, employers without known job openings, or networking contacts. Let's briefly look at each.

Employers with Job Openings

If you've mailed your resume in response to an advertised job opening, there's no need to call the employer. Your resume will be considered along with the others received, and the employer will call you if an interview is desired.

In their ads, some employers explicitly state you should not call. Follow their wishes. Nothing will doom your application faster than violating the employer's guidelines.

If the ad doesn't specifically prohibit calling, you may call once—but only once. State that you're calling to follow up on the resume you sent a few days earlier, and were wondering whether there is any other information you can supply that would be useful. That's it unless the person you're speaking to volunteers more. Don't ask when the interviews will be conducted, when a final decision will be made, or whether you're likely to be interviewed. All such questions are pushy.

Some folks think that calling an employer several times a day will show initiative and put them at the head of the pack. All it really shows is that you're a pain in the neck.

Employers without Known Job Openings

Always call to follow up on resumes sent to employers without known job openings, because they have little incentive to contact you. When you call, remember that you'll likely reach a gatekeeper who screens calls for the person you're trying to reach. Be polite and professional to these people and never, ever do anything to anger them. They can be your strongest allies or your fiercest enemies, depending on how you treat them.

When you reach your contact, say that you're following up on the resume you sent a few days earlier. Explain that you're aware there aren't any current job openings but that you'll be in Washington on X date and were hoping to arrange a brief interview so you can learn more about the organization. If the person balks, thank the person for his or her time and move on to your next contact.

Networking Contacts

I discussed the need to call networking contacts in the earlier section about networking. Networking contacts won't expect to call you—they'll expect that you'll call them to follow up on your resume.

With networking contacts, it's important to stress that you only want a few minutes of their time. Folks in Washington are terribly busy, and will be much more responsive if you acknowledge this fact.

So now you've mailed out the resumes, you've made the follow-up calls, and you've scheduled a variety of appointments. It's time to go to Washington.

2

How to Search
for a Washington Job:
In the City

Although you can conduct most of your Washington job search from anywhere in the country, near the end it's really essential for you to travel to Washington. Very few employers will hire you sight unseen—nor should they.

By the same token, you shouldn't accept a job without first seeing the workplace, meeting your boss, and getting a hands-on feel for whether the job would suit you. Thus you get just as many benefits from your trip to Washington as do your potential employers.

How you get to Washington is usually up to you. Most employers won't pay your travel costs, especially if you're applying for an entry-level position. If you live far away, two ways to save money are to find others who are driving to the East Coast and sharing travel costs with them or arranging a joint trip with friends where you all look for jobs in Washington. Other creative solutions also are possible depending on your circumstances.

In Washington, you'll need a place to stay. The best short-term accommodations—because they're likely to be free—are on a spare couch at the home of a relative, friend, friend of a friend, and so on. For more leads on accommodations, read the box titled "Where to Stay in Washington."

By the time you arrive, you should have at least one interview scheduled—and preferably more. It's unwise to arrive in town without any interviews lined up because it could take days, weeks, or even months for you to get the necessary appointments. That wait can get mighty long if you're sleeping on your aunt's couch or your cash is getting low.

Preparing for Interviews

The best way to ensure you have a great interview is to prepare, prepare, prepare. You may be tempted to wing it. Don't. Preparation is the key to a successful interview.

WHERE TO STAY IN WASHINGTON

If you can't find a couch to crash on in Washington, lots of other housing options exist. The good news is that because of Washington's high turnover—especially among interns and other short-timers—housing is generally available. The bad news is that it's not cheap.

Rents for shared apartments run $350–650 per month in Washington and $300–500 per month in the suburbs, according to the off-campus housing office at George Washington University. Efficiencies run $650–750 in the city and $550–700 in the suburbs, and one-bedroom apartments usually cost $750–1,000 in Washington and $650–900 in the suburbs.

If you're planning to be in Washington just for the summer, some of your best housing options are provided by local universities that throw open their dorms to nonstudents. Dorm rooms typically rent for $20 to $35 per night, and meal plans are usually available for an added fee.

One crucial tip: If you come to Washington in the summer, make absolutely sure that your accommodations have air conditioning. Otherwise, you'll learn what fried chicken is like from the chicken's perspective.

Summer rooms are available from the following universities:

American University
202-885-3370

Catholic University
202-319-5615

George Washington University
202-994-9193

Georgetown University
Telephone: 202-687-4560
Web address: http://www.georgetown.edu/housing/OHCS

Georgetown University Law Center
Telephone: 202-662-9290
Web address: http://www.law.georgetown.edu/reslife/index.html

Howard University
202-806-5661

If you're going to be in Washington during the school year—or you can't bear the thought of living in a dorm room in the

(Box continues)

summer—three universities offer Internet databases listing off-campus housing that's available to anyone. Typically, you can search the databases by housing type, price, neighborhood, whether it's near public transportation, date available, and other factors. One caution: The listings are provided by landlords and not checked by the universities, so proceed with your eyes open.

Perhaps the best off-campus housing database is provided by American University (http://www.ngen.com/housing/american). It's especially strong in listings for rooms in group houses. Georgetown University also has a good database with lots of listings (http://data.georgetown.edu/student-affairs/och), and George Washington University provides a smaller database (http://www.och.gwu.edu).

Another good source for lower priced housing is the classified ads in the *Washington City Paper*, Washington's alternative newspaper (http://www.washingtoncitypaper.com/class/classifieds.html). It has dozens of listings of rooms in group houses, sublets, and other housing options.

Three sources for housing listings that aren't necessarily aimed at student budgets are

Washington Post classified ads
http://www.washingtonpost.com/wp-adv/classifieds/realestate/front.htm

Yahoo! Classifieds
http://rentals.classifieds.yahoo.com/washingtondc/rentals

Rent.Net
http://www.rent.net

Start by finding out everything you can about your potential employer. If you're interviewing for a job in a congressional office, check out the member's voting record, positions on issues, accomplishments, major initiatives, and so forth. If you're interviewing with a public interest group, learn about its major projects and how it operates. Such research is easier than ever before because just about everyone in Washington has a Web site. You can supplement your online efforts through library research in directories, magazines, and newspapers and by calling people who might know something about the employer and its reputation.

The interviewer will invariably be impressed that you took the initiative to research the employer. And you'll also be prepared to ask specific, on-target questions during the interview.

The next step is to learn about yourself. That may sound stupid, but it isn't. Few people can spontaneously rattle off short, pithy answers to dozens of questions about their backgrounds, goals, and dreams—especially under the pressure of an interview.

It helps to figure out answers to common questions ahead of time in a mock interview, either in your own head or with a friend asking you questions. The point isn't to memorize word-for-word answers to questions. You don't want to do that because you'll sound robotic. Instead, the point is to get comfortable giving direct, focused answers to many of the questions that you'll be asked.

Here are some common interview questions that you should be prepared to answer:

- Why did you apply for this job?

- What do you know about this organization or the job?

- Why did you choose this career?

- Why should I hire you?

- How would you describe yourself?

- What would you like to tell me about yourself?

- What are your major strengths?

- What are your weaknesses?

- What type of work do you like to do most?

- What type of work do you like to do least?

- What kinds of accomplishments give you the most satisfaction?

- Can you give me an example from school or a previous job where you showed initiative?

- What was your worst mistake at work or in school?

- What courses did you like best or least in school?

- What did you like most or least about your last job?

- Why did you leave your last job?

- How does your education or experience relate to this job?

- What are your goals and how do you plan to reach them?

- What do you hope to be doing in five years? In ten years?

- What are your salary expectations?

Especially if you're new to Washington, you may want to do a dry run to the interview location sometime before your appointment. Few things are worse than arriving at an interview frazzled—and possibly late—because you got lost. A dry run is particularly important if you're driving to the interview, because Washington has some of the worst traffic in the nation and severely limited parking throughout most of the city.

The Interview

Take care when choosing the clothes for your interview. Washington is a conservative town, so you should dress appropriately. Business suits are preferred for men, although a nice sports coat and tie will do. Business suits also are the preferred attire for women, although a dress (nothing flashy) is fine as well. Leave the jeans, sneakers, and nose rings at home for your nighttime visits to Dupont Circle or Georgetown.

Even if you've already sent the employer a resume, take along a few more copies just in case. Also take your list of references and any appropriate work samples.

You want to arrive at the interview in the best shape possible, so you may wish to consider blowing a few bucks on a cab. Washington has a great public transportation system that will take you just about anywhere, but cabs deliver you to the front door fresh (assuming it isn't summer and you get stuck with one of Washington's many cabs that lack air conditioning) and relaxed (or at least as relaxed as you can be before an interview).

Be sure to arrive at your interview a few minutes early. This helps create a good first impression. Some people take this advice to an extreme and show up an hour early. This does *not* create a good first impression. If you get to the interview location too early, walk around the block, get a cup of coffee, or find some other way to kill the time.

You'll probably be nervous at the interview. Try to relax as much as possible, and keep in mind that the interviewer may be just as nervous as you. Why is the interviewer nervous? Because he or she has just as much at risk as you. The interviewer doesn't want to hire the wrong person—someone who won't fit in, will cause problems, or can't do the work. The interviewer also has very little information on which to make a decision: just some resumes and a few face-to-face interviews. The interviewer also wants to make a good impression so that if you're offered the job, you'll accept. And finally, the interviewer is typically under time pressure to fill the position, because the previous occupant is either already gone or leaving soon.

In the cover letter that helped land the interview, you stressed how hiring you benefits the employer. Do the same thing in the interview. As you answer the questions, focus on describing how you can

GETTING AROUND WASHINGTON

One of the great things about interning or working in Washington is that you really don't need a car. The region's Metro train and bus system will take you just about anywhere you want to go.

Metrorail trains are clean and safe. They run from 5:30 A.M. to midnight weekdays, and 8 A.M. to midnight weekends. The trains cover much of Washington itself, and also go to many suburbs. Fares depend on the time of day and how far you travel.

The Metrobus system largely picks up where the trains leave off. Buses run twenty-four hours a day, seven days a week.

Rail and bus timetables, maps of the subway system, fare information, and details about parking at Metro stations are available at the Washington Metropolitan Area Transportation Authority's Web site (http://www.wmata.com). You can even order various rail and bus passes and fare cards online. Answers to all of your rail and bus questions also are available by calling the WMATA at 202-637-7000.

One of the best resources to help you navigate the Metrorail system is actually located in France. The Subway Navigator (http://metro.ratp.fr:10001/bin/select/english/usa/washington) lets you enter the names of any two Metrorail stations and then will compute your route.

apply your background and skills to meet the employer's specific needs.

No matter what the interviewer does, don't let it throw you. Some will keep you waiting well past the scheduled time for your interview to see how you respond to stress. Others will pause a long time after you answer a question, seeing if the silence will make you uncomfortable. Just keep your calm no matter what happens.

Some interviewers will stray from the standard questions to get a better idea of how your head works. The interviewer may describe a problem and ask how you would solve it. There isn't a "right" answer to the question—the interviewer just wants to see your thinking process in action.

For example, I know a library director who has a favorite question when interviewing candidates for reference librarian positions: "If the building caught on fire, which five reference books would you grab on your way out the door and why?" There are an infinite number of answers to this question, and none is "right." The library director just wants to see how the candidates work through problems—and how they respond to questions for which they probably haven't prepared.

The interviewer may ask something like, "What kind of a salary are you looking for?" Try to avoid a specific answer. The proper time to discuss salary is when you receive a job offer, not before. If asked to name a salary, you can say, "I don't yet know enough about the position's duties to give a proper answer." Or you can turn the question around: "Is there a standard salary or salary range for this position?"

Many interviewers conclude with this question: "Do you have anything you'd like to ask me?" You'd better be prepared for this, because if you just say "no" you'll look stupid and uninterested in the job. This is *not* the time to ask about money or the amount of vacation you'd get. Such questions make it appear you're just interested in money and time off, not working for the employer.

Instead, use your questions to learn more about the job and to discreetly show the amount of research you've done about the employer. Here are some examples:

- What would a day in this job be like?

- To whom would I report?

- How does this job fit into the office's functioning?

- What training programs are offered?

- What opportunities for advancement are available?

- Why did the last person leave this job?

- What is that person doing now?

- What is this job's greatest challenge?

- How do you expect the (recent political event) to affect the organization's work?

Sometimes you'll be interviewed by a personnel officer instead of by the person who would be your immediate supervisor. In these cases, always try to meet the person who would be your boss. It's important to get a sense of the chemistry between you, because your boss can make your life either glorious or miserable.

At the end of the interview, ask when the employer expects to make a hiring decision. This will help with your planning, especially if you're interviewing for more than one position.

Once you return home and take a breath or two, write the interviewer a thank-you note. Besides thanking the interviewer for taking the time to meet with you, you also can summarize the interview's highlights, mention anything that you forgot to bring up during the interview, and once again express your enthusiasm for the employer.

TEMP WORK FOR POLICY WONKS

Need to make a few bucks in Washington while waiting for your dream job to come through? You might want to consider PoliTemps, a Washington company that supplies temporary workers to nonprofit groups, public affairs and lobbying firms, associations, political consultants, and others in the political field.

"Temporary staffing is an opportunity for people to work in a variety of positions in Washington," said Chris Jones, the company's president and CEO. "What we ask is that people look at it as a bridge to a permanent job, whether a monetary bridge or a learning bridge."

The temporary jobs aren't necessarily glamorous. "The biggest problem I see is people come straight out of college and they want to work at the mid- and senior-level policy and research jobs without the educational or work experience," Jones said. "Unfortunately, there is a lot to be said for paying your dues."

Jones said about 75 percent of PoliTemps's placements involve administrative duties such as answering the telephone, entering data onto a spreadsheet, producing memos, faxing, and filing. The typical pay is $7 to $13 per hour.

Assignments through PoliTemps are perfect for recent college graduates, Jones said. "It's a great opportunity for someone to get their start in the work world, to know what it's like to be on an assignment and to be in a professional atmosphere," Jones said.

To be considered for PoliTemps assignments, you need at least a political science degree. Jones especially likes candidates who also have legislative, campaign, public relations, or media experience.

A good attitude and professional bearing are critical for success with PoliTemps, Jones said. "The thing that puts people over the edge is to have a couple of software packages under their belt," he said. Some of the best packages to know: Microsoft Word, WordPerfect, Access, and Excel.

Many people end up with permanent jobs at the offices where they temp, Jones said. With a client list that includes Common Cause, Edelman Public Relations, EMILY's List, Fleishman Hillard, Ketchum Public Relations, National Conference of State

(Box continues)

Legislators, Ogilvy Public Relations Worldwide, People for the American Way, Planned Parenthood, Sprint, the Democratic Leadership Council, and others, PoliTemps provides an excellent way to get your foot in the door.

Jones, who has held several political and public relations jobs in Washington, offers this final advice for job seekers: "One of the important things in Washington is to network, network, network. Regularly keep in touch with your contacts, whether you're down or whether you're up. And never burn your bridges."

PoliTemps
1244 19th St., N.W.
Washington, DC 20036
Telephone: 202-785-8500
Web address: http://www.politemps.com
E-mail: info@politemps.com

The Job Offer

The telephone rings. On the line is an employer calling to offer you a job. Your first inclination is to leap in the air with joy. That's fine—just don't overdo it. When I received a job offer by telephone once, I leaped so high that I clunked my head on a chandelier.

Your second inclination will likely be to immediately accept the job and agree to any terms the employer offers. Will you work for free? Sure. Will you give the employer your first-born child? You bet. Anything to get a job.

Don't do it. Always request at least twenty-four hours to consider any job offer, no matter how good it sounds, and try to get more time if you can. You need the time to calm down and evaluate the offer rationally.

In evaluating a job offer, you must ask yourself a number of questions. The first one is a biggie: Do I really *want* this job? To get a grip on this big question, you may want to consider some smaller ones:

- Does the work look like it will be interesting and meaningful?

- Does the work environment appear congenial?

- Does the person who will be my supervisor seem reasonable?

- If the employer has made promises about the type of work I'll do or other matters, can I reasonably expect that they'll be honored?

- Will the job be a good stepping stone to other jobs with more responsibility?

- Does the job fit into my long-term goals?

- Will the job provide opportunities to learn and grow?

- If the job's hours are long or variable, will I be able to handle this?

- Is the equipment that I'll work with top of the line?

- Is the salary reasonable?

- Is the benefits package (especially the health insurance) good? If I want to continue my education while working, does the employer offer tuition reimbursement?

Your own situation and values dictate which of these questions receive the highest priority. Nonetheless, try to focus on the big picture: Will you learn something? And will what you learn help you further your career?

If this will be your first job, your decision is doubly important. Not because a bad first job will harm you—it may slow you down a tad, but it won't do any long-term harm. The reason the first job is important is that a good one can help set you on the fast track to success and achievement of your goals.

One other piece of advice: Keep in mind that few people start out at their dream job. You need to realistically assess your abilities and qualifications (setting aside all ego considerations), and decide whether the job is as good as you're likely to be offered at this stage in your career.

Ultimately, your decision about whether to accept a job should rely largely on what your gut tells you. Always remember this bottom line: If you accept a job and it doesn't work out, after a reasonable amount of time you can move on. Even if you make a bad decision in accepting a job—as many people do—no job lasts forever.

Assuming that you want the job, you next need to answer another question: Are the terms I'm being offered adequate, or do I need to negotiate to improve them? Many job applicants think that if they accept the job, they automatically accept the terms as well. That's not true.

From a practical perspective, most of the major terms—such as your health insurance benefit—are probably set by company policy. Nonetheless, you may be able to negotiate on smaller issues such as your exact working hours.

The biggest issue you typically can negotiate is salary. Some employers play games with salary offers, "low-balling" you with a first offer to see if you'll bite but going higher if you flinch. Others are straightforward and offer you what they believe the job is worth from the beginning. Teasing out how the employer works can be tricky. One way is to ask questions. When the employer floats a number, you might ask, "Is that the ceiling for this position?" or "Is that number negotiable?" Based on the employer's response, you can decide how hard to push.

Don't feel bad about asking for more money than the employer initially offers. The only one who has your self-interest at heart is you, so stick up for yourself. At the same time, keep in mind that entry-level policy jobs in Washington typically pay very modest salaries. By all means ask for more money—but don't be disappointed if you don't get it.

When negotiating a salary, also remember that Washington is one of the most expensive cities in which to live. In Washington, a $20,000 salary doesn't go nearly as far as it does in Des Moines.

But what if, after carefully considering everything, you decide you don't want the job? Then you must contact the employer to say no. This is probably best done by telephone, although a letter also works. Be vague about your reasons for turning down the job. You can say something like, "After careful consideration, I've decided that the job doesn't fit closely enough with my career objectives." Be sure to thank the employer for considering you and for the job offer.

There are three reasons for turning down a job offer gently:

- Simple politeness.

- You don't want to burn any bridges. Life can take lots of crazy turns, and you never know when you might need the employer—or the specific hiring official—who you're rejecting.

- Washington is a small town in many ways. If you burn the employer, word can get around.

Juggling Multiple Job Opportunities

If you're talented and work hard on your job search, you may end up juggling multiple job opportunities or offers. That's a great boost to your ego and to your chances of ultimately landing the best job possible. But it's also a potential mine field if you handle it wrong.

Let's say you had two outstanding interviews, and are under active consideration at Office 1 and Office 2. You liked Office 1 best, but Office 2 calls first to offer you a job. What do you do?

First, ask Office 2 for as much time as possible to make a decision. Then immediately call Office 1 to see if they're willing to make an offer within the time frame you have available. You can say, "I have received a job offer, and must make a decision by X date. I was very impressed by your office, and you're my first choice of employer if there's any way you can make a decision by X date."

There's nothing unethical about doing this. However, avoid playing one office against another by saying something like, "The other guys

offered me X dollars. If you can top them, I'll go with you instead."
That's unethical—and may get you dropped from consideration by both
employers.

Of course, Office 1 may say, "Gee, we like you a lot. Unfortunately,
we're still interviewing and won't be making an offer by the date you
have to make a decision." In this case, you have to make a tough choice:
Is it better to take the offer from Office 2, or to reject it on the chance
that Office 1 might offer you a job? Largely, you have to rely on your gut
instinct to tell you what to do.

In a slight variation, you may be in the happy position of getting multiple job offers almost simultaneously. You would not believe how often
this happens: You've given up all hope because your telephone hasn't
rung in weeks, and then all of a sudden two employers call in one day to
offer jobs.

Making a choice between multiple job offers usually involves weigh-
ing the pros and cons of each position. To help with your thinking, you
may want to write down the pros and cons of each job on paper and then
compare how they stack up.

If you have multiple job offers, you'll have to gently turn down those
that you don't choose. You might say, "I'm very sorry, but after careful
consideration I've decided that another job offer I've received fits better
into my career plans. I'm sorry that I won't be able to work with you, and
am flattered by your job offer." Do not say, "I got a better offer somewhere else, so I'm not going to take your job." Remember: politeness
counts for a lot, and you don't want to burn any bridges in Washington.

Once you accept a job, inform any other organizations where you're
being actively considered so they can remove you from the candidate list.
But what if Office 1, your first choice, suddenly offers you a job after
you've accepted the offer from Office 2? Too bad. You've made a commitment to Office 2, and must stick with it. Backing out after you've
accepted the job will look very, very bad.

This also is the time to get in touch with all the people who helped
with your job search, usually by writing them notes. Let them know
where you ended up, and thank them again for their help. Besides being
polite, these notes will help create a good lasting impression on your contacts—who you may need during your next job search. With the speed at
which people change jobs in Washington, that could end up being very
soon.

3

Working in Washington: Internships

The misadventures of Monica Lewinsky notwithstanding, participating in a Washington internship can be a great way to put your career on the fast track. That's true whether you plan to stay in Washington after the internship ends or to pursue employment elsewhere.

If Washington were a limousine, interns would be its tires. They do lots of the dirty work, their jobs are not glamorous, and they receive little recognition. Yet they're essential to the limo's functioning, and when one goes bad the limo tends to crash (just ask President Clinton).

On any given day, Washington probably has more interns per square foot than any other city on the planet. Thousands of college students and recent graduates flock to the city each year, drawn by unparalleled opportunities to observe the political process up close and, not incidentally, to buff up their resumes.

Washington employers love interns. Interns are young, enthusiastic, and work for free (usually). Many employers use internships to check out people they may later be interested in hiring full time.

Washington internships also present great opportunities for you, no matter what your major is or what you plan to do after graduation. A Washington internship can:

- Introduce you to the working world.

- Give you a break from the classroom.

- Provide a first-hand look at how the political system works.

- Let you explore career options by giving you a look at a particular field without having to make a long-term commitment.

- Help you develop a network of valuable contacts.

- Help you find permanent employment by providing an excellent credential for your resume.

PROFILE: BRIAN WALTERS

If you want to intern on Capitol Hill, should you head for the Senate or the House? Brian Walters has interned at both and said the two institutions provide different kinds of experiences.

"The overall atmosphere of the two is very different," Walters said. "The Senate is very fast paced like the House, but in the House there's a sense of urgency that's not present in the Senate. I think that has a lot to do with length of term."

Which does he recommend? "It definitely depends on what you're looking for," said Walters. "If you want a wider exposure, I would suggest the Senate. But because the House is specialized, if you can find a congressman who specializes in an issue that you care about, you can learn a lot more about the particulars and nuances of things in the House than you can in the Senate."

Walters, who is from Arizona, interned while pursuing a bachelor's degree in political science and a master's degree in public administration at George Washington University in Washington, D.C. He recommends applying for Hill internships with the members of Congress who represent your home district and state. "Senators and congressmen definitely prefer people who come from their districts," he said.

Walters followed his own advice, interning first with Rep. Matt Salmon, R-Ariz., and next with Sen. Jon Kyl, R-Ariz. He handled a wide range of duties during his internships, including conducting tours, drafting correspondence, answering telephones, and delivering documents. One of his favorite jobs during his Senate internship was delivering draft bills to the Senate legal office, allowing him to see the bills before they were introduced on the Senate floor. The Senate internship also led to Walters's being offered a staff job in Kyl's Phoenix office during the summer, where he did research on the Y2K problem.

Walters "absolutely" recommends Capitol Hill internships—"especially for people who are interested in politics and the political process. It's incredible to see what happens behind the scenes and also to get a feel about whether this is for you or not."

What did Walters learn from his internships? "My first one taught me the importance of staff, and how much of a senator or congressman's work is done by staff," he said. "It also taught me what Hill life is like.

"The second one taught me a lot about the legal ramifications of decisions. I also got to see what the life of a politician is like. And as a citizen, it taught me how hard it is to do the job that we expect our congressmen and senators to do."

After attending law school, Walters plans to practice corporate law. And does he have aspirations to run for Congress himself some day? "Who knows?" he said. "Maybe after I'm retired."

• Provide you the opportunity during your internship to show a potential full-time employer what you can do.

Perhaps most important in today's highly competitive job market, an internship gives you demonstrated work experience. To get the best jobs, a degree isn't enough anymore. An internship gives you the extra edge that helps you stand out when you apply for your first professional job.

The Downsides of Internships

Although Washington internships can be great experiences overall, they have two major downsides. The first—and most important—is that most of them don't pay anything. This is especially true of congressional internships. The lack of pay is a major hindrance, particularly with the high cost of living in Washington.

Most internships don't pay for one simple reason: They don't have to. The supply of interns seems inexhaustible, so why pay when you can get help for free? This is called exploitation. Consider it part of your learning experience.

Some internships offer a salary. But even if you get a salary, it will likely be too small to cover your expenses. This means you need to do some financial planning before tackling an internship. As part of that planning, you might want to consider getting a part-time job in Washington in addition to your internship.

The second downside to a Washington internship is that almost invariably, the bulk of your work will be less than exciting. Forget your dreams of relaxing in a plush office, regaling a tableful of senators at lunch with your wit, and drafting legislation. In many offices you won't even have your own desk, and you'll likely eat many lunches out of pizza delivery boxes—usually shared with other interns, not the senators you all work for.

And the work? If you're interning in a senator's office, you'll probably become better acquainted with the stapler than the senator. Wherever you work, the bulk of your duties are likely to be clerical—opening and sorting mail, answering telephones, making photocopies, sending faxes, and running errands. You'll also likely get a few substantive assignments, but you're not going to save the Republic during your semester in Washington.

With any luck, your office will not be one of those that shamelessly exploits interns by tethering them to the photocopier eight hours a day, day in and day out. In a minute I'll explain how to avoid Internships from Hell in the first place, how to improve a bad situation if you get trapped, and how to make the best of even the worst experience.

INTERNSHIP MISUNDERSTANDINGS AND DISAPPOINTMENTS

Interns frequently arrive in Washington with "serious misunderstandings about what the job involves," according to the Republican Policy Committee in the U.S. Senate. To help set interns straight, the committee—chaired by Sen. Larry Craig, R-Idaho—lists some common intern misunderstandings and disappointments on its Web site:

Common Misunderstandings of Interns

- *I'll become personal friends with the Senator, see him every day, have lunch with him, exchange jokes with him.* Sorry. Although Senator Craig makes an effort to get acquainted with interns and commits to at least one meeting with them each semester, every Senator's schedule is necessarily so tight that much regular personal contact is simply not possible.

- *I'll be advising the Senator on how to vote on critical issues, or I'll be advising RPC Staff on areas on which I am an expert.* Truth is, no one is an expert when they first come to town. Spend your time listening, learning, observing and absorbing.

- *I'll be writing speeches and drafting bills.* There are some opportunities along these lines such as background research, but for the most part, that is the job of the Staff and your job will be to help them however possible.

- *I'll be doing detailed research on particular issues.* The Senate has access to the best researchers in the world at the Congressional Research Service, and Washington is the information capital of the world. Your job may entail pulling together research which has already been done, perhaps distilling it to a readable level.

- *I'll have a big desk, an office, a secretary, and lots of perks.* Office space is crowded in Washington, and designated space for interns is limited. You will also work around the office at whatever table happens to be free, and you'll do all your own typing, as all staffers do.

- *I'll be a key player in the decision-making process.* The goal of the internship is to learn what the Republican policy-making process is, how it works, who is involved in it. This knowledge will help you become a key player later on.

Some Disappointments Interns Experience

- *I spend a lot of time stuffing envelopes, folding and filing letters, and doing pure "grunt work."* All of us do the same, including the Staff Director. Politics is 90% pure grunt work. Don't concentrate on the

(Box continues)

routine nature of your tasks; think of it as the price you pay for the learning opportunity.

- *There isn't enough time to attend hearings, lectures, and fun events, even though I'm required to do so.* One thing you have to learn about the political life is that you have to make days last 36 hours, not 24. If you're the clock-punching type who wants to go home at 5:00 every day, you'll never experience all Washington has to offer.

- *I don't get to offer my opinion on issues, or speak out at staff meetings.* There may be MUCH more to any issue or discussion than you realize. So be realistic about the reason you are here. Your purpose is to learn.

- *People give me piles of work and don't explain how to do it, or even where to find answers.* This happens because everyone else is so busy there isn't time to explain everything to you. They won't know you're lost unless you say so. Ask questions whenever you don't know something.

How to Find an Internship

There's no central clearinghouse for Washington internships, or even for internships in Congress. This means you have to poke around a lot to learn what's available and which internships best suit your interests.

Start your internship planning early. The reason is that many Washington internships are highly competitive—especially during the summer months—so getting your application in early gives you a better chance of landing your first choice. Make sure you apply at least three months before your internship would start.

The first step is to decide when you want to come to Washington. Most Washington internships are available during the fall and spring semesters and during the summer, although a few are only offered during limited periods.

Most interns come to Washington in the summer. It's a convenient time for many, because they can still take classes during the fall and winter semesters. But in several ways it's the worst time to intern in Washington. Here's why:

- Washington's political scene is far less active in the summer than during the fall and spring. In the summer Congress takes a long break, life typically slows down at other political organizations, a good chunk of the populace heads for the beaches, and tourists take over the town. This means you'll likely see and experience far less than if you come during the academic year.

- Because most interns come in the summer, competition for internships is stiffer than during other seasons. For example, the Judicial Intern Program at the Supreme Court typically receives 100 applications for its summer session and only hires two or three interns. However, it also hires two or three interns for its fall and winter sessions—but only draws about twenty applicants for each period.

- Washington's heat and humidity often reach epic levels in the summer, whereas the other months of the year are usually quite nice. The temperature was 101° on the July day when I moved to Washington more than ten years ago. That was the start of a string of thirty-one straight days where the daily high was 90° or higher. It's the kind of thing you remember.

Once you decide when you want to intern, the best starting point for your internship search is your own campus. Many colleges and universities have Washington internship programs or are affiliated with a program. Participating in an established program has two major advantages: (1) a lot of the legwork involved in finding internship opportunities, locating housing, and so on will likely already be done, and (2) your school will already have in place a system for granting academic credit for your internship.

To learn about Washington internship opportunities available through your campus, you may want to start by talking to your academic adviser. Your school's career counselors also are valuable sources of information.

Don't worry if your school lacks a Washington internship program. You should be able to hook up with one of the established programs listed at the end of this chapter or to create your own internship. Just make sure that your school will grant you academic credit for the experience so it will count toward your degree.

When most people think of a Washington internship, they envision working on Capitol Hill. It's true that Congress offers an enormous number of internship opportunities. However, valuable experiences also are available at federal agencies and departments, interest groups, think tanks, trade associations, labor unions, news outlets, and other organizations. To increase your chances of landing a worthwhile internship, explore all of the opportunities that Washington offers. Reading this book should give you lots of ideas for internship possibilities.

The Internet is a great tool for tracking down an internship. Some sites described at the end of this chapter have listings for dozens or hundreds of internships. In addition, many Washington organizations post information about their own internship opportunities on their Web sites. Typically, an organization's Web site will describe the intern's duties, explain how to apply, and tell you who to contact for more information.

PROFILE: NATIONAL ORGANIZATION FOR WOMEN (NOW) INTERNSHIPS

Interns at the National Organization for Women learn "grassroots organizing from the very core," according to AnitaMarie Murano, the group's intern and volunteer coordinator.

NOW typically has twelve to eighteen interns at a time, Murano said. She usually receives 50 applications for the fall semester, 50–80 for the spring semester, and 80–150 for the summer.

Interns are not paid, although college credit can be arranged. NOW prefers full-time interns, but also offers part-time internships during the fall and spring semesters requiring two days a week and during the summer requiring three days a week.

Murano chooses a wide range of interns—from students who are already feminist leaders on their campuses to those who are just starting to think about feminist issues. "I look for people who need an education, who can give an education, and who are excited and enthusiastic," Murano said. "My favorite word is flexible."

Gender doesn't matter when it comes to choosing interns at NOW. "You just have to be a feminist," she said. "I don't care if you're a man or a woman or even transgendered."

NOW offers internships in five areas. Here's how NOW describes them on its Web site:

- *Government Relations/Public Policy Team:* Characterized by lobbying, legislative research and writing, and political campaign work.

- *Field Organizing Team:* Get involved in the nuts and bolts of grassroots organizing for NOW's broad range of priority issues. Work on pickets, campaigns, conferences/summits, speaking tours and materials development.

- *Direct Mail, Fundraising, and Membership Team:* Characterized by excellent opportunities for experience in marketing, business administration, and computer science.

- *Communications Team:* Research and write articles for the *National NOW Times,* assist in maintaining press clips, draft press releases, field press calls, design and edit web pages.

- *Political Action Committee:* Assist with NOW/PAC organizing, including meeting with candidates, processing endorsement requests, and managing Federal Election Commission materials.

The work is generally 75 percent substantive and 25 percent clerical, Murano said. Interns also receive lots of political training and chances to organize and attend congressional hearings, press conferences, demonstrations, and rallies.

To apply, submit a cover letter describing why you want to intern for NOW, a resume, two letters of recommendation, and an application form. The application form and more details about NOW's internships are available at its Web site.

How do you stand out from the crowd when applying? "Be creative," Murano said. "Don't tell me what you think I want to hear—tell me what you really feel. I want to see your conviction."

AnitaMarie Murano
Intern/Volunteer Coordinator
National Organization for Women
1000 16th St. N.W., Suite 700
Washington, DC 20036
Telephone: 202-331-0066
Web address: http://www.now.org/organiza/intern.html
E-mail: volunteer@now.org

Does the place where you'd like to work lack an intern program? Don't let that discourage you. Simply write to the organization about why you want to work there and what you can do. Many will be responsive, especially if you'll work for free.

If you'd like to intern in Congress, start with the member of the House of Representatives who represents your district and the two senators for your state. Most members of Congress prefer interns from their district or state who presumably know the region and its issues, so you'll have your best chance with those who represent you.

As you consider various internship possibilities, make sure your political views are compatible with the office where you'd be working. For example, if you're a liberal Democrat you probably wouldn't be happy working for conservative senator Jesse Helms of North Carolina, and if you oppose abortion you'd be out of place at the National Organization for Women. If you have questions about the political views of a particular office, check the Web site operated by the member of Congress or organization to learn more.

Another factor to consider is the size of the office where you'd be working. Some interns who want to work in Congress automatically gravitate toward the Senate, because it's the senior chamber of Congress and has a tad more prestige than the House of Representatives. What prospective interns sometimes fail to consider is that some Senate offices have dozens of interns at a given time, whereas most House offices only have a few. In terms of opportunities, it's sometimes best to be a big fish in a little pond instead of competing with dozens of others for choice assignments.

PROFILE: THE CAPITOL HILL INTERNSHIP EXPERIENCE

What's it really like to be a congressional intern? And what is it that interns actually do? Here's how three congressional offices describe the internship experience on their Web sites:

Rep. Tom Lantos, D-Calif.

Each intern's experience is unique, but there are some things that can be expected from each internship. A significant amount of clerical work will be expected of all interns. You will be asked to assist in processing incoming mail and phone calls, receive visitors to the office and do some general filing and organization. While these may seem like mundane tasks, handling both the mail and the visitors that come into and out of a congressional office are excellent ways to gain familiarity with the issues the office handles daily.

In addition, interns may be called upon to do a significant amount of research and writing. This is commonly in connection with responding to constituent inquiries, but can also entail issue briefs, commemorative speeches, statements on particular issues for the Congressional Record, or hearing summaries. Research is conducted with the resources of the Congressional Research Service of the Library of Congress, by attending committee hearings and markups, and by analysis of floor debate in the House of Representatives.

During the internship, interns are encouraged to take advantage of the resources and opportunities for learning on Capitol Hill. In Washington, committee hearings are frequently held on a whole range of issues, and interns are encouraged to attend those of interest to them. The Library of Congress is a resource for students who wish to pursue specific areas of study. Since the internship is primarily an educational experience, the office will be flexible to allow you to attend events outside of the office.

Like any college course, you will get out of an internship what you put into it. If you are able to keep organized and alert and maintain your common sense, you will emerge from your internship with a wealth of knowledge about the legislative process and the work of a congressional office.

Rep. Fred Upton, R-Mich.

Representative Upton views internships as mutually beneficial. Interns who work in the Washington office carry out a combination of administrative duties. While some responsibilities are clerical in nature, there are opportunities to conduct substantive research, attend staff meetings, and Congressional hearings. It must be emphasized that this internship is not guided so much by the staff or intern coordinator as it is by the intern.

The general responsibilities of the Congressional intern are:

- Answering the telephone
- Data entry

- Assisting with special projects, including legislative research
- Drafting constituent letters
- Answering constituent requests
- Attending Congressional hearings and other miscellaneous tasks, as required

. . . Because interns are viewed as part of the staff for the period they are affiliated with Representative Upton, it is vital that they possess professionalism and maturity. The staff and Mr. Upton realize that the internship may be the intern's first career-oriented work experience job and there is a lot to learn. However, the fast-paced nature of the office dictates that interns must be "on their toes" and aware that staff will not always have time to organize the intern's day. Therefore, the intern who is a self-starter and relies on his/her sense of good judgment, common sense, and listening skills is extremely valuable in the Upton office.

Sen. Christopher Bond, R-Mo.

There are two types of internships in Senator Bond's office—Legislative Intern and Press Intern. The following is a breakdown of just some duties that an intern will encounter as either a legislative or a press intern.

Legislative Intern

- Mail Sort—Involves opening and separating constituent mail into general issue areas by legislative correspondent.

- Drafting letters—Generally one of two different types of responses is given to letter writers: the standard form letter and the special tailor-made or priority letter. The standard letters are often sent in response to constituents who wrote along with thousands of other Missourians on a particular bill or issue. Thus, the standard form letter states how the Senator stands or feels on the subject or explains the bill or issue. A special or priority letter response is sent to those constituents who are writing on a previously unaddressed issue or all casework responses.

- Attend Hearings/Special Meetings—Interns are often sent to "sit in" on a few hearings or press conferences during the legislative session. These can range from foreign affairs to Senator X's resignation.

- Distribute "Dear Colleague" letters/Deliver messages—An intern is usually the bearer of hand-delivered messages. A "Dear Colleague" is a letter from one Senator directed to his peers with the purpose of obtaining their support in a particular endeavor.

- Order Official Documents—As requested by any Bond staffer. These "documents" could include material from the Library of Congress, any federal agency, or a hard copy of a piece of legislation.

- Facts and Figures Research—Any request from a staffer or constituent involving "how, what, when, where, why or who." Interns are often

(Box continues)

expected to try to find the answers to these requests using various Congressional information resources.

- Special Legislative Projects—This could be anything from helping a Legislative Assistant obtain sponsors for a commemorative to looking up and recording every vote the Senator made concerning any given issue.

Press Intern

- Press Releases—Assist Communications staff in issuing releases and reports on the Senator's activities and stances on certain issues.

- Fax Machine—Interns usually operate the fax machines in the Press section. Involves sending and receiving material for staff members.

- News Clippings—Compiles daily news clippings from state and nationwide periodicals involving Missouri happenings and the Senator's activities. Copies and distributes for staff use.

- Radio Show—Press interns help the Communications staff prepare the Senator's radio program.

- Requests from the Communications Director—Press interns handle any requests or errands needed by the Press section.

How to Apply for an Internship

Applying for an internship is just like applying for a job—because that's what an internship is. There may be no pay and the position may only last a few months, but an internship is a job nonetheless. You have to conduct yourself accordingly when applying.

Most of all, you have to be professional. Written application materials that you submit should be carefully written and free of typos or other mistakes. You also should handle yourself professionally during any telephone calls or interviews with the office where you're applying. If you need advice about how to apply for a job and prepare application materials, turn back to Chapter 1 for tips.

Exactly what you must do to apply for an internship varies. If you're applying through your school, you'll likely need to submit a transcript, a letter of application, and perhaps some letters of recommendation to the appropriate office. If you're directly applying for a Washington internship, you may have to fill out an application form and submit other types of materials. To learn the exact requirements, check the Web site operated by the organization where you're applying or call to inquire.

It's best to apply for several internships because competition—especially for the most coveted spots—can be tough. It's fine to consider one

PROFILE: STATE DEPARTMENT INTERNSHIPS

If you're interested in learning about foreign affairs, an internship with the U.S. Department of State could provide a marvelous opportunity. Internships are offered to juniors, seniors, and graduate students—but only those who will be returning to school when the internship ends.

The department selects about 800 interns annually from more than 4,000 applicants. About half work at the State Department in Washington, and the other half work at U.S. embassies and consulates overseas.

The department seeks interns with a variety of backgrounds and majors. For example, it commonly chooses students with majors in business or public administration, social work, economics, information management, journalism, and the biological and physical sciences, in addition to those with majors that are traditionally identified with international affairs.

Interns' duties vary depending on the State Department bureau where they work. At its Web site, the department provides a helpful document describing its bureaus and the internships each of them offers. The document is available at http://www.state.gov/www/careers/internbureau. html. You must choose either one or two bureaus where you'd like to work.

The vast majority of State Department internships are unpaid. When funds are available, students who can demonstrate financial need are provided paid internships. However, fewer than 5 percent of the department's interns typically receive paid positions. Interns who serve overseas are frequently—but not always—provided housing, but most pay their own travel expenses to and from their posts.

To apply, you must submit an application form, a one-page statement of interest, a college transcript, an employment data form, and a financial aid form (only if you're applying for a paid internship). The necessary forms are available on the department's Web site, by writing to the department, or from your campus placement office. Extensive information about the program and the exact application procedures is available at the department's Web site. Application deadlines are:

- Summer internship: November 1
- Fall internship: March 1
- Spring internship: July 1

U.S. Department of State
Intern Coordinator
Recruitment Division
P.O. Box 9317
Arlington, VA 22219
Web address: http://www.state.gov/www/careers/rinterncontents.html

of the internships your first choice, but be sure that you have backups in case it doesn't come through.

Offices vary in how they select interns. Some choose based solely on the written materials that you submit. Most, though, require an interview of some sort. Interviews are usually done by telephone, especially if you don't live close to Washington, D.C.

Don't miss the opportunity presented by the interview to ask questions yourself. Although the interview's primary focus will be on the potential employer learning more about you, you also should use it to learn more about the employer. This is your best chance to avoid the Internship from Hell. Here are some questions you might want to ask:

- How would I be supervised?

- How often would I be expected to meet with my supervisor?

- What types of tasks does an intern typically perform in your office?

- Do you have any special projects in mind for my internship?

- What types of people seem to have the best internship experiences in your office?

- Will you be providing any kind of training for the interns?

How the employer answers these questions should help you determine whether the internship would be a good fit for you.

How to Have a Successful Internship

When you first start the internship, sit down with your supervisor to make sure you're on the same page about what the internship will entail. This is the best way to avoid frustrations and disappointments. If you already discussed work issues during the interview, use this meeting just to quickly reaffirm your earlier conversation.

You'll likely feel lost during your first days and weeks at the internship. Everything is new—Washington, the place you're living, the office buildings, the subway system, your coworkers, the work—and you may feel overwhelmed at first. The sense of being overwhelmed can be especially strong if this is your first work experience.

Just take a deep breath and plunge in. One of the points of an internship is to have new experiences, and you should have a zillion of them in Washington. Most will be good and a few may be bad, but you'll learn from all of them.

Your first task is to fit into your office and its routine as quickly and seamlessly as possible. The best way to do this is to keep your eyes and ears open to learn how people dress, whether they address each other formally or informally, how the chain of command works, and the office's

PROFILE: REP. RON KIND, D-WIS.

When Ron Kind was elected to Congress in 1996, he didn't need the tour of Capitol Hill offered to new lawmakers. That's because he'd already learned his way around a decade earlier as a Hill intern.

Kind, who represents Wisconsin's third congressional district, got his start in Washington as an intern for William Proxmire, the legendary Wisconsin senator. Kind interned during the summer after his junior year of college, and remembers it as "a wonderful opportunity to get a real hands-on look at what goes on here in Washington."

During his internship, Kind did lots of practical things like helping constituents, writing letters, researching issues, and drafting speeches. "I was in college studying government and economics with no real intent at the time to run for office myself," Kind said. "It certainly sparked an interest in keeping an open mind toward public service."

Kind finished his undergraduate degree, got master's and law degrees, practiced law for two years at a private firm, and became a county prosecutor in his hometown of La Crosse. Then he started thinking about returning to Washington and sought out his old boss, Senator Proxmire. Proxmire's advice "played a part in terms of the ultimate decision to run," said Kind, who considers Proxmire a role model.

In his own office today, Kind tries to make interns' experiences interesting and diverse. Interns attend committee hearings and bill markups and work on substantive issues in addition to the standard clerical duties, Kind said. "They're very important to our office, but it ultimately comes down to how an individual office utilizes them," he said.

As a former Senate intern and a current House member, Kind is reluctant to recommend one chamber over the other for interns. The key is finding an individual office that fits well, he said. "During the interview process, they should be confident enough to fire questions back," Kind said. "They should be interviewing the office at the same time to find out about the kind of experience they'll be allowed to have."

Interns can't be shy if they want to get the most out of the experience, Kind said. "It's good if they have the confidence to take the initiative on certain things, not to be afraid to speak to the member or the chief of staff," he said.

"Take advantage of all the different events that take place on Capitol Hill and in other parts of the District [of Columbia]. If they see a hearing they'd be interested in, speak up and say 'I'd like to attend the hearing.' Or if they're interested in a particular bill, ask to go over to the House floor or the Senate floor to watch the debate."

other nuances. Each office has a personality, and the sooner you learn your office's personality the better off you'll be.

The best way to make a good impression at your internship is to handle each assignment pleasantly and professionally, no matter how menial it may be. A good attitude is critical to success. There's no faster way to torpedo your internship than to sit around whining that the work is beneath you and a waste of your tremendous talents.

To help keep your attitude on track, it sometimes helps to put yourself in the other person's shoes. For example, say you're working in a senator's office and you're assigned to conduct a tour of the Capitol for a family visiting from the senator's state—a common job for interns. You may have already conducted dozens of such tours and be bored to death at the thought of another one.

It should help, though, to remember that this may be the family's first trip to Washington, their first chance to see their government in action, and—most important—their first direct contact with the senator. For them, walking through the halls of power may be a profound experience. And the impression you make on them directly reflects on your senator— for good or for bad. It better be for good.

If you intern at a trade association, you may be asked to track down some government publications that an association member has requested. This may not strike you as thrilling work, but to the member who made the request it's very important. It's also important to the association, because it wants to serve members properly and keep them happy.

As an intern, you must be willing to tackle any assignment (as long as it's legal and ethical). Your cheerful attitude and superb work ethic will make you stand out, and should help get you assignments that are more challenging. But remember: Even at the best internship, a lot of your work is likely to be clerical. If you can't handle that, don't apply.

But what if all your assignments for weeks have been menial, and you've been given no substantive work at all? Then it's time to talk to your supervisor. Don't do it in a whiny or confrontational manner. Don't say: "All this crummy work you've given me is garbage and a waste of my considerable talents. I demand something better!" Instead, you might want to say something like, "I appreciate all the assignments I've been given, and hope that I've done them well. However, much of my recent work has been clerical in nature, and I was hoping to get a few assignments with more substance to help round out my internship. Do you have anything that might be appropriate for me?"

Another way to get better work is to be proactive and create opportunities for yourself. Don't wait for things to be handed to you. Instead, keep your eyes and ears open and offer your assistance on any projects that sound interesting. Let your colleagues know—without being a pain—that you're available and willing to help.

PROFILE: CONGRESSIONAL RESEARCH SERVICE INTERNSHIPS

Internships at the Congressional Research Service don't pay anything, but they're among the most coveted positions in Washington. Why? Because they provide a substantive experience and look really good on a resume.

The CRS, which as its name implies conducts research for Congress, is one of the world's leading public policy research organizations. Its research covers the whole gamut of public policy issues.

CRS interns work directly with staff members to perform research and answer reference queries from congressional offices. "This is different than many other internship opportunities," said Warren Lenhart, head of the CRS intern program. "It's very substantive, doing some first-hand research and writing."

The highly competitive program is open to everyone from college undergraduates to professionals seeking first-class work experience. Most interns are graduate students who have gained public policy experience during a previous internship elsewhere, Lenhart said.

Lenhart receives more than 1,000 applications annually, but can only place fifty to seventy-five interns. He accepts applications year round, but recommends applying for positions during the academic year rather than the summer because there's less competition.

Lenhart looks for people "who have good writing and analytical skills, and who have an understanding of Congress and how Congress operates." In judging candidates, he examines the academic record and recommendations, but most importantly looks for evidence of "a student's passion for public policy work and public service—not just saying they want to do it, but demonstrated experience is very important."

When interns leave CRS, they have a top credential. "They'll have some substantive experience to show on the resume," Lenhart said. "It's an eye-catcher on the resume."

A strong internship credential is critical in today's job market. "Internships today are more important than they've ever been, because to be competitive in jobs you have to have demonstrated experience," Lenhart said. "It's not enough to just get a degree anymore."

Applicants should submit a resume, a writing sample, and a cover letter with dates of availability and areas of interest or expertise. Be sure to submit the application at least four to eight weeks before your proposed starting date. More information about the internship program is available at the CRS Web site.

Warren W. Lenhart
Library of Congress, CRS/LM-205
101 Independence Ave., S.E.
Washington, DC 20540-7000
Telephone: 202-707-7641
Web address: http://lcweb.loc.gov/crsinfo/crsvolteer.html

PROFILE: LEAGUE OF CONSERVATION VOTERS INTERNSHIPS

The League of Conservation Voters is often referred to as "the political arm of the environmental movement" because it focuses on electing members of Congress who are responsive to environmental concerns.

The league may be best known for its annual National Environmental Scorecard, which grades all members of Congress based on their environmental voting records. It also provides financial and in-kind help to congressional candidates with strong environmental records.

The league offers three types of internships:

- Political Action Internship: Research congressional voting records, follow and research important environmental legislation, study and report on congressional candidates, and assist in other political work.

- Communications Internship: Research stories for news reporters, draft press releases, and help with other media work. Depending on skills, other projects may include desktop publishing, creating electronic versions of league publications for the Internet, and helping engineer the league's connection to the Internet.

- Grassroots Internship: Work with the field staff of the league's Education Fund, which seeks to build the capacity of environmental groups across the country. Interns develop grassroots organizing materials and oversee the operations of the field staff.

Each internship lasts six months, is full time, and pays $950 per month. Most interns are recent college graduates.

League interns meet lots of people involved in the environmental movement both in Washington and around the country, said Lydia Vermilye, the league's internship coordinator and a former intern herself. "There are a tremendous number of political and environmental contacts to be made through the league," she said. Many interns get full-time jobs on Capitol Hill or in other environmental organizations, Vermilye said, and some go on to graduate school.

The league usually has between two and eight interns at any one time, Vermilye said. Interns are hired as needed—not on a regular schedule—so the best way to learn about current openings is to check the league's Web site.

Applicants must submit a cover letter explaining their interest in working for the league, a resume, a one-page writing sample, and two letters of reference.

Lydia Vermilye, Internship Coordinator
League of Conservation Voters
1707 L St., N.W., Suite 750
Washington, DC 20036
Telephone: 202-785-8683
Web address: http://www.lcv.org/aboutlcv/internships.htm

This advice is particularly important if you're given little to do in your internship. Most Washington offices are extremely busy, and supervisors typically don't have much time to give direction. This means you can get lost in the shuffle. Don't sit around whining about how little you have to do. Instead, find out about interesting projects that are underway and ask the people in charge, "Is there anything I can do to help?" Nine times out of ten, your extra pair of hands will be most welcome.

How to Survive the Internship from Hell

Thankfully, the vast majority of Washington internships do not merit the title "Internship from Hell." But a few do, and if you're unlucky enough to get stuck in one you need to know how to survive and make the most of the experience.

In this circumstance, your first step is to try to turn things around. For instance, if you hate your internship because your boss is a jerk, you might consider quietly asking your colleagues if they have any tips for dealing with the boss. Or you can try to hook yourself to projects being directed by people in the office who you like.

If your internship is awful because you're given nothing but menial tasks, ask your boss if there might be a few more substantive projects you could add to the mix. And keep alert for interesting projects around the office where you might be able to lend a hand.

If your efforts to improve things don't work, try to find other activities outside of the office that will make your time in Washington worthwhile. Spend some time using the resources of the Library of Congress to get a head start on your upcoming thesis research, lose yourself in Washington's fantastic museums, learn from the city's many cultural offerings, and so on. Washington has an enormous amount to offer outside of your internship.

Keep in mind, too, that you can learn even under the worst conditions. Even at the Internship from Hell, you can see what kinds of work you do and do not like, learn how to deal with coworkers (even those who are abrasive), and learn how to fit into an office environment. Your office may be the most dysfunctional place you've ever seen, but that in itself leads to learning opportunities: What makes the office dysfunctional? What are people doing that makes the office dysfunctional? Look beyond the obvious (my boss is a jerk) to some of the more subtle things. By watching carefully, you can learn what not to do when you start working full time.

One last thought also may be of some comfort: An internship does not last forever. You may be stuck for a few weeks or even a few months, but there's an end to this experience. And even if your experience is awful, it still will look mighty fine on your resume.

PROFILE: U.S. SUPREME COURT INTERNSHIPS

If you're interested in law, management, and social sciences, the Judicial Internship Program at the Supreme Court may be worth considering.

Interns in the program, which is open to advanced undergraduates and graduating seniors, work in the Office of the Administrative Assistant to the Chief Justice. Interns do not work on cases pending before the Supreme Court. Instead, they focus on issues related to judicial administration.

Interns perform tasks such as clipping and copying news articles, preparing memoranda and correspondence, conducting background research for speeches, and reviewing legislation about the federal judicial system. They also participate in both short-term and long-term research projects. Some of the past research topics have included alternatives to litigation, problems of civil procedure, international law, and judicial relations.

Interns also can observe Supreme Court sessions, attend outside lectures and conferences, and participate in educational luncheon meetings sponsored by the office with Supreme Court justices, government officials, and academic experts, among others.

Interns are not paid. However, if funding is available, interns can receive a $1,000 scholarship.

The program offers three sessions:

- Fall (September–December). Application deadline: June 1
- Winter (January–May). Application deadline: October 10
- Summer (June–August). Application deadline: March 10

Two interns are selected for each session. About 100 people typically apply for the summer session, and 20 people usually apply for each of the fall and winter sessions.

To apply, you must submit a resume, an official transcript, a written statement about why you're applying, a separate writing sample, three letters of recommendation, and a two-page essay about the importance of the American constitutional system. More information is available in a brochure about the program, which you can obtain by calling the number below.

Judicial Internship Program
Judicial Fellow
Office of the Administrative Assistant to the Chief Justice
Supreme Court of the United States
Room 5
Washington, DC 20543
Telephone: 202-479-3415

PROFILE: U.S. GENERAL ACCOUNTING OFFICE INTERNSHIPS

The General Accounting Office is commonly known as "the investigative arm of Congress." It audits and evaluates federal programs in such areas as financial institutions and markets, tax policy and administration, education, employment, health care financing, public health, defense acquisitions, international relations and trade, national security, environmental protection, agriculture, housing, and transportation, among others.

The agency hires about one hundred interns annually, most of whom work at its office in Washington, D.C. Internships also are available at regional GAO offices in Atlanta, Boston, Chicago, Dallas, Denver, Kansas City, Los Angeles, Norfolk, San Francisco, and Seattle. Intern appointments are for sixteen weeks, and most are in the summer.

The GAO hires both graduate students and those undergrads who have completed at least sixty semester hours of classes. The agency particularly seeks students majoring in accounting, business administration, public policy and administration, computer science, management information systems, economics, or the social sciences, although students with other majors also are considered. Interns are paid between $1,400 and $2,500 per month, with the amount depending on how many semester hours the intern has completed.

Interns handle a variety of tasks, including determining information needs; collecting information through record searches, automated data retrieval, interviewing, and questionnaires; analyzing information and developing recommendations; and writing reports and briefings.

Applicants must submit a resume, college transcripts, a list of courses and credit hours in which they are currently enrolled, the dates they're available for employment and expect to return to school, and a supplemental form available at the agency's Web site that requests basic contact information.

U.S. General Accounting Office
Office of Recruitment
Room 1165
441 G St., N.W.
Washington, DC 20548
Telephone: 1-800-WORK-GAO or 202-512-6092
Web address: http://www.gao.gov/jobs
E-mail: recruit@gao.gov

This advice about surviving the Internship from Hell is good except in one very rare circumstance: if some aspect of your internship places you in danger. For example, say that your boss makes it clear he expects you to perform sexual favors. In cases like this, get out of the internship immediately and do whatever you must to ensure your safety.

How to End the Internship

Most people put lots of effort into finding and working at an internship, but don't give a thought to concluding it properly. That's a serious mistake.

Try to arrange an exit interview with your supervisor. Use this opportunity to get as much feedback as possible about your performance. What did you do well? What areas might you focus on improving? Because the supervisor has seen you in action, you also can seek recommendations for career options based on your performance.

You also want to leave people in the office with a good impression. Besides just being the right thing to do, it also helps ensure they'll remain valuable contacts when you're looking for a full-time job or need a good reference. To help with this, at the end of the internship send thank-you notes to your supervisor and anyone else in the office who was particularly helpful.

Once you leave, stay in touch with folks at your old office. Don't be a pest, but keep your network connections open. You never know when they might be handy.

A Final Word

Don't forget to enjoy yourself while you're in Washington. Sure, internships are serious work, but they also should be fun. Take advantage of Washington's parks, museums, cultural performances, monuments, sporting events, restaurants, clubs, and everything else the city has to offer. They're all part of your learning experience, so don't spend all your time sitting at a desk.

Internship Contacts

The Washington Center for Internships and Academic Seminars
Telephone: 800-486-8921
Web address: http://www.twc.edu
E-mail: info@twc.edu

The Washington Center provides a structured program in conjunction with participating colleges and universities that places interns in a variety of Washington offices. The program also includes seminars, social and cultural events, and housing.

Institute for Experiential Learning
Telephone: 800-IEL-0770
Web address: http://www.ielnet.org
E-mail: info@ielnet.org

The Institute for Experiential Learning offers two different internship programs. The Capital Experience places interns throughout Washington, and the Embassy and Diplomatic Scholars Internship Program places interns with foreign embassies, international organizations, and federal foreign policy agencies. Both programs also provide seminars and housing. Tuition for the semester-long programs ranges from $1,950 to $2,500, and housing costs between $1,500 and $1,950.

Washington Intern Foundation
Web address: http://www.interns.org
E-mail: intern@erols.com

The Washington Intern Foundation's Web site typically has listings for more than 200 Washington internships offered by everyone from trade associations to congressional offices. You can search the listings by keyword or browse them by category. Some of the categories with the most listings include advertising and public relations, advocacy, communications and marketing, environment, government affairs and trade associations, health care, international and human rights, legal, U.S. House of Representatives, and U.S. Senate. You also can sign up to receive free e-mail notices about new internships posted at the Web site. And finally, you can post your resume for free.

Nonprofit Internships
Web address: http://www.idealist.org/IS/intern_search.html

This site offers information about dozens of Washington-based internships with nonprofit organizations. For each internship, it provides a brief description, information about whether it's paid or unpaid, and contact details. Organizations that list openings at the site include the Union of Councils for Soviet Jews, Union of Concerned Scientists, Leadership Conference on Civil Rights, American Rivers, Benton Foundation, Environmental Defense Fund, Families USA Foundation, National Campaign for Freedom of Expression, U.S. Term Limits, National Whistleblower Center, Landmine Survivors Network, International Human Rights Law Group, National Sleep Foundation, Public Citizen's Critical Mass Energy Project, Gay and Lesbian Victory Fund, Center on Budget and Policy Priorities, League of Women Voters of the United States, and Zero Population Growth, among many others. The site is operated by Action without Borders.

Internships Directory
Web address: http://www.feminist.org/911/internship/internship.html

The Internships Directory from the Feminist Majority Foundation lists dozens of internships in the Washington area. Information is provided about internships with the Alliance for Justice, Bread for the World, Democratic National Committee, EMILY's List, the Feminist Majority, National Abortion and Reproductive Rights Action League, National Lesbian and Gay Health Association, National Foundation for Women Legislators, National Organization for Women, People for the Ethical Treatment of Animals, Planned Parenthood Federation, Save America's Forests, Zero Population Growth, and many other groups.

Uncle Sam: Student Internships from the Feds
Web address: http://www.lib.memphis.edu/gpo/intern.htm

Uncle Sam has links to internship information provided by more than twenty federal agencies and departments, including the Administration on Aging, Central Intelligence Agency, Environmental Protection Agency, National Archives and Records Administration, Securities and Exchange Commission, State Department, and the White House, among others.

U.S. Senate
Telephone: 202-224-3121 (U.S. Capitol switchboard)
Web address: http://www.senate.gov

If you're looking for an internship with the U.S. Senate, the Senate's Web site is a good place to start. It has links to sites operated by senators and committees, many of which offer information about internship opportunities.

U.S. House of Representatives
Telephone: 202-224-3121 (U.S. Capitol switchboard)
Web address: http://www.house.gov

The House Web site is a gateway into information about internships in the U.S. House of Representatives. It has links to sites operated by the representatives and committees, but unfortunately you must check each separately to find internship information.

Internship Resources on the Web
Web address: http://www.cc.colorado.edu/CareerCenter/
SummerJobsAndInternships/Intern.html

This site from the Colorado College Career Center has links to internship information across the Internet. The sites provide general information about internships, national listings of internship opportunities, and listings of internships in specific subject areas.

4

Working in Washington: Congress

According to an old saying, there are two things you should not watch being made: sausage and laws. Yet the process of making the nation's laws is so endlessly fascinating that many relish the idea of having a front-row seat as a congressional staffer.

Many, too, are drawn to congressional staff jobs by a desire to help people—whether that help involves writing a new piece of legislation that benefits the entire country or solving an individual constituent's problem in getting Social Security benefits.

The largest survey of congressional staffers ever conducted found that they overwhelmingly enjoy their jobs. Seventy-six percent of staffers agreed with the statement "I like my job," and only 8 percent disagreed and 16 percent had no opinion.

"They enjoy the nature of their work, its challenge and variety, as well as the autonomy with which they are allowed to perform it," according to *Working in Congress: The Staff Perspective* (1995, p. 7), a report of the survey's findings by the Congressional Management Foundation, a nonprofit group. "They see the opportunity for ongoing learning in their jobs and feel that they work alongside high-quality colleagues. Perhaps most surprising in these somewhat cynical times is the fact that staff strongly wish to help people and contribute to the public good and are very satisfied with their ability to do so through their jobs in Congress."

Congressional staff jobs do have frustrations that help cause a high turnover rate. I'll discuss some of those problems in a minute. But first, let's look at what staffers actually do in Congress.

Who Runs Congress?

More than perhaps any other Washington institution, Congress is run by its staffers. The reason is simple: With Congress tackling hundreds of different issues in a typical session, no individual member of Congress can keep up alone. Nor can any individual member of Congress respond personally to the thousands of constituent requests that flood the typical congressional office or to the tens of thousands of letters that must be answered.

This means that members of Congress must delegate much of their work—and with it, some of their power—to staffers. The typical member of the House of Representatives has eight staffers in the Washington office, and the typical senator has twenty-two.

How much power an individual staffer wields largely depends on his or her job in the congressional office. Most offices are divided into two parts in response to Congress' dual functions: responding to constituents' requests and passing legislation.

Constituents' requests are called *casework,* and those who handle them are caseworkers. Caseworkers solve constituents' problems in dealing with federal agencies. They may help a constituent appeal a denial of Social Security benefits, assist a member of the military service in getting a hardship discharge, or help someone track down information from a federal agency. Caseworkers have quite a bit of power in attending to the needs of individuals—because they contact agencies on behalf of their member of Congress—but little power overall.

The staffers with power work on the legislative side of the office, studying legislation introduced by other members of Congress, writing legislation to be introduced by their own members, lining up outside support for legislation, and negotiating with staff members in other offices about provisions in bills. These staffers play a central role in the legislative process, and can wield enormous power by pressing their own legislative priorities, shaping legislation offered by others, helping to block legislation they oppose, and initiating investigations of federal agencies.

"There are thousands of nonvoting lawmakers on Capitol Hill," wrote political scientists Roger Davidson and Walter Oleszek in *Congress and Its Members* (1981, p. 235):

> The unelected staff aides of committees and members constitute a behind-the-scenes "shadow government" that shapes the nation's policies. Legislative employees process Congress' workload, suggest policy initiatives, mobilize public opinion, advise legislators how to vote, serve constituents, and review agency implementation of laws.

Congressional staffers are like Santa's elves: They do all their work behind the scenes and are totally anonymous. They may write an important bill, but the representative they work for will introduce it and the staffers will receive no credit. They may solve a constituent's problem with a federal agency, but the letter to the constituent announcing the solution will be signed by the member of congress. Congressional staff work is not for glory hounds or those who seek the limelight.

PROFILE: SHANNON TESDAHL

Shannon Tesdahl's trial by fire came the week before President Clinton's impeachment trial started in the Senate. Senators were arguing about how the trial should be conducted, and Tesdahl's boss, Sen. Tom Harkin, D-Iowa, was in the thick of it.

Tesdahl is the number-three person in Harkin's press office, but that week her two senior colleagues were off on other assignments. Suddenly, as chaos erupted in the office, Tesdahl became press secretary for the week.

"I was the only one here," she said, "and that entire week the phone never stopped ringing." Calls came in from Russian television, the BBC, CNN, and lots of other media outlets, all wanting comments from Harkin for stories. Tesdahl credits her colleagues in the office with helping her get through the week. "That's something I'll carry with me for the rest of my life," she said. "It was a really phenomenal experience."

Normally, her job as press assistant is a bit quieter. She writes media advisories, writes a Q&A column with Harkin for weekly newspapers in Iowa, helps produce a cable show, clips newspapers, and assists with related tasks.

While growing up in Cedar Rapids, Iowa, Tesdahl's interests were politics and journalism. She moved to Washington, D.C., to attend George Washington University, where she majored in political communication. She also embarked on a series of internships and short-term paid positions as soon as she hit the city.

She started by sending her resume to Iowa's two senators and the representative from her home district. Harkin replied first, and she started in his office as a scheduling intern. That led to more internships and paid positions in Harkin's office and on his campaign staff, culminating in Tesdahl doing advance work for Harkin's reelection campaign back in Iowa. She next tackled an internship at C-SPAN and work at a public relations firm, all while finishing her degree.

As Tesdahl approached graduation, the deputy press secretary in Harkin's office called to say that a press job would be opening. But a staff assistant job answering telephones opened first in Harkin's office, and Tesdahl faced a dilemma: Should she take the staff assistant job, which wasn't her first choice, to get her foot in the door? Or should she wait to see whether the press job panned out? She decided to accept the staff assistant position, and three months later was able to move to the press job.

Tesdahl calls working on Capitol Hill "absolutely wonderful. Often I will stand back a little from a work situation and think I'm so lucky to work with such energetic, caring, hard-working people of so many ages and so many interests."

Her advice for others who might want to follow in her footsteps? "You have to be willing to accept anything, and then use whatever position you may receive. Just work as hard as you can and try to learn from everything. And contacts are really important."

Who's Who in a Congressional Office

Every congressional job has a title, and they can be mighty confusing if you don't know the lingo. For example, if you read an employment ad that says a member of Congress is looking for an "A.A.," it means the member is seeking an administrative assistant—not a member of Alcoholics Anonymous.

Exactly how titles and duties are assigned varies from office to office. But the following scorecard should help you keep the major players straight—and determine which congressional jobs might be right for you:

- Administrative Assistant ("A.A.") or Chief of Staff: The A.A. is the top staff person and runs the office. The A.A. typically supervises senior staff members and assigns them work, hires and fires all staff members, determines legislative priorities in consultation with the member of Congress, tracks political developments in the home district and on Capitol Hill, and represents the member at various meetings that he or she cannot attend in person.

- Legislative Director ("L.D.") or Chief Legislative Assistant: The L.D. is in charge of all activities related to legislation. The L.D. supervises legislative assistants, may oversee committee work for the member, helps set legislative priorities, tracks legislation on the Hill, briefs the member regarding the pros and cons of upcoming bills, and reviews constituent mail relating to legislation.

- Legislative Assistant ("L.A."): The number of L.A.'s varies among offices. Typically, an L.A. is responsible for legislation on certain topics or from certain committees on which the member sits. L.A.'s in the House handle numerous topics or committees, and those in the Senate are usually able to specialize. In connection with their topics, L.A.'s track legislation, oversee the member's legislative program, write speeches and legislation, meet with constituents, and answer constituent mail.

- Legislative Correspondent ("L.C."): An office may have several L.C.'s who respond to constituent letters about legislative issues. On common issues, an L.C. simply cranks out a computer-generated response. But on more complex issues, the L.C. will conduct research and draft an original letter for the member's signature.

- Caseworker: Caseworkers help constituents solve problems with federal agencies, ranging from expediting passport requests to assisting in an appeal when Social Security benefits are denied. The caseworker identifies the problem, contacts the appropriate agency to arrange a resolution, and prepares correspondence about the issue.

- Press Secretary or Communications Manager: The press secretary responds to requests from the news media, arranges radio and TV appearances, monitors media coverage of the member, and writes and distributes press releases, newsletters, newspaper columns, and speeches.

- Office Manager: The office manager is responsible for day-to-day operation of the office—everything from ordering supplies to managing office expense accounts to supervising clerical staff. In many offices, the manager also oversees the intern program.

How to Find a Hill Job

The good news for job seekers is that Capitol Hill has a high turnover rate, meaning there are always lots of job openings. The bad news is there's lots of competition for those openings—especially the entry-level positions. So how do you learn about openings and land a job?

The key is networking, networking, and more networking. Many Hill jobs are never advertised, so networking is the only way you'll learn about them. If you need some tips, turn back to Chapter 1.

It's also critical to explore all the available opportunities. Although member offices are the most obvious places to look, Congress offers lots of other great staff jobs to those who dig a bit deeper.

Some of the most interesting staff jobs are with the dozens of committees and subcommittees that serve the House and Senate. These committees handle such topics as agriculture, education, energy and natural resources, environment and public works, government reform, intelligence, international relations, national security, and science.

Other job opportunities are available at the General Accounting Office, which is the investigative arm of Congress; the Congressional Budget Office, which analyzes and reports on budget issues; the Congressional Research Service, a branch of the Library of Congress that conducts research for members of Congress; political party committees, such as the Democratic Congressional Campaign Committee and the National Republican Senatorial Committee; and various caucuses, including the House Democratic Caucus and the House Republican Conference.

One of the best ways to land a full-time Hill job is to start out as an intern. An internship provides you with that key asset when seeking a full-time job in Congress: Hill experience. It doesn't matter that all you did at your internship was spend four months licking envelopes—it still counts as Hill experience and puts you far ahead of those without it. A Hill internship also has two other advantages if you want to work there full time:

- If you do outstanding work at your internship, your office may promote you to a staff job when the internship ends.

CONGRESSIONAL INFORMATION ONLINE

Just about anything you need to know about Congress—the addresses of specific congressional offices, definitions of the arcane terms used on Capitol Hill, or descriptions of exactly how laws are made—is available on the Internet. Here are some of the key sites:

United States Legislative Branch
http://lcweb.loc.gov/global/legislative/congress.html
This Library of Congress page is a meta directory of other Internet sites about the U.S. Congress. It has links to sites that provide official congressional information, e-mail addresses, congressional schedules and calendars, details about floor proceedings, legislation, the U.S. Code, House and Senate Rules, the *Congressional Record,* roll call votes, congressional news, the history of Congress, visitor information, and more.

Federal Government Resources: Legislative Branch
http://www.lib.umich.edu/libhome/Documents.center/fedlegis.html
This page from the University of Michigan Documents Center has links to dozens of Internet sites that provide information about Congress. It's a fantastic place to start a search for congressional information on the Internet.

The United States Senate
http://www.senate.gov
The Senate Web site has records of how senators voted (arranged by bill), schedules of upcoming committee meetings and hearings, the Senate legislative calendar, reports about Senate floor activity, contact information for senators, links to the homepages of those senators and committees that are online, and background information about the Senate.

U.S. Senators
http://lcweb.loc.gov/global/legislative/senators.html
The Library of Congress provides this page, which has links to dozens of other sites about the U.S. Senate. The sites have directories of senators, photographs of senators, congressional e-mail addresses, biographical information about senators, committee assignments, voting records, and more.

Standing Rules of the Senate
http://www.senate.gov/learning/learn_rules.html
The official rules of the U.S. Senate are provided at this page. Some of the topics covered include order of business, voting procedures, amendments and motions, debate, precedence of motions, committee procedures, public financial disclosure, gifts, outside earned income, conflict of interest, and foreign travel.

U.S. House of Representatives
http://www.house.gov

A wealth of information about Congress is provided by the House Web site. It has up-to-the-minute reports about current actions on the House floor, schedules of upcoming floor and committee votes and hearings, records of roll call votes, links to Web pages operated by House members and committees, background about how laws are made, information about touring Capitol Hill, and maps of Washington, D.C., and of the city's subway system.

U.S. House Members
http://lcweb.loc.gov/global/legislative/house.html

This page from the Library of Congress provides links to dozens of Web sites about the U.S. House of Representatives. The sites provide directories of House members, lists of e-mail addresses, directories of House leaders, biographies and background information about House members, committee assignments, and voting records.

Rules of the U.S. House of Representatives
http://lcweb.loc.gov/global/legislative/hrules/106/hrulestoc.html

The Library of Congress operates this page, which has the official rules of the House of Representatives. The rules cover such topics as organization of committees, order and priority of business, motions and amendments, decorum and debate, voting and quorum calls, limitations on outside income and acceptance of gifts, and financial disclosure.

Enactment of a Law
http://thomas.loc.gov/home/enactment/enactlawtoc.html

The Senate parliamentarian wrote this publication, which explains the legislative process. Some of the subjects discussed include contrasting procedures of the Senate and the House, motions and quorums, committee rules, amendment, engrossment and transmittal, messages and amendments between the houses, and conference committees and reports.

How Our Laws Are Made
http://thomas.loc.gov/home/lawsmade.toc.html

This publication, which was written by the House parliamentarian, complements the previously mentioned document, *Enactment of a Law.* It covers such topics as sources of legislation, forms of congressional action, consideration by committee, reported bills, legislative oversight by standing committees, and House debates, among others.

Congressional Research Service Reports
http://www.house.gov/rules/crs_reports.htm

This page, which is operated by the House Rules Committee, offers more than three dozen reports from the Congressional Research Service about how Congress operates. Many will be extremely valuable if you get a job on Capitol Hill. Some of the titles include *Legislative Research in Congressional Offices: A Primer; How to Follow Current Federal*

(Box continues)

Legislation and Regulations; The Committee System in the U.S. Congress; Hearings in the House of Representatives; Floor Procedure in the House of Representatives; How Measures Are Brought to the House Floor; The Amending Process in the House of Representatives; and *Voting and Quorum Procedures in the House of Representatives.*

Learning about the Senate
http://www.senate.gov/learning/learn_glossery_more.html
Is your head swimming with the jargon of Capitol Hill—terms like *cloture, engrossed bill,* and *pocket veto?* This page at the Senate Web site defines them all, along with more than 100 others that can bedevil new Hill employees.

Congressional Quarterly VoteWatch
http://cnn.com/ALLPOLITICS/cq/resources/votewatch
At this site you can examine the voting record of any member of Congress. The site is a project of CNN and Congressional Quarterly. If you want to check votes by your own member of Congress, you can search by the representative's last name, your Zip Code, or your voting district. You also can search by popular bill name or subject. Each vote listing links to an article that describes the bill. The site also has stories about the latest key votes in the House and Senate, along with details about how representatives or senators voted.

THOMAS
http://thomas.loc.gov
The highlight of THOMAS, which is operated by the Library of Congress, is its collection of searchable databases. They offer the full text of all bills introduced in Congress, information about the status of bills, reports by House and Senate committees, and the full text of the *Congressional Record.* It also has links to other congressional Web sites.

Map of the U.S. Capitol Complex
http://www.house.gov/house/Maps.html
Capitol Hill can be a tough place to navigate without a map. This page from the House Web site offers a map that shows the locations of all the House and Senate office buildings, the U.S. Capitol, the Library of Congress, and streets in the area.

- During your internship you'll make lots of contacts that should give you the inside track on job openings—especially for the "hidden" jobs that are never advertised.

As mentioned in Chapter 3, the biggest downside of Hill internships is that most don't pay. But you wanted to go on a diet anyway, didn't you?

A key starting place for a Hill job search is the offices of the three members of Congress who represent you: the representative who serves your home district and the two senators who serve your state. Members

---

GUIDES TO CONGRESS

Even in this electronic age, two books still provide the best guides to Congress available anywhere. They can be a great help in determining whether a particular congressional office might be a comfortable place for you to work.

The books are *Politics in America,* published by Congressional Quarterly, and *The Almanac of American Politics,* published by National Journal. Both books are published every two years and contain extensive information about the members of Congress.

For each member, the books provide information about the district or state represented, biographical information, committee assignments, votes on key issues, interest group ratings, election results, contact information, and more.

Both books should be available in your college or public library.

---

of Congress like to hire people from their district or state, so you should at least receive serious consideration for any openings. Even if you don't want to work for your representative or senator, letting their offices know that a constituent is looking for a Hill job can be a key piece of networking. Next, take advantage of the services for job seekers provided by the House Office of Human Resources and the Senate Placement Office.

House Office of Human Resources

The highlight is the Human Resources Job Line (202-226-6731), a tape-recorded service that offers brief descriptions of current job openings in various House offices. The jobs are divided into three categories: vacancies in member and committee offices, computer and technical support openings, and other administrative jobs. An important note: the member and committee category also lists lots of internship openings.

On the tape, jobs are identified by a vacancy announcement number. Applicants are asked to send a cover letter that identifies the position by title and vacancy announcement number, a resume, salary requirements (although you should think twice before doing this), and any other relevant information. If you apply for more than one job, you must send a separate packet for each position. You can fax your materials to 202-226-0098 or mail them to:

Office of Human Resources
Room 263, Cannon House Office Building
Attn: CAOKEF
Washington, DC 20515-6610

The office also operates the House Resume Referral Service. You can submit a resume and a cover letter stating the type of position you want and your salary requirements. When a House office wants to hire, it can call the referral service and ask for the resumes of appropriate candidates. However, not all House offices use the referral service when hiring. You can fax your materials to 202-226-0098 or mail them to:

House Resume Referral Service
Room 263, Cannon House Office Building
Washington, DC 20515-6610

The referral service keeps your materials for three months. If you haven't found a job in that period and want to remain in the system, you must submit an updated resume and cover letter.

Senate Placement Office

The Senate Placement Office offers slightly more extensive services than the House Office of Human Resources. The highlight is the Senate Employment Bulletin (202-228-5627), a tape-recorded message that lists job openings in the Senate. The openings are divided into four categories: legislative, administrative, press, and miscellaneous. The tape is updated every Friday afternoon.

Each job on the tape has a referral number, and you must write this number on your mailing envelope and resume when applying. If you apply for more than one job, you must submit a separate resume for each position. Send your resume, cover letter, and any other materials to:

Senate Employment Bulletin
Senate Placement Office
Room SH-142, Hart Senate Office Building
Washington, DC 20510

The placement office also operates a resume bank. To submit a resume you must visit the Senate Placement Office in Room 142 of the Hart Senate Office Building. While you're at the office, be sure to also fill out an application, check its listings of federal government and private sector job openings, and have an informational interview with a counselor. One of the biggest advantages of registering with the resume bank is that you'll be considered for Senate jobs that aren't advertised.

You can drop off your resume from 8:30 A.M. to 5:30 P.M. Monday through Friday, although interviews are only conducted Monday through Thursday from 10:00 A.M. to noon and 1:00 P.M. to 3:00 P.M. and on Fridays from 10:00 A.M. to noon and 1:00 P.M. to 2:00 P.M. Services are provided on a walk-in basis, so you don't need an appointment. You can learn more about the placement office's services by calling its main telephone number (202-224-9167).

Here are two other methods for finding a Hill job:

- Check the employment ads in the two newspapers that serve Capitol

Hill: *Roll Call* and *The Hill*. Both papers put their classified ads on-line. For details, see the box titled "Capitol Hill Newspapers Online."

- Blanket Capitol Hill with resumes. This usually isn't very effective, especially in relation to the amount of work involved. It's far better to target your efforts at a few jobs or offices. However, every once in a while a blanketing campaign works, so don't automatically drop the idea from consideration.

The Downsides of Working on Capitol Hill

Most congressional staffers do not make a career out of working on Capitol Hill. The reasons are varied—some leave because their congressional experience has made them very valuable in the private sector. But a good share leave because of dissatisfaction with various aspects of their jobs. Here are some of the factors they cite most often:

- The work hours are unpredictable. The congressional schedule can change weekly, daily, or even hourly, depending on the press of legislation, world events, and other factors. This makes it next to impossible for staffers to plan their lives.

- The work hours are long. More than half of all congressional staffers work more than fifty hours a week, according to a survey by the Congressional Management Foundation.

- Staffers feel overwhelmed by the huge amount of work, and frequently feel they must sacrifice quality just to get all the work done.

CAPITOL HILL NEWSPAPERS ONLINE

Two newspapers devoted to Capitol Hill offer electronic versions that are excellent sources for ads listing Hill jobs and other public policy positions. The two papers also offer much of their editorial content online, providing useful information for anyone thinking about working in Congress.

Roll Call (http://www.rollcall.com) is the older of the two, having been published since 1955. The biweekly newspaper posts its top stories online every Monday and Thursday, along with editorials, election news, commentary, cartoons, and the classified ads. The paper's Web site also offers a searchable congressional directory.

The Hill (http://www.hillnews.com), a weekly paper published each Wednesday, is a relative upstart. On its Web site, the paper offers news stories, columns, articles about political campaigns, and classified ads.

- Many congressional offices are poorly managed, creating chaos that interferes with staffers' ability to do their work.

- Staffers have little job security. If your boss loses an election, you're out of a job (although you can frequently move to another congressional office).

- Congressional staffers generally make less money than people working in the executive branch or the private sector. For example, Senate staffers with bachelor's degrees make 27 percent less than other workers nationally who have the same level of education, according to a study by the Congressional Management Foundation. According to the most recent data from the foundation, the average House staffer in Washington made $42,558 in 1998 and the average Senate staffer made $42,343 in 1997. However, these averages are boosted significantly by the amounts made by high-level staffers, which mask the low pay received by most. For example, the foundation found that in the House the average pay was $34,275 for a legislative assistant, $24,048 for a legislative correspondent, and $21,762 for a staff assistant. In the Senate, the average pay was $32,548 for a correspondence manager, $24,585 for a research assistant, and $24,209 for a legislative correspondent.

- Stress levels are high and are exacerbated by the heavy amount of work and unpredictable schedules.

- No matter how powerful you may become, you're always a surrogate for someone else—and that someone else always gets the credit for your work.

All this dissatisfaction creates lots of turnover. In the House, 29 percent of staffers have worked in Congress less than one year, the foundation reported. The average House staffer has worked in Congress for just five years. Things are at least as bad in the Senate. The foundation's latest survey found that 39 percent of chiefs of staff, 53 percent of legislative directors, and 62 percent of legislative assistants have been in their current jobs for two years or less.

"What we see is that staff love working in Congress, but the schedule, the pressure, and the salary make it tougher to work there for a long time," Rick Shapiro, the foundation's executive director, told the *Washington Post* on release of the foundation's latest congressional salary survey.

The statistics sum up standard operating procedure on Capitol Hill: hire staffers young, give them an incredible opportunity like none available anywhere else, work them nonstop until they burn out, then ship them on to jobs in corporate law, lobbying, government contracting, and other professions. The ride may be short, but what a heck of a ride it can be.

Capitol Hill Contacts

ONLINE DIRECTORIES

Congressional Quarterly's Rate Your Rep

http://www-cgi.cnn.com/cgi-bin/election/raterep/raterep.sh

Don't know who represents you in Congress? Just type your Zip Code into this page and it will return the names of your two senators and your member in the House of Representatives.

U.S. House of Representatives Member Office Web Services

http://www.house.gov/house/MemberWWW.html

This page links you to Web sites operated by individual members of the House of Representatives. It's an excellent starting place for finding names of staff contacts, office telephone numbers, and other information about member offices.

U.S. Senators

http://www.senate.gov/senators/index.cfm

This page provides links to Web sites operated by individual members of the U.S. Senate. Through the links, you can quickly find detailed information about each Senate office.

(For additional online Capitol Hill directories, see the box titled "Congressional Information Online," p. 58.)

CAUCUSES AND PARTY ORGANIZATIONS

Congressional Black Caucus Foundation, 1004 Pennsylvania Ave. S.E., Washington, DC 20003; (202) 675-6730. Fax (202) 547-3806, Web http://www.cbcfonline.org. Adjoe Aiyetero, director of administration; Edwin Makhutela, intern coordinator.

Conducts research and programs on public policy issues of concern to African Americans. Sponsors fellowship programs in which professionals and academic candidates work on congressional committees and subcommittees. Sponsors internship and scholarship programs.

Congressional Hispanic Caucus Institute, 504 C St. N.E., Washington, DC 20002; (202) 543-1771. Fax (202) 546-2143. Ingrid Duran, executive director; Silvia Golombek, programs director.

Addresses issues of concern to Hispanic Americans and fosters awareness of the contributions of Hispanics to American society. Develops programs to familiarize Hispanic students with policy-related careers and to encourage their professional development.

Congressional Hunger Center, 229¹/₂ Pennsylvania Ave. S.E., Washington, DC 20003; (202) 547-7022. Fax (202) 547-7575, e-mail nohungr@aol.com, Web http://www.hungercenter.org. John Morrill, executive director.

Works to increase public awareness of hunger in the United States and abroad. Develops strategies to combat hunger and facilitates collaborative efforts between organizations.

House Democratic Caucus, Longworth House Office Building, Room 1420, Washington, DC 20515; (202) 226-3210. Fax (202) 225-0282, Web http://www.dcaucus.gov. Jennifer Dean, office manager.

Membership: House Democrats. Selects Democratic leadership, formulates party rules and floor strategy, and considers caucus members' recommendations on major issues.

House Democratic Policy Committee, The Capitol, Room H302, Washington, DC 20515; (202) 225-6760. Fax (202) 226-0938, Web http://www.house.gov/democrats. Craig Hannah, executive director; Daniel Nazisky, staff assistant.

Studies and makes recommendations to the Democratic leadership on party policy and priorities.

House Republican Conference, Longworth House Office Building, Room 1010, Washington, DC 20515; (202) 225-5107. Fax (202) 225-0809. Terri Hasdorff, deputy director; Amy Lorenzini, conference coordinator.

Membership: House Republicans. Selects Republican leadership, formulates party rules and floor strategy, and considers party positions on major legislation.

House Republican Policy Committee, Rayburn House Office Building, Room 2471, Washington, DC 20515; (202) 225-6168. Fax (202) 225-0931, Web http://policy.house.gov. Benedict Cohen, executive director; Lance Larson, intern coordinator.

Studies legislation and makes recommendations on House Republican policies and positions on proposed legislation.

Senate Democratic Conference, The Capitol, Room S309, Washington, DC 20510; (202) 224-3735. Martin P. Paone, secretary for the minority.

Membership: Democratic senators. Selects Democratic leadership, formulates party rules and floor strategy, and considers party positions on major legislation.

Senate Democratic Policy Committee, The Capitol, Room S118, Washington, DC 20510; (202) 224-3232. E-mail postmaster@dpc.senate.gov. Carolyn Chambers, staff director; Sue Christenson, office manager.

Studies and makes recommendations to the Democratic leadership on legislation for consideration by the Senate.

Senate Republican Conference, Hart Senate Office Building, Room 405, Washington, DC 20510; (202) 224-2764. Lee Johnson, staff director; Al Rowell, intern coordinator.

Membership: Republican senators. Serves as caucus and central coordinating body of the party. Staff provides various support and media services for Republican members.

Senate Republican Policy Committee, Russell Senate Office Building, Room 347, Washington, DC 20510; (202) 224-2946. Kelly Oliver, staff assistant; Wes Harris, intern coordinator.

Studies and makes recommendations to the majority leader on the priorities and scheduling of legislation on the Senate floor; prepares policy papers and develops Republican policy initiatives.

CONGRESSIONAL SUPPORT AGENCIES

Congressional Budget Office, Ford Building, Room 402, Washington, DC 20515; (202) 226-2700. Fax (202) 225-7509, Web http://www.cbo.gov. Jan Bohren, personnel coordinator.

Nonpartisan office that provides the House and Senate with budget-related information and analyses of alternative fiscal policies.

General Accounting Office, 441 G St. N.W., Washington, DC 20548; (202) 512-5500. Fax (202) 512-5507, Web http://www.gao.gov, personnel office (202) 512-4500, job line recording (202) 512-6092. David M. Walker, comptroller general; Madelyn Daniels, internship program director.

Independent, nonpartisan agency in the legislative branch. Serves as the investigating agency for Congress; carries out legal, accounting, auditing, and claims settlement functions; makes recommendations for more effective government operations; publishes monthly lists of reports available to the public.

Library of Congress, Congressional Research Service, 101 Independence Ave. S.E., Washington, DC 20540; (202) 707-5775. Fax (202) 707-2615, job line recording (202) 707-4315. Daniel P. Mulhollan, director; Leon Turner, co-op program manager.

Provides members of Congress and committees with general reference assistance; prepares upon request background reports, analytical studies, reading lists, bibliographies, and pros and cons of policy issues; conducts public issue seminars and workshops for committees, members, and staffs; makes available the services of subject specialists.

CONGRESSIONAL COMMITTEES

House Committees

Agriculture Committee, Longworth House Office Building, Room 1301, Washington, DC 20515; (202) 225-0029. Web http://www.house.gov/agriculture. Bill O'Conner, staff director; Stephen Haterius, minority staff director; Tom Sell, deputy staff director.

Jurisdiction summary: Agriculture, forestry, farm credit, meat and seafood inspections, human nutrition, and rural development.

Appropriations Committee, The Capitol, Room H-218, Washington, DC 20515; (202) 225-2771. Web http://www.house.gov/appropriations. James W. Dyer, clerk and staff director; R. Scott Lilly, minority staff director.

Jurisdiction summary: Appropriation of revenue for the support of the government.

Armed Services Committee, Rayburn House Office Building, Room 2120, Washington, DC 20515; (202) 225-4151. Web http://www.house.gov/hasc. Andrew K. Ellis, majority staff director; Thomas Glakas, minority staff director.

Jurisdiction summary: General defense issues, military applications of nuclear energy, working conditions of defense personnel, and Selective Service System.

Banking and Financial Services Committee, Rayburn House Office Building, Room 2129, Washington, DC 20515; (202) 225-7502. Web http://www.house. gov/banking. Anthony F. Cole, staff director; Angela Gambo, intern coordinator.

Jurisdiction summary: Banks and banking, economic stabilization, financial aid to commerce and industry, international finance, public and private housing, and urban development.

Budget Committee, Cannon House Office Building, Room 309, Washington, DC 20515; (202) 226-7270. Web http://www.house.gov/budget. Wayne Struble, staff director; Monica Murphy, intern coordinator.

Jurisdiction summary: Congressional budget process and the Congressional Budget Office.

China Investigation Committee, Longworth House Office Building, Room 1036, Washington, DC 20515; (202) 226-3511. Dean McGrath, staff director.

Jurisdiction summary: Inquiry on the transfer of technology, information, advice, goods, or services to the People's Republic of China that might have enhanced its development of missiles, weapons of mass destruction, or other weapons.

Commerce Committee, Rayburn House Office Building, Room 2125, Washington, DC 20515; (202) 225-2927. Web http://www.house.gov/commerce. Gabriel Glynn, personnel specialist; Marie Burns, intern coordinator.

Jurisdiction summary: Interstate and foreign commerce, biomedical research and development, consumer affairs and consumer protection, health and health facilities, national energy policy, securities and exchanges, and travel and tourism.

Education and the Workforce Committee, Rayburn House Office Building, Room 2181, Washington, DC 20515; (202) 225-4527. Web http://www.house.gov/ed_workforce. Bob Baylor, assistant to the staff director; Deborah Samantar, office manager.

Jurisdiction summary: Education, labor, school food programs, and vocational rehabilitation.

Government Reform Committee, Rayburn House Office Building, Room 2154, Washington, DC 20515: (202) 225-5074. Web http://www.house.gov/reform. Grace Washbourne, administrative officer; Robin Butler, office manager.

Jurisdiction summary: Civil service, federal paperwork reduction, government operations, Postal Service, public information and records, and the relationship of the federal government to the states and municipalities.

House Administration Committee, Longworth House Office Building, Room 1309, Washington, DC 20515; (202) 225-8281. Web http://www.house.gov/cha. Cathy Abernathy, staff director; Christy Kirschenamm, staff assistant.

Jurisdiction summary: Federal elections, Library of Congress, Smithsonian Institution, travel by House members, campaign finances of House candidates, and House employment.

International Relations Committee, Rayburn House Office Building, Room 2170, Washington, DC 20515; (202) 225-5021. Web http://www.house.gov/international_relations. Richard J. Garon Jr., chief of staff; Jill Weber, senior staff associate.

Jurisdiction summary: Relations of the United States with foreign nations, export controls, foreign loans, international commodity agreements, declarations of war, commercial relations with foreign nations, international economic policy, protection of American citizens abroad, and UN organizations.

Judiciary Committee, Rayburn House Office Building, Room 2138, Washington, DC 20515; (202) 225-3951. Web http://www.house.gov/judicary. John Dudas, staff director; Michele Manon-Utt, administrative assistant.

Jurisdiction summary: Civil and criminal judicial proceedings, bankruptcy, civil liberties, constitutional amendments, immigration and naturalization, national penitentiaries, patents, copyrights, trademarks, presidential succession, and subversive activities affecting the internal security of the United States.

Resources Committee, Longworth House Office Building, Room 1324, Washington, DC 20515; (202) 225-2761. Web http://www.house.gov/resources. Lloyd Jones, chief of staff; Chris Kennedy, chief clerk.

Jurisdiction summary: Fisheries and wildlife, forest reserves and national parks, international fishing agreements, irrigation, Indians and Indian lands, mineral resources on public lands, and oceanography.

Rules Committee, The Capitol, Room H-312, Washington, DC 20515; (202) 225-9191. Web http://www.house.gov/rules. Vince Randazzo, majority staff director; George C. Crawford, minority staff director; Danielle Simonetta, staff assistant/intern coordinator.

Jurisdiction summary: Rules of the House.

Science Committee, Rayburn House Office Building, Room 2320, Washington, DC 20515; (202) 225-6371. Web http://www.house.gov/science/welcome.htm. Tisch Schwartz, chief clerk.

Jurisdiction summary: Energy and environmental research and development, astronautical and civil aviation research and development, marine research, and the National Weather Service.

Select Intelligence Committee, The Capitol, Room H-405, Washington, DC 20515; (202) 225-4121. John I. Millis, staff director; Michael W. Sheehy, minority staff director.

Jurisdiction summary: Legislative and budget authority over the National Security Agency and the director of central intelligence, the Defense Intelligence Agency, the National Security Agency, intelligence activities of the Federal Bureau of Investigation, and other components of the federal intelligence community.

Small Business Committee, Rayburn House Office Building, Room 2361, Washington, DC 20515; (202) 225-5821. Web http://www.house.gov/smbiz. Mark Strand, director; Bridget Luketin, staff assistant.

Jurisdiction summary: Assisting small business and participation of small businesses in federal procurement and government contracts.

Standards of Official Conduct Committee, The Capitol, Room HT-2, Washington, DC 20515; (202) 225-7103. Web http://www.house.gov/ethics. Robert Walker, staff director and chief counsel.

Jurisdiction summary: Measures relating to the Code of Official Conduct.

Transportation and Infrastructure Committee, Rayburn House Office Building, Room 2165, Washington, DC 20515; (202) 225-9446. Web http://www.house. gov/transportation. Carol Wood, administrator; Cheryl McCullough, intern coordinator.

Jurisdiction summary: Transportation and transportation safety, the Coast Guard, federal management of emergencies and natural disasters, navigation, pollution of navigable waters, road construction, and bridges and dams.

Veterans' Affairs Committee, Cannon House Office Building, Room 335, Washington, DC 20515; (202) 225-3527. Web http://veterans.house.gov. Carl Commenator, staff director; Mary McDermott, intern coordinator.

Jurisdiction summary: Veterans' issues, including military cemeteries, vocational rehabilitation, education, pensions, and veterans' hospitals.

Ways and Means Committee, Longworth House Office Building, Room 1102, Washington, DC 20525: (202) 225-3625. Web http://www.house.gov/ ways_means. A. L. Singleton, chief of staff; Janice A. Mays, minority chief counsel.

Jurisdiction summary: Revenue issues, reciprocal trade agreements, customs, Social Security, and tax-exempt foundations and charitable trusts.

Joint Committees

Joint Library of Congress Committee, Longworth House Office Building, Room 1309, Washington, DC 20515; (202) 225-8281. Catherine Fanucchi, House staff contact; Ed Edens, Senate staff contact; Christy Kirschenmann, intern coordinator.

Jurisdiction summary: Library of Congress and the Botanic Garden.

Joint Printing Committee, Hart Senate Office Building, Room 818, Washington, DC 20510: (202) 225-8281. Cathy Abernathy, staff director.

Jurisdiction summary: Printing of federal government publications.

Joint Taxation Committee, Longworth House Office Building, Room 1015, Washington, DC 20515; (202) 225-3621. Web http://www.house.gov/jct. Lindy Paull, chief of staff; Michael Born, administrative assistant.

Jurisdiction summary: The federal system of internal revenue taxes.

Senate Committees

Agriculture, Nutrition, and Forestry Committee, Russell Senate Office Building, Room 328A, Washington, DC 20510; (202) 224-2035. Web http://www.senate.gov/~agriculture. Robert Sturm, chief clerk.

Jurisdiction summary: Agricultural and food issues, including soil conservation, farm credit, food stamp programs, forestry, human nutrition, meat inspection, rural development, and school nutrition programs.

Appropriations Committee, The Capitol, Room 128, Washington, DC 20510; (202) 224-3471. Web http://www.senate.gov/~appropriations. Donna Pate, chief clerk.

Jurisdiction summary: Appropriation of revenue.

Armed Services Committee, Russell Senate Office Building, Room 228, Washington, DC 20510; (202) 224-3871. Web http://www.senate.gov/~armed_ services. Romie L. Brownlee, staff director; David Lyles, minority staff director. Jurisdiction summary: Defense and defense policy.

Banking, Housing, and Urban Affairs Committee, Dirksen Senate Office Building, Room 534, Washington, DC 20510; (202) 224-7391. Web http://www. senate.gov/~banking. Wayne Abernathy, staff director; Steven Harris, minority staff director.

Jurisdiction summary: Banking and financial institutions, price controls, economic stabilization and growth, export and foreign trade promotion, federal monetary policy, international economic policy, public and private housing, and urban development and mass transit.

Budget Committee, Dirksen Senate Office Building, Room 621, Washington, DC 20510; (202) 224-0642. Web http://www.senate.gov/~budget. G. William Hoagland, staff director; Bruce King, minority staff director; Maureen O'Neill, intern coordinator.

Jurisdiction summary: The federal budget.

Commerce, Science, and Transportation Committee, Dirksen Senate Office Building, Room 508, Washington, DC 20510; (202) 224-5115. Web http://www. senate.gov/~commerce. Mark Buse, staff director; Ivan A. Schlager, minority staff director; Virginia Pounds, professional staff member.

Jurisdiction summary: Interstate commerce and transportation, coastal zone management, inland waterways, nonmilitary aeronautical and space sciences, regulation of consumer products and services, science and technology research and development, and sports.

Energy and Natural Resources Committee, Dirksen Senate Office Building, Room 304, Washington, DC 20510; (202) 224-4971. Web http://www.senate. gov/~energy. Andrew Lundquist, staff director; Robert Simmon, minority staff director; Allyson Kennett, executive assistant.

Jurisdiction summary: Energy policy, solar energy, mining, nonmilitary development of nuclear energy, national parks, wild and scenic rivers, public lands and forests, and historic sites.

Environment and Public Works Committee, Dirksen Senate Office Building, Room 410, Washington, DC 20510; (202) 224-6176. Web http://www.senate. gov/~epw. Jimmie Powell, majority staff director; J. Thomas Sliter, minority staff director; Amy Dunatham, professional staff.

Jurisdiction summary: Environmental policy, including air and water pollution, toxic substances, fisheries and wildlife, ocean dumping, solid waste disposal and recycling, and water resources, in addition to public works, bridges and dams, and regional economic development.

Finance Committee, Dirksen Senate Office Building, Room 219, Washington, DC 20510; (202) 224-4515. Web http://www.senate.gov/~finance. Carol Petty, finance committee.

Jurisdiction summary: Taxes and other revenue measures, customs, and Social Security.

Foreign Relations Committee, Dirksen Senate Office Building, Room 450, Washington, DC 20510; (202) 224-4651. Web http://www.senate.gov/~foreign. Susan Oursler, special assistant to staff director.

Jurisdiction summary: Relations of the United States with foreign nations, including economic and military assistance, international aspects of nuclear energy, intervention abroad and declarations of war, national security, foreign trade, international environmental and scientific affairs, and the United Nations.

Governmental Affairs Committee, Dirksen Senate Office Building, Room 340, Washington, DC 20510; (202) 224-4751. Web http://www.senate.gov/~gov_ affairs. Dee Kefalaf, executive assistant.

Jurisdiction summary: Census and statistics, federal civil service, congressional organization, government information, District of Columbia, Postal Service, and government efficiency and effectiveness.

Health, Education, Labor, and Pensions Committee, Dirksen Senate Office Building, Room 428, Washington, DC 20510; (202) 224-5375. Web http://www. senate.gov/~labor. Mark Powden, staff director; Michael Myers, minority staff director.

Jurisdiction summary: Education, labor, health, aging, arts and humanities, biomedical research and development, equal employment opportunity, handicapped people, occupational safety and health, public health, and student loans.

Indian Affairs Committee, Hart Senate Office Building, Room 838, Washington, DC 20510; (202) 224-2251. Web http://www.senate.gov/~scia. Paul Moorehead, staff director; Patricia Zell, minority staff director.

Jurisdiction summary: Indian issues, including Indian land management, education, health, and loan programs.

Judiciary Committee, Dirksen Senate Office Building, Room 224, Washington, DC 20510; (202) 224-5225. Web http://www.senate.gov/~judiciary. Manus Cooney, chief counsel and staff director; Katharine Dillingham, office manager.

Jurisdiction summary: Civil and criminal judicial proceedings, penitentiaries, bankruptcy, civil liberties, constitutional amendments, government information, immigration and naturalization, patents, copyrights, trademarks, and monopolies and unlawful restraints of trade.

Rules and Administration Committee, Russell Senate Office Building, Room 305, Washington, DC 20510; (202) 224-6352. Web http://www.senate.gov/~rules. Tamara Somerville, staff director; Nan Mosher, office manager.

Jurisdiction summary: Senate administration, federal elections, presidential succession, Government Printing Office, the Capitol, the Library of Congress, the Smithsonian Institution, and the Botanic Garden.

Select Ethics Committee, Hart Senate Office Building, Room 220, Washington, DC 20510; (202) 224-2981. Victor M. Baird, staff director and chief counsel.

Jurisdiction summary: Standards and conduct of Senate members and employees.

Select Intelligence Committee, Hart Senate Office Building, Room 211, Washington, DC 20510; (202) 224-1700. Nick Rostow, majority staff director; Art Grant, minority staff director.

Jurisdiction summary: Legislative and budgetary authority over the Central Intelligence Agency, Defense Intelligence Agency, National Security Agency, and intelligence activities of the Federal Bureau of Investigation and other components of the federal intelligence community.

Small Business Committee, Russell Senate Office Building, Room 428A, Washington, DC 20510; (202) 224-5175. Web http://www.senate.gov/~sbc. Emilia DiSanto, staff director and chief counsel; Patricia Forbes, minority staff director; Theresa Hoggard, office manager.

Jurisdiction summary: The Small Business Administration and problems of small business.

Special Committee on Aging, Dirksen Senate Office Building, Room G31, Washington, DC 20510; (202) 224-5364. Web http://www.senate.gov/~aging. Ted Totman, staff director; Michelle Prejean, minority staff director; Patricia Hameister, office manager.

Jurisdiction summary: Problems and opportunities of older people, including health, income, employment, housing, and care and assistance.

Special Committee on the Year 2000 Technology Problem, Dirksen Senate Office Building, Room B40, Washington, DC 20510; (202) 224-5224. Web http://www. senate.gov/~y2k. Robert Cresanti, majority staff director; Wilke Green, minority staff director.

Jurisdiction summary: Study of the effects of the year 2000 technology problem on the executive and judicial branches of the federal government, state governments, and private-sector operations in the United States and abroad.

Veterans' Affairs Committee, Russell Senate Office Building, Room 412, Washington, DC 20510; (202) 224-9126. Web http://www.senate.gov/~veterans. C. Charles Battaglia, staff director; James R. Gottlieb, minority staff director.

Jurisdiction summary: Veterans' issues, including national cemeteries, pensions, veterans' hospitals, medical care, vocational rehabilitation, and education.

5

Working
in Washington:
Federal Agencies and
Departments

An aura of mystery surrounds the hiring process at federal agencies and departments. It's hard to know why, because today it's easier than ever to learn about federal vacancies and apply for jobs. Most likely, the aura is a carryover from the days—not so long ago—when federal hiring was a convoluted process.

However, the system today still has its quirks that make applying for a job at federal agencies or departments—all of which are part of the executive branch—different from applying for a job in the private sector or even in Congress. To successfully apply for a federal job, you must know how the system works: how jobs are advertised, how to create federal-style application documents, and how to determine exactly what kinds of documents you must submit. This chapter will tell you everything that you need to know.

Working for the federal government has many advantages. Here are just a few:

- The federal government is the nation's largest employer, and has *lots* of jobs. In January 1999, in the Washington area the executive branch employed 293,584 people—and that's just civilians. Between January 1998 and January 1999, federal agencies and departments together hired an average of 3,272 new employees *each month* in the Washington area.

- Federal jobs provide excellent job security. It's true that the federal government has been on a "downsizing" kick in recent years, but the vast majority of the job cuts have occurred through attrition and buyouts, not layoffs. The downsizing trend has now largely tapered off. In fact, between January 1998 and January 1999, the number of executive branch employees in the Washington area actually *grew* by 4,254.

- In general, federal wages and benefits are good, and are comparable to those in the private sector. Federal workers in the Washington area got a 3.68 percent pay hike in January 1999, raising the salary of the average white-collar employee to $59,307.

- Workers who retire from the federal government receive excellent pension benefits.

FEDERAL EMPLOYEE JOB ATTITUDES (IN PERCENTAGES)

Question	Favorable	Unfavorable	No Opinion
How would you rate the overall quality of work being done in your work group?	72	8	20
Supervisors/team leaders understand and support employees' family/personal life responsibilities.	65	19	17
Differences among individuals are respected and valued.	62	18	19
Considering everything, how satisfied are you with your job?	62	25	13
A spirit of cooperation and teamwork exists in my immediate work unit.	60	27	13
Employees receive the training they need to perform their jobs.	54	30	16
Overall, how good a job do you feel is being done by your immediate supervisor/team leader?	52	25	23
At the place I work, my opinions seem to count.	51	33	16
How satisfied are you with the recognition you receive for doing a good job?	42	42	16
Recognition and rewards are based on merit.	32	46	21
Creativity and innovation are rewarded.	30	45	25
Corrective actions are taken when employees do not meet performance standards.	28	44	28

Source: National Partnership for Reinventing Government.

Note: This table reproduces selected questions from a random survey of nearly 14,000 employees at forty-eight federal agencies and departments. The survey was conducted by the National Partnership for Reinventing Government, the Office of Personnel Management, the Merit Systems Protection Board, and the Federal Aviation Administration. The results were announced in December 1998. Totals do not always add to 100 percent because of rounding.

Perhaps most important, working for the federal government gives you a hands-on chance to make a difference. Federal workers are often portrayed as faceless, paper-pushing bureaucrats, but that's not fair. They truly are the lifeblood of our governmental system, providing the services and benefits that citizens of the United States have come to expect.

The federal government touches nearly every aspect of our lives today, giving federal workers a huge role in our society. They determine what new drugs can be brought to market, help domestic victims of natural disasters, inspect workplaces for safety, operate public assistance programs, protect our national parks, enforce food safety regulations, investigate discrimination against minorities, protect national security, administer U.S. foreign policy, and much more.

While performing all these jobs, they also establish public policy. Sometimes their role in creating policy is open and direct, such as when a federal agency drafts legislation that it then asks Congress to pass. Often, though, the federal workers' role in creating policy is more subtle and not widely known. Typically, they become most involved *after* Congress passes a bill and public debate over an issue has quieted.

They become involved because most bills Congress passes are fairly vague about implementation. The bill usually states a goal—X shall be accomplished—but leaves it to subject experts at agencies and departments to work out the details.

As the old saying goes, "The devil is in the details." The working out of those details—the nitty-gritty of how a law will be implemented and enforced—can give workers at federal agencies and departments tremendous power.

Usually the details are spelled out in "rules" written by the agencies and departments. Take the Clean Air Act of 1990. Although Congress spent thirteen years writing and arguing about the bill before finally passing it, the law lacked many details. Shortly after passage, the Environmental Protection Agency predicted that it would have to write between *300 and 400* rules to implement the single law. Those rules ultimately determined who had to do what to make the air cleaner, and today have a tremendous impact on everyone from motorists to large industrial plants.

Rule making by federal agencies is an essential component of the U.S. governmental system, according to political scientist Cornelius M. Kerwin. "Rulemaking is a significant government function that has, since the start of the Republic, played an increasingly pivotal role in the definition of American public policy and law," he wrote in his book *Rulemaking: How Government Agencies Write Law and Make Policy* (1999, p.36).

Federal agencies and departments also exert tremendous power by deciding how laws and rules will be enforced. For example, the Occupational Safety and Health Administration enforces a huge number of workplace safety laws and rules. The agency has limited resources, so it must decide which laws and rules receive the most enforcement attention. This setting of priorities means that certain laws and rules are thoroughly enforced, and others receive little attention. OSHA employees make those decisions—not members of Congress.

Qualifications and Salaries for Federal Jobs

Federal agencies and departments need workers with a huge variety of backgrounds. To get some ideas about the kinds of federal jobs that your specific major might qualify you for, turn to Appendix B, titled "Federal Jobs by College Major." You'll see that any major qualifies you for some jobs, although others require specific majors. Some federal jobs don't even require a college degree.

However, college degrees do make a difference in qualifying you for a higher starting salary. Most federal salaries are set by the General Schedule, which has 15 grades. Assuming you have no work experience, here's where you'd start on the scale in Washington based on various diplomas and degrees:

- High school diploma: GS-2. Salary in 1999: $16,205.

- Undergraduate degree: GS-5. Salary in 1999: $22,208.

- Undergraduate degree with a B average or above: GS-7. Salary in 1999: $27,508.

- Master's degree: GS-9. Salary in 1999: $33,650.

- Doctoral degree: GS-11. Salary in 1999: $40,714.

Nearly all federal jobs are awarded based on merit, not your political support of the current administration. That's unlike the old days, when patronage ruled and jobs were handed out based on political allegiance. The patronage system thrived until 1881, when a disgruntled job seeker assassinated President James Garfield after Garfield refused to give him a job. Shortly thereafter, Congress reformed the civil service system.

Today, only about 3,000 executive branch positions go to political appointees. These are sensitive positions that involve working closely with the president and his cabinet members.

How to Search for a Federal Job

Unfortunately, there's no central place where you can submit your resume to be considered for job openings at all federal agencies and departments. But you don't need to trudge from agency to agency inquiring about vacancies—all executive branch openings aside from political appointments are posted together and are easily accessible from anywhere in the world.

With that said, there are advantages to actually being in Washington when you're hunting for an executive branch job. If you're in Washington, you can seek informational interviews at agencies of particular interest and you can network—a useful component in any Washington job search. But the announcements of federal job openings, which tell you everything you need to apply for specific positions, can be accessed from anywhere.

Executive branch job openings are described in formal documents called vacancy announcements. Each job opening gets it own announcement, which can run to several pages. Written in typically leaden government prose, the announcements list the job title, grade and pay levels, application opening and closing dates, number of vacancies for the position, job location, job duties, general and special requirements, application procedures, and person to contact for additional information.

Vacancy announcements for federal agencies and departments are distributed by the U.S. Office of Personnel Management, which provides access through four different electronic systems. Here are brief descriptions of each:

- The USAJOBS Web site (http://www.usajobs.opm.gov) is the best way to gain access to the job listings because of its completeness and ease of use. The job listings are divided by category: professional career, entry-level professional, senior executive, worker-trainee, series, clerical and technician, trades and labor, agency job search, summer, and alphabetical job search.

  Within each category you can search for job openings by a number of variables. These differ somewhat among the categories, but you often can search by job type, keyword, geographic region, state, salary, and experience level.

  Best of all, for most of the jobs the full text of the vacancy announcement is provided online. The announcement tells you everything you need to know to apply for a job, and having it available online saves you the trouble of calling the agency to request a copy.

  A particularly handy feature is an online resume builder that you can use to create a federal-style resume. Once you complete the resume online, you can print it or save it to the system for future editing.

  Finally, the Web site also has lots of general information about federal salary and benefits, veterans preferences, student employment, the Presidential Management Intern Program, federal job scams, and related topics.

- The USAJOBS Electronic Bulletin Board (telnet://fjob.opm.gov or 912-757-3100) is available on the Internet through telnet or as a dial-in bulletin board system. It has many similar features to the Web site—searchable job listings, general federal employment information, and the full text of many vacancy announcements—but it's not as easy to use. You also must register online before using the system, although registration is free. Bulletin board files also are available through FTP at ftp://ftp.fjob.opm.gov, although the job listings are not searchable at the FTP site.

* USAJOBS by Phone (912-757-3000, TDD 912-744-2299) offers telephone access to job listings, information about federal salaries and benefits, and related information. The system does not provide the text of vacancy announcements, although you can leave a message asking that an announcement be mailed to you.

    Local telephone numbers for USAJOBS by Phone are available in more than a dozen cities:

> Alabama (Huntsville): 205-837-0894
> California (San Francisco): 415-744-5627
> Colorado (Denver): 303-969-7050
> District of Columbia: 202-606-2700
> Georgia (Atlanta): 404-331-4315
> Hawaii (Honolulu): 808-541-2791
> Illinois (Chicago): 312-353-6192
> Michigan (Detroit): 313-226-6950
> Minnesota (Minneapolis-St. Paul): 612-725-3430
> Missouri (Kansas City): 816-426-5702
> North Carolina (Raleigh): 919-790-2822
> Ohio (Dayton): 937-225-2720
> Pennsylvania (Philadelphia): 215-597-7440
> Texas (San Antonio): 210-805-2402
> Virginia (Norfolk): 757-441-3355
> Washington (Seattle): 206-553-0888

* Federal job information kiosks are available at federal office buildings and other locations around the country. These touch-screen computers provide job listings and general information about working for the federal government. They do not provide the full text of vacancy announcements, although you can use the kiosk to order copies of vacancy announcements. For a list of the locations of federal job information kiosks, see the sidebar titled "Kiosks Provide Federal Job Information."

How to Decipher Federal Vacancy Announcements

Federal vacancy announcements may be some of the most boring, poorly written documents produced by the federal government—and that's saying a lot. But carefully reading the documents and following their

KIOSKS PROVIDE FEDERAL JOB INFORMATION

Touch-screen computers at kiosks around the country provide listings of federal job openings from the U.S. Office of Personnel Management. They also have information about working for the federal government, and let you request application packages. The job information is similar to that provided through OPM's Internet sites, bulletin boards, and dial-in telephone systems.

Most states have at least one kiosk, and the computers are generally available Monday through Friday during normal business hours. Kiosks are available at the following locations:

Alabama
520 Wynn Dr., N.W.
Huntsville

Alaska
Federal Building
222 W. 7th Ave.
Room 156
Anchorage

Arizona
VA Medical Center
650 E. Indian School Rd.
Building 21, Room 141
Phoenix

Arkansas
Federal Building
700 W. Capitol, 1st Floor Lobby
Little Rock

California
801 I St.
Sacramento

Colorado
Department of Social Services
Employment Center
2200 West Alameda Avenue, #5B
Denver

Connecticut
Federal Building
450 Main St., Lobby
Hartford

District of Columbia
Theodore Roosevelt Federal Building
1900 E St., N.W., Room 1416
Washington, DC

Florida
Downtown Jobs and Benefits Center
Florida Job Service Center
401 N.W. 2nd Ave., Suite N-214
Miami

Florida Job Service Center
1001 Executive Center Drive
First Floor
Orlando

Georgia
Richard B. Russell Federal Building
Main Lobby, Plaza Level
75 Spring St., S.W.
Atlanta

Hawaii
Federal Building, Room 5316
300 Ala Moana Blvd.
Honolulu

Department of Army
Army Civilian Personnel Office
Army Garrison, Building T-1500
Fort Shafter

Illinois
77 West Jackson Blvd.
1st Floor Lobby
Chicago

Indiana
Minton-Capehart Federal Building
575 N. Pennsylvania St., Room 339
Indianapolis

Louisiana
Federal Building
423 Canal St., 1st Floor Lobby
New Orleans

Maine
Federal Office Building
40 Western Ave.
Augusta

Maryland
George H. Fallon Building
Lombard St. & Hopkins Plaza, Lobby
Baltimore

Massachusetts
Thomas P. O'Neill Jr. Federal Building
10 Causeway St., 1st Floor
Boston

Michigan
477 Michigan Ave.
Room 565
Detroit

Minnesota
Bishop Henry Whipple Federal Building
1 Federal Dr., Room 501
Ft. Snelling

Missouri
Federal Building
601 E. 12th St., Room 134
Kansas City

New Hampshire
Thomas McIntyre Federal Building
80 Daniel St., 1st Floor Lobby
Portsmouth

New Jersey
Peter J. Rodino Federal Building
970 Broad St.
2nd Floor near Cafeteria
Newark

New Mexico
New Mexico State Job Service
501 Mountain Rd. N.E., Lobby
Albuquerque

New York
Leo W. O'Brian Federal Building
Clinton Ave. & North Pearl
Basement Level
Albany

Thaddeus T. Dulski Federal Building
111 West Huron St., 9th Floor
Buffalo

Jacob K. Javits Federal Building
26 Federal Plaza, Lobby
New York City

World Trade Center
Cafeteria
New York City

James M. Hanley Federal Building
100 S. Clinton St.
Syracuse

Ohio
Federal Building
200 W. 2nd St., Room 509
Dayton

Oklahoma
Career Connection Center
7401 N.E. 23rd St.
Oklahoma City

Oregon
Federal Building
1220 S.W. Third Ave., Room 376
Portland

Bonneville Power Administration
905 N.E. 11th Ave.
Portland

Dept. of Army & Corps of Engineers
Duncan Plaza
Portland

(Box continues)

Pennsylvania
Federal Building
228 Walnut St., Room 168
Harrisburg

William J. Green Jr. Federal Building
600 Arch St., 2nd Floor
Philadelphia

Federal Building
1000 Liberty Ave., 1st Floor Lobby
Pittsburgh

Reading Postal Service
2100 N. 13th St.
Reading

Puerto Rico
U.S. Federal Building
150 Carlos Chardon Ave., Room 328
San Juan

Rhode Island
380 Westminster
Mall Lobby
Providence

Tennessee
Naval Air Station Memphis
Transition Assistance Center
7800 3rd Ave., Building South 239
Millington

Texas
Federal Building, 1st Floor Lobby
1100 Commerce St.
Dallas

Federal Building
700 East San Antonio St., Lobby
El Paso

Mickey Leland Federal Building
1919 Smith St., 1st Floor Lobby
Houston

Federal Building
1st Floor Lobby
727 East Durango
San Antonio

Utah
Utah State Job Service
720 South 2nd East, Reception Area
Salt Lake City

Vermont
Federal Building
11 Elmwood Ave., 1st Floor Lobby
Burlington

Virginia
Federal Building
200 Granby St.
Norfolk

Washington
Federal Building
915 Second Ave., Room 110
Seattle

instructions to the letter is essential to getting a federal job.

One of the reasons to carefully study the documents is to pick up on the language they use. You'll want to parrot some of these words in your application materials to make it clear you meet the job requirements.

To help you decipher federal vacancy announcements—and create the strongest possible application—I'll briefly describe the sections found in a typical announcement. If you'd like to see samples of actual announcements, turn to Appendix C, titled "Federal Government Vacancy Announcements":

- Summary: Before the actual vacancy announcement begins, there are usually several paragraphs—typically all in capital letters—that summarize some of the announcement's most important details. In this section you'll commonly find the job title, the open period (the dates during which you can apply), the "grade" on the federal government pay scale, the salary, the job's promotion potential on the federal government pay scale, the announcement number, and the name and telephone number of a contact at the hiring agency, among other information. Pay special attention to a paragraph in this section labeled "Remarks." This summarizes the application procedure and the documents you must submit.

- Heading: This section typically repeats information from the summary, including the job title, the grade on the federal government pay scale, the announcement number (which you need to include on your cover letter, resume, and mailing envelope), the open period, and the basic application procedure. Take special note of the last date in the open period. Typically, applications must be received—not mailed—by this date. Open periods commonly last just two to four weeks, so you have to move quickly. Also check the line titled "Area of Consideration." If it says "all sources," anyone can apply. However, sometimes only people from a particular region or with particular characteristics are allowed to apply, and that's indicated in this section.

- Duties: Read this section very carefully, because you'll want to clearly state in your application materials how your skills and experiences qualify you to handle the job's duties.

- Qualification Requirements: This section describes any special qualifications you must have to be considered for the job. Usually the qualifications involve degrees or work experience in areas related to the job.

- Basis of Rating: You'll learn what factors the hiring agency will consider when evaluating candidates in this section. By carefully studying these factors, you can learn what aspects of your background, education, and experience to stress the most in your application materials.

- Knowledge, Skills, and Abilities (KSAs): KSAs are supplemental statements you write about specific aspects of your ability to perform the job. This section of the announcement will tell you what to write about. Some topics are broad: "Ability to meet and deal tactfully with other professionals." Others are quite specific: "Ability to apply auditing procedures to financial investigations." Most vacancy announcements have five KSA topics. You're not required to write KSAs, but failing to do so dramatically hurts your chances of getting the job. I'll have more to say about how to write KSAs later in this chapter.

- Significant Working Conditions: This section will tell you about any unusual working conditions for the job, such as a requirement that you travel.

- How to Apply: Finally, you get the details about exactly how to apply. This section describes what materials you must submit and provides the address where you send them.

How to Prepare Your Federal Application Materials

For most jobs in the private sector, you have quite a bit of flexibility in deciding what information to include on your application materials. This is *not* true when applying for a federal job. Federal jobs have very precise application requirements, and if you fail to meet any of them your stuff will be trashed. That's why it's so important to carefully study the vacancy announcement to find out exactly what's required.

The first step is to create the main document about your background. For most federal jobs, you have three options: Standard Form 171, Optional Form 612, or a resume—but not just any resume (more about this in a minute).

Standard Form 171 used to be the standard application form for federal government jobs. It's a lengthy form with lots and lots of little boxes, and can run to dozens of pages when you add all the supplementary materials it requires. It's no longer officially used, and you don't want to fool with it unless you're currently a federal employee and already have one filled out from a previous job.

Optional Form 612 is shorter and more flexible. You can tailor it at least somewhat to the job for which you're applying, which is helpful. Optional Form 612 is reproduced in Appendix D and you can obtain a copy from the USAJOBS Web site (http://www.usajobs.opm.gov/b1a.htm #OF612).

If you choose to submit a resume instead of Optional Form 612, it must contain specific information. You can't just submit your standard resume. Your federal resume must contain:

- The vacancy announcement number, along with the title and grade(s) of the job for which you're applying.

- Your full name and mailing address (with Zip Code), and your day and evening telephone numbers (with area codes).

- Your Social Security number.

- Your country of citizenship.

- Your veterans' preference (if you qualify).

- Your reinstatement eligibility (if you're a former federal employee).

- The highest federal civilian grade you've held (if you're a current or former federal employee). Also include the job series and the dates you held the job.

- The name, city, and state of your high school (and its Zip Code if you know it), along with the date of your diploma or GED.

- For each college or university attended, the name, city, and state (and Zip Code if you know it), your majors, and the type and year of any degrees you received. If you didn't get a degree, list the total credits earned and whether they're semester or quarter hours.

- For each paid and nonpaid work experience related to the job for which you're applying, the job title (including the series and grade if a federal job), duties and accomplishments, employer's name and address, supervisor's name and telephone number, starting and ending dates (month and year), number of hours per week, and salary.

- Indicate whether your current supervisor can be contacted.

- Any job-related training courses you've taken; include the title and year.

- Any job-related skills you possess, such as foreign languages, computer software or hardware, or special tools.

- Job-related certificates and licenses you've received (current only).

- Job-related honors, awards, and special accomplishments such as publications, memberships in professional or honor societies, leadership activities, public speaking, and performance awards.

When writing your federal resume, tailor it as much as possible to the specific job for which you're applying. This is where the vacancy announcement can be a big help. Feel free to copy its language where applicable.

Don't worry about keeping your federal resume to one page—with all the information required, it will be next to impossible. Most federal resumes run several pages.

Like I said earlier, for most federal jobs you can submit either the Optional Form 612 or the federal-style resume. So which should you use? There aren't any hard and fast rules. One good idea is to call the contact person listed on the vacancy announcement and ask if he or she prefers one or the other. Some federal hiring officials love forms (because they're standard and can be easily scored), although others prefer to see what you can do with a resume. If the contact doesn't have a preference, choose the format that best showcases your skills.

When you finish the Optional Form 612 or federal-style resume, you should turn to the KSAs listed in the vacancy announcement. These are the statements you write about your special knowledge, skills, and abilities related to the job. Use a separate sheet of paper for each KSA (there are usually five listed in the vacancy announcement), and write a maximum of one page for each.

The KSAs are your chance to stand out, to show how your training and experience specially qualify you for the job. Describe any applicable projects you've directed, classes you've taken, awards you've won, or anything else that shows you can do the job. Remember: Just like with your resume, detail your accomplishments instead of just listing your job duties.

Last—but certainly not least—you need to write a strong cover letter. You might want to focus on your greatest strength and explain how it applies to the job duties listed in the vacancy announcement. For more details about how to write cover letters, turn back to Chapter 1.

Once you finish writing the cover letter, the KSAs, and your Optional Form 612 or federal-style resume, carefully proofread everything several times and ask your roommate/significant other/spouse/friend/parent/sibling to do likewise. Then put everything in an envelope and send it to the address listed in the vacancy announcement. It's a good idea to include the announcement number on the envelope.

One word of caution: There are stiff penalties if you lie in any of your federal application materials. Your application can be rejected if the lie is found during the hiring process, you can be fired if it's found after you're hired, and you can be fined or even jailed at any time. So resist any urge to "embellish."

If you're selected for an interview, don't worry about having to take a civil service test. The government no longer has a general civil service test. Tests are only given to applicants for certain types of positions, usually clerical jobs.

Moving Beyond Vacancy Announcements

If you're interested in working for the executive branch, don't limit yourself to responding to vacancy announcements. Like with any job search, you also need to network and to do as many informational interviews as possible.

It's a good idea to call the personnel offices at agencies and departments of particular interest. Explain that you're interested in working for the agency, and ask if there's anything special you should know about how it announces job openings, inquire about any special hiring programs it may offer, and ask any other questions you have.

Most important, try to arrange an informational interview. During this interview you can ask about the agency's mission, the kinds of jobs that are available, how people are typically hired, and much more. Even if the agency doesn't have any current openings, you'll learn a lot about the agency and make some networking contacts that could be very useful down the road.

The Presidential Management Intern Program

If you're a graduate student, one of the best ways to get a federal job is through the Presidential Management Intern (PMI) Program. Competition for PMI positions is stiff, but if you win one your federal career will get a strong jump start.

The program, which started in 1977, is aimed at attracting outstanding graduate students to the federal service. Students who are selected participate in a two-year internship program, after which many are offered permanent government positions.

Students from all academic disciplines are eligible. The only requirement is that you have a commitment to a career in analyzing and managing public policies and programs.

Graduate schools and university placement offices receive applications in September. To be considered, you must be nominated by the dean, chair, or program director of your graduate program. You can't be nominated by an individual professor, advisor, or placement counselor. Each school devises its own competitive process to select PMI nominees.

All nominees attend regional interviews, and finalists are notified in March. Each finalist receives a handbook that lists PMI positions and contact points in federal agencies, but the student must arrange for his or her own position. All federal departments and more than fifty agencies have hired Presidential Management Interns.

Presidential Management Interns are paid. They start at the GS-9 grade level, which in 1999 translated into a salary of $33,650 in Washington. Those who successfully complete the first year are promoted to the GS-11 level, which in 1999 paid $40,714. And those who are offered permanent jobs after their internship can be promoted to the GS-12 level, which paid $48,796 in 1999.

Presidential Management Interns start at a given job in an agency, but during their internship rotate to other parts of their agency, other agencies, or even other branches of the federal government. They also attend seminars, briefings, and conferences, and receive special training.

To read an interview with a Presidential Management Intern at the U.S. Agency for International Development, see the box titled "Profile: Aparna Mohan."

How to Avoid Federal Job Scams

You may have seen newspaper classified ads or Internet sites that promise to help you find and apply for federal jobs—for a fee. You need to check

PROFILE: APARNA MOHAN

Aparna Mohan's career is on the fast track, thanks to her selection as a Presidential Management Intern. Only a few months into her two-year paid internship at the U.S. Agency for International Development (USAID), she's already been offered a full-time job at the agency when her internship ends. And after that, the possibilities are limitless.

Mohan works in the Asian–Near East Bureau at USAID, which administers the U.S. foreign economic assistance program. She's up to her neck in hot issues: the Asian financial crisis, a Mideast trade and investment initiative, and efforts to stop trafficking in women and children. "What's especially exciting for me is hearing on the news every night the fruits of my daily endeavors," Mohan said.

Mohan received her undergraduate degree in international studies at Johns Hopkins University, and stayed at Hopkins's School of Advanced International Studies to get a master's degree in international conflict management and international economics. She never thought she'd end up working for the federal government.

"I had always sworn that I did not ever want to grow up and become a bureaucrat," she said. "But the more I learned about my field of international development and conflict, whatever I did was going to have some collaboration with USAID and the U.S. government." She wanted to learn about the government perspective, and her PMI stint gives her a chance "at seeing what goes on behind closed doors," she said. "There's no other way to get this kind of education about what the U.S. government does than to get in the thick of it."

When Mohan was interviewed for this book, her work primarily involved supporting USAID programs overseas. But shortly after the interview, she was scheduled to travel to New Delhi, India, for three months to work on child labor and information technology initiatives.

With a career slot waiting for her, Mohan plans to remain at USAID for at least a while after her internship ends. After that, she expects to move around and shift directions frequently. "I don't think anybody in our generation starts out in a job and expects to be there for thirty years like people did in past generations," she said. Mohan is especially interested in pursuing opportunities at the United Nations or the World Bank.

But in the meantime, Mohan is happy in her work with USAID. "I have a good conscience every day when I go home," she said. "I think I'm making a contribution and a difference."

these carefully before sending along your money, because many are scams.

Be especially wary of any company that tries to confuse you by using a name like "U.S. Agency for Career Advancement." It sounds like a federal agency, but it's not.

Some legitimate companies "add value" to the basic government job listings and charge for the service. For example, some search the U.S. Office of Personnel Management Web site and send you e-mail messages about any openings that meet your criteria. If you don't want to search the site yourself, such a service may be worthwhile.

So how do you identify the scammers? The Federal Trade Commission and the Office of Personnel Management offer these tip-offs:

- The classified ad or oral sales pitch implies an affiliation with the federal government, guarantees jobs or high test scores, or states that "no experience is necessary."

- The ad claims to offer information about "hidden" or unadvertised federal jobs.

- The ad provides a toll-free telephone number. When you call, in many cases the operator will encourage you to buy a "valuable" booklet with job listings and practice test questions.

- The ad lists a pay-per-call number that you must dial to receive more information.

The bottom line: All information about federal job openings is available for free from the U.S. Office of Personnel Management. If you buy job information from a private company, make sure you're getting something valuable for your money.

Executive Branch Contacts

ONLINE DIRECTORIES

Executive Office of the President Current Competitive Vacancies
http://www.whitehouse.gov/Jobs

Want to work at the White House? This page lists vacancies in the Executive Office of the President, which includes the Council of Economic Advisers, Council on Environmental Quality, Office of Administration, Office of Management and Budget, Office of National Drug Control Policy, Office of Science and Technology Policy, and Office of United States Trade Representative. The page usually lists just a few jobs.

Federal Job Source
http://www.statejobs.com/fed.html

This site provides links to jobs pages at Web sites operated by dozens of federal agencies and departments. Some of the links duplicate those at Uncle Sam (next listing), but others are unique. The Federal Job Source also has links to some congressional job sites.

Uncle Sam: Employment Opportunities with the Feds
http://www.lib.memphis.edu/gpo/employ.htm
This site from the University of Memphis Library has links to jobs pages at Web sites operated by dozens of federal agencies and departments. The pages typically list job openings, application instructions, and information about working for the agency.

USAJOBS
http://www.usajobs.opm.gov
This site from the U.S. Office of Personnel Management is the best online source for executive branch job listings. You can search the job openings by numerous variables, and the full text of the vacancy announcement is provided for most jobs. For more information about USAJOBS, see p. 78.

DEPARTMENTS

Agriculture Dept., 1400 Independence Ave. S.W., Washington, DC 20250; (202) 720-3631. Fax (202) 720-2166, Web http://www.usda.gov, personnel office (202) 720-5781. Dan Glickman, secretary; Lynn Campbell, personnel assistant.
Serves as principal adviser to the president on agricultural policy; works to increase and maintain farm income and to develop markets abroad for U.S. agricultural products.

Commerce Dept., 14th St. and Constitution Ave. N.W., #5854, Washington, DC 20230; (202) 482-2112. Fax (202) 482-2741, Web http://www.doc.gov, personnel office (202) 482-5138 (recording). William M. Daley, secretary; Theresa Tolson, intern coordinator.
Acts as principal adviser to the president on federal policy affecting industry and commerce; promotes national economic growth and development, competitiveness, international trade, and technological development; provides business and government with economic statistics, research, and analysis; encourages minority business; promotes tourism.

Defense Dept., The Pentagon 20301-1000; (703) 695-5261. Fax (703) 697-9080, Web http://www.defenselink.mil, civilian personnel office (703) 696-2720. William S. Cohen, secretary.
Civilian office that develops national security policies and has overall responsibility for administering national defense; responds to public and congressional inquiries about national defense matters.

Education Dept., 400 Maryland Ave. S.W., Washington, DC 20202; (202) 401-3000. Fax (202) 401-0596, Web http://www.ed.gov, personnel office (202) 401-0553, job line recording (202) 401-0559. Richard W. Riley, secretary.
Establishes education policy and acts as principal adviser to the president on education matters; administers and coordinates most federal assistance programs on education.

Energy Dept., 1000 Independence Ave. S.W., Washington, DC 20585; (202) 586-6210. Fax (202) 586-4403, Web http://www.doe.gov, personnel office (202) 586-2731. Bill Richardson, secretary.

Decides major energy policy issues and acts as principal adviser to the president on energy matters, including trade issues, strategic reserves, and nuclear power.

Health and Human Services Dept., 200 Independence Ave. S.W., #615F, Washington, DC 20201; (202) 690-7000. Fax (202) 690-7203, Web http://www.os. dhhs.gov, personnel office (301) 504-3301. Donna E. Shalala, secretary; Evelyn Brockington, director of personnel.

Acts as principal adviser to the president on health and welfare plans, policies, and programs of the federal government. Encompasses the Health Care Financing Administration, the Administration for Children and Families, the Public Health Service, and the Centers for Disease Control and Prevention.

Housing and Urban Development Dept., 451 7th St. S.W., #10000, Washington, DC 20410; (202) 708-0417. Fax (202) 619-8365, Web http://www.hud.gov, personnel office (202) 708-0408, job line recording (202) 708-3203. Andrew M. Cuomo, secretary; Gwen Dickson, intern coordinator.

Responsible for federal programs concerned with housing needs, fair housing opportunity, and improving and developing the nation's urban and rural communities.

Interior Dept., 1849 C St. N.W., #6156, Washington, DC 20240; (202) 208-7351. Fax (202) 208-6956, Web http://www.doi.gov, personnel office (800) 336-4562 (recording). Bruce Babbitt, secretary; Delores Chacon, intern coordinator.

Principal U.S. conservation agency. Manages most federal land; responsible for conservation and development of mineral and water resources; responsible for conservation, development, and use of fish and wildlife resources; operates recreation programs for federal parks, refuges, and public lands; and preserves and administers the nation's scenic and historic areas.

Justice Dept., 950 Pennsylvania Ave. N.W., #5111, Washington, DC 20530; (202) 514-2001. Fax (202) 514-4371, Web http://www.usdoj.gov, personnel office (202) 514-6877. Janet Reno, attorney general; Angelina Thomas, intern coordinator.

Investigates and prosecutes violations of federal laws; represents the government in federal cases and interprets laws under which other departments act. Supervises federal corrections system; administers immigration and naturalization laws.

Labor Dept., 200 Constitution Ave. N.W., #S2018, Washington, DC 20210; (202) 693-6000. Fax (202) 219-8822, Web http://www.dol.gov, personnel office (202) 219-6646 (recording). Alexis Herman, secretary.

Promotes and develops the welfare of U.S. wage earners; administers federal labor laws; acts as principal adviser to the president on policies relating to wage earners, working conditions, and employment opportunities.

State Dept., Main State Bldg., 2201 C St. N.W., Washington, DC 20520; (202) 647-5291. Fax (202) 647-5939, Web http://www.state.gov, personnel office (202) 647-7284 (civil service recording), (703) 875-7490 (foreign service recording). Madeleine K. Albright, secretary.

Directs and coordinates U.S. foreign relations and interdepartmental activities of the U.S. government overseas.

Transportation Dept., 400 7th St. S.W., Washington, DC 20590; (202) 366-1111. Fax (202) 366-7202, Web http://www.dot.gov, personnel office (202) 366-9392, job line recording (202) 366-9391. Rodney Slater, secretary.

Deals with most areas of transportation.

Treasury Dept., 1500 Pennsylvania Ave. N.W., #3330, Washington, DC 20220; (202) 622-1100. Fax (202) 622-0073, Web http://www.ustreas.gov, personnel office (202) 622-1029. Lawrence H. Summers, secretary.

Serves as chief financial officer of the government and adviser to the president on economic policy. Formulates and recommends domestic and international financial, economic, tax, and broad fiscal policies; manages the public debt.

Veterans Affairs Dept., 810 Vermont Ave. N.W., Washington, DC 20420; (202) 273-4800. Fax (202) 273-4877, Web http://www.va.gov, personnel office (202) 273-4901. Togo D. West Jr., secretary; Kim Broden, staff assistant.

Administers programs benefiting veterans, including disability compensation, pensions, education, home loans, insurance, vocational rehabilitation, medical care at veterans' hospitals and outpatient facilities, and burial benefits.

INDEPENDENT ESTABLISHMENTS AND GOVERNMENT CORPORATIONS

African Development Foundation, 1400 Eye St. N.W., 10th Floor, Washington, DC 20005; (202) 673-3916. Fax (202) 673-3810, Web http://www.adf.gov. Connie Smith-Field, personnel director.

Established by Congress to work with and fund organizations and individuals involved in development projects at the local level in Africa. Gives preference to projects involving extensive participation by local Africans.

Central Intelligence Agency, CIA Headquarters, Langley, VA; (703) 482-1100. Fax (703) 482-6790, Web http://www.cia.gov. George J. Tenet, director.

Coordinates the intelligence functions of government agencies as they relate to national security and advises the National Security Council on those functions; gathers and evaluates intelligence relating to national security and distributes the information to government agencies in the national security field.

Commission on Civil Rights, 624 9th St. N.W., #700, Washington, DC 20425; (202) 376-7700. Fax (202) 376-7672, Web http://www.usccr.gov. Myrna Hernandez, personnel officer.

Assesses federal laws and policies of government agencies and studies legal developments to determine the nature and extent of denial of equal protection under the law on the basis of race, color, religion, sex, national origin, age, or disability in many areas, including employment, voting rights, education, administration of justice, and housing.

Commodity Futures Trading Commission, 3 Lafayette Center, 1155 21st St. N.W., Washington, DC 20581; (202) 418-5030. Fax (202) 418-5525, Web http://www.cftc.gov, personnel office (202) 418-5010 (recording). Keith Ross, recruitment; Frank Alston, intern coordinator.

Enforces federal statutes relating to commodity futures and options, including gold and silver futures and options.

Consumer Product Safety Commission, 4330 East-West Hwy., Bethesda, MD 20814; (301) 504-0990. Fax (301) 504-0281, e-mail info@cpsc.gov, Web http://www.cpsc.gov, personnel office (301) 504-0100. Jackie Taylor, human resources specialist.

Establishes and enforces product safety standards; collects data; studies the causes and prevention of product-related injuries; identifies hazardous products and recalls them from the marketplace.

Corporation for National Service, 1201 New York Ave. N.W., Washington, DC 20525; (202) 606-5000. Fax (202) 565-2784, Web http://www.cns.gov, personnel office (202) 606-5000, ext. 330. Crystal Cooper, human resources assistant; Tara West, assistant to chief of staff.

Independent corporation that administers federally sponsored domestic volunteer programs to provide disadvantaged citizens with services. Programs include AmeriCorps, AmeriCorps-VISTA (Volunteers in Service to America), AmeriCorps-NCCC (National Civilian Community Corps), Learn and Serve America, and the National Senior Service Corps.

Defense Nuclear Facilities Safety Board, 625 Indiana Ave. N.W., #700, Washington, DC 20004; (202) 694-7000. Fax (202) 208-6518, Web http://www.dnfsb.gov. Susan Dickerson, head of personnel.

Independent board created by Congress and appointed by the president to provide external oversight of Energy Dept. defense nuclear facilities and make recommendations to the secretary of energy regarding public health and safety.

Environmental Protection Agency, 401 M St. S.W., Washington, DC 20460; (202) 260-4700. Fax (202) 260-0279, Web http://www.epa.gov, personnel office (202) 260-3267 (recording). Carol Browner, administrator; Yvonne Robinson, intern coordinator.

Administers federal environmental policies, research, and regulations; provides information on environmental subjects, including water pollution, pollution prevention, hazardous and solid waste disposal, air and noise pollution, pesticides and toxic substances, and radiation.

Equal Employment Opportunity Commission, 1801 L St. N.W., Washington, DC 20507; (202) 663-4001. Fax (202) 663-4110, Web http://www.eeoc. gov, personnel office (202) 663-4337. Arlethia Monroe, assistant director of personnel.

Works to end job discrimination by private and government employers based on race, color, religion, sex, national origin, or age. Works to protect employees against reprisal for protest of employment practices alleged to be unlawful in hiring, promotion, firing, wages, and other terms and conditions of employment.

Export-Import Bank of the United States, 811 Vermont Ave. N.W., Washington,

DC 20571; (202) 565-3500. Fax (202) 565-3505, Web http://www.exim.gov, personnel office (202) 565-3300. Nancy Leighow, personnel assistant.

Independent agency of the U.S. government. Aids in financing exports of U.S. goods and services; offers direct credit to borrowers outside the United States; guarantees export loans made by commercial lenders, working capital guarantees, and export credit insurance; conducts an intermediary loan program.

Farm Credit Administration, 1501 Farm Credit Dr., McLean, VA 22102-5090; (703) 883-4007. Fax (703) 734-5784, e-mail info-line@fca.gov, Web http://www.fca.gov, personnel office (703) 883-4139 (recording). Marsha Pyle Martin, chair.

Examines and regulates the cooperative Farm Credit System, which comprises federal land bank associations, production credit associations, federal land credit associations, agriculture credit associations, farm credit banks, and banks for cooperatives.

Federal Communications Commission, 445 12th St. S.W., Washington, DC 20554; (202) 418-1000. Fax (202) 418-2801, Web http://www.fcc.gov, personnel office (202) 418-0130, job line recording (202) 418-0101. Mary Beth Richards, deputy under managing director.

Regulates interstate and foreign communications by radio, television, wire, cable, microwave, and satellite.

Federal Deposit Insurance Corp., 550 17th St. N.W., Washington, DC 20429; (202) 898-6974. Fax (202) 898-3778, Web http://www.fdic.gov, personnel office (202) 942-3311. Donna Tanoue, chair; Joyce Orr, personnel specialist.

Insures deposits in national banks, state banks, and savings and loans. Conducts examinations of insured state banks that are not members of the Federal Reserve System.

Federal Election Commission, 999 E St. N.W., Washington, DC 20463; (202) 694-1000. Fax (202) 219-3880, Web http://www.fec.gov, personnel office (202) 694-1080. Scott E. Thomas, chair.

Formulates, administers, and enforces policy with respect to the Federal Election Campaign Act of 1971 as amended, including campaign disclosure requirements, contribution and expenditure limitations, and public financing of presidential nominating conventions and campaigns.

Federal Emergency Management Agency, 500 C St. S.W., Washington, DC 20472; (202) 646-3923. Fax (202) 646-3930, Web http://www.fema.gov, personnel office (202) 646-4040. Sheryl Wither, personnel staffing specialist.

Assists state and local governments in preparing for and responding to natural and other emergencies. Coordinates emergency preparedness and planning for all federal agencies and departments.

Federal Housing Finance Board, 1777 F St. N.W., Washington, DC 20006; (202) 408-2587. Fax (202) 408-1435, Web http://www.fhfb.gov. Barbara Fisher, director of human resources.

Regulates and supervises the credit and financing operations of the twelve Federal Home Loan Banks, which provide a flexible credit reserve for member institutions engaged in home mortgage lending.

Federal Labor Relations Authority, 607 14th St. N.W., #410, Washington, DC 20424-0001; (202) 482-6500. Fax (202) 482-6635, Web http://www.flra.gov, personnel office (202) 482-6660. Sheyla White, personnel management specialist.

Oversees the federal labor-management relations program; administers the law that protects the right of federal employees to organize, bargain collectively, and participate through labor organizations of their own choosing.

Federal Maritime Commission, 800 N. Capitol St. N.W., #1046, Washington, DC 20573; (202) 523-5725. Fax (202) 523-0014, Web http://www.fmc.gov, personnel office (202) 523-5773. Harold J. Creel Jr., chair.

Regulates foreign ocean shipping of the United States; reviews agreements on rates, schedules, and other matters filed by common carriers for compliance with antitrust laws and grants antitrust immunity.

Federal Mediation and Conciliation Service, 2100 K St. N.W., Washington, DC 20427; (202) 606-8100. Fax (202) 606-4251, Web http://www.fmcs.gov, personnel office (202) 606-5460. Bill Carlisle, director of human resources; Cheryl Louer, personnel management specialist.

Assists labor and management representatives in resolving disputes in collective bargaining contract negotiation through voluntary mediation and arbitration services.

Federal Mine Safety and Health Review Commission, 1730 K St. N.W., #600, Washington, DC 20006; (202) 653-5660. Fax (202) 653-5030. Richard Baker, executive director.

Holds fact-finding hearings and issues orders affirming, modifying, or vacating the labor secretary's enforcement actions regarding mine safety and health.

Federal Reserve System, 20th and C Sts. N.W., Washington, DC 20551; (202) 452-3201. Fax (202) 452-3819, personnel office (202) 452-3880, job line recording (202) 452-3038. Kathy Cimral, manager.

Sets U.S. monetary policy. Supervises the Federal Reserve System and influences credit conditions through the buying and selling of treasury securities in the open market, by fixing the amount of reserves depository institutions must maintain, and by determining discount rates.

Federal Retirement Thrift Investment Board, 1250 H St. N.W., #200, Washington, DC 20005; (202) 942-1600. Fax (202) 942-1676. Roger W. Mehle, executive director.

Administers the Thrift Savings Plan, a tax-deferred, defined contribution plan that permits federal employees to save for additional retirement security under a program similar to private 401(k) plans.

Federal Trade Commission, 6th St. and Pennsylvania Ave. N.W., Washington, DC 20580; (202) 326-2100. Web http://www.ftc.gov, personnel office (202) 326-2021 (recording). Del Smith, intern coordinator.

Promotes policies designed to maintain strong competitive enterprise within the U.S. economic system. Monitors trade practices and investigates cases involving monopoly, unfair restraints, or deceptive practices. Enforces Truth in Lending and Fair Credit Reporting Acts.

General Services Administration, 1800 F St. N.W., #6137, Washington, DC 20405; (202) 501-0800. Web http://www.gsa.gov, personnel office (202) 501-0370. David J. Barram, administrator.

Establishes policies for managing federal government property, including construction and operation of buildings and procurement and distribution of supplies and equipment.

Inter-American Foundation, 901 N. Stuart St., 10th Floor, Arlington, VA 22203; (703) 306-4301. Fax (703) 306-4363, Web http://www.iaf.gov. Marcia Savoie, personnel manager; Bob Sogge, intern coordinator.

Quasi-governmental organization. Supports small-scale Latin American and Caribbean social and economic development efforts through grassroots development programs, grants, and fellowships.

Merit Systems Protection Board, 1120 Vermont Ave. N.W., Washington, DC 20419; (202) 653-7101. Fax (202) 653-7130, Web http://www.mspb.gov, personnel office (202) 653-5916. Ben Erdreich, chair.

Independent quasi-judicial agency that handles hearings and appeals involving federal employees; protects the integrity of federal merit systems and ensures adequate protection for employees against abuses by agency management.

National Aeronautics and Space Administration, 300 E St. S.W. (mailing address: NASA Headquarters, Mail Code A, Washington, DC 20546); (202) 358-1801. Fax (202) 358-2811, Web http://www.nasa.gov, personnel office (202) 358-1543. Daniel Goldin, administrator.

Conducts research on problems of flight within and outside the earth's atmosphere; develops, constructs, tests, and operates experimental aeronautical and space vehicles; conducts activities for exploration of space.

National Archives and Records Administration, 8601 Adelphi Rd., #4200, College Park, MD 20740-6001; (301) 713-6410. Fax (301) 713-7141, e-mail inquire@nara.gov, Web http://www.nara.gov, jobline (800) 827-4898, personnel office (301) 713-6760. Mary Rephlow, intern coordinator.

Identifies, preserves, and makes available federal government documents of historic value; administers a network of regional storage centers and archives and operates the presidential library system.

National Capital Planning Commission, 801 Pennsylvania Ave. N.W., #301, Washington, DC 20576; (202) 482-7200. Fax (202) 482-7272, Web http://www. ncpc.gov. Theresa Jackson, administrative officer.

Central planning agency for the federal government in the national capital region, which includes the District of Columbia and suburban Maryland and Virginia.

National Credit Union Administration, 1775 Duke St., Alexandria, VA 22314-3428; (703) 518-6300. Fax (703) 518-6319, Web http://www.ncua.gov, personnel office (703) 518-6510. Janis Lomax, personnel assistant; Claire Whiting, personnel management specialist.

Regulates all federally chartered credit unions; charters new credit unions; supervises and examines federal credit unions and insures their member accounts up to $100,000. Insures state-chartered credit unions that apply and are eligible.

National Foundation on the Arts and the Humanities, 1100 Pennsylvania Ave. N.W., Washington, DC 20506; (202) 682-5400. Fax (202) 682-5603. Phillis Littles, personnel specialist.

Encourages national progress in the arts and humanities. Consists of the National Endowment for the Arts, the National Endowment for the Humanities, the Federal Council on the Arts and the Humanities, and the Institute of Museum Services.

National Labor Relations Board, 1099 14th St. N.W., Washington, DC 20570-0001; (202) 273-1790. Fax (202) 273-4276, Web http://www.nlrb.gov, personnel office (202) 273-3980. Emma Johnson, assistant chief of personnel.

Works to prevent and remedy unfair labor practices by employers and labor unions; conducts elections among employees to determine whether they wish to be represented by a labor union for collective bargaining purposes.

National Mediation Board, 1301 K St. N.W., #250E, Washington, DC 20572; (202) 692-5000. Fax (202) 692-5080, personnel office (202) 523-5010. June King, chief financial officer.

Mediates labor disputes in the railroad and airline industries; determines and certifies labor representatives for those industries.

National Railroad Passenger Corp. (Amtrak), 60 Massachusetts Ave. N.E., Washington, DC 20002; (202) 906-3960. Fax (202) 906-2850, Web http://www.amtrak.com. Loraine Green, head of human resources.

Quasi-public corporation created by the Rail Passenger Service Act of 1970 to improve and develop intercity passenger rail service.

National Science Foundation, 4201 Wilson Blvd., Arlington, VA 22230; (703) 306-1234. Fax (703) 306-0109, e-mail info@nsf.gov, Web http://www.nsf.gov, personnel office (703) 306-1182. Rita R. Colwell, director.

Sponsors scientific and engineering research; develops and helps implement science and engineering education programs; fosters dissemination of scientific information; and assists with national science policy planning.

National Transportation Safety Board, 490 L'Enfant Plaza East S.W., Washington, DC 20594; (202) 314-6010. Fax (202) 314-6018, Web http://www.ntsb.gov, personnel office (202) 314-6230. James E. Hall, chair.

Promotes transportation safety through independent investigations of accidents and other safety problems. Makes recommendations for safety improvement.

Nuclear Regulatory Commission, 11555 Rockville Pike, Rockville, MD 20852; (301) 415-1759. Fax (301) 415-1672, e-mail opa@nrc.gov, Web http://www.nrc.gov, personnel office (301) 415-7400. Alison Hoffman, human resources specialist.

Regulates commercial uses of nuclear energy. Monitors and regulates the import and export of nuclear material and equipment.

Occupational Safety and Health Review Commission, 1120 20th St. N.W., 9th Floor, Washington, DC 20036-3419; (202) 606-5374. Fax (202) 606-5050. Christine McKenzie, personnel specialist.

Independent agency that adjudicates disputes between private employers and the Occupational Safety and Health Administration arising under the Occupational Safety and Health Act of 1970.

Office of Government Ethics, 1201 New York Ave. N.W., #500, Washington, DC 20005-3917; (202) 208-8000. Fax (202) 208-8037, Web http://www.usoge.gov. Stephen D. Potts, director.

Administers executive branch policies relating to financial disclosure, employee conduct, and conflict-of-interest laws.

Office of Personnel Management, 1900 E St. N.W., Washington, DC 20415; (202) 606-1000. Fax (202) 606-2573, Web http://www.opm.gov, personnel office (202) 606-2424 (recording). Terri Coleman, recruitment.

Administers civil service rules and regulations; sets policy for personnel management, labor-management relations, work force effectiveness, and employment within the executive branch; manages federal personnel activities, including recruitment, pay comparability, and benefit programs.

Office of Special Counsel, 1730 M St. N.W., #300, Washington, DC 20036-4505; (202) 653-7122. Fax (202) 653-5151, Web http://www.osc.gov. Timothy Hanmatel, deputy special counsel.

Investigates allegations of prohibited personnel practices and prosecutes individuals who violate civil service regulations. Receives and refers employee disclosures of waste, fraud, inefficiency, mismanagement, and other violations in the federal government.

Panama Canal Commission, 1825 Eye St. N.W., #1050, Washington, DC 20006-5402; (202) 634-6441. Fax (202) 634-6439, Web http://www.pananet.com/pancanal. William J. Connolly, secretary.

Independent federal agency that manages, operates, and maintains the Panama Canal and its complementary works, installations, and equipment.

Peace Corps, 1111 20th St. N.W., Washington, DC 20526; (202) 692-2100. Fax (202) 692-2101, Web http://www.peacecorps.gov. Theresa Spikes, personnel management specialist.

Promotes world peace and mutual understanding between the United States and developing nations. Administers volunteer programs to assist developing countries in education, the environment, health, small business development, agriculture, and urban development.

Pension Benefit Guaranty Corp., 1200 K St. N.W., #210, Washington, DC 20005-4026; (202) 326-4010. Fax (202) 326-4016. Sharon Barbee-Fletcher, director of human resources.

Self-financed U.S. government corporation. Insures private-sector, defined-benefit pension plans; guarantees payment of retirement benefits subject to certain limitations established in the Employee Retirement Income Security Act of 1974 (ERISA).

Postal Rate Commission, 1333 H St. N.W., #300, Washington, DC 20268-0001; (202) 789-6800. Fax (202) 789-6886. Cyril Pittack, personnel officer; Margaret Crenshaw, intern coordinator.

Submits recommendations to the governors of the U.S. Postal Service concerning proposed changes in postage rates, fees, and mail classifications.

Securities and Exchange Commission, 450 5th St. N.W., Washington, DC 20549; (202) 942-0100. Fax (202) 942-9646, Web http://www.sec.gov, personnel office (202) 942-4150 (recording). Jennifer Scardino, chief of staff; Veronica Gillette, support staff.

Requires public disclosure of financial and other information about companies whose securities are offered for public sale, traded on exchanges, or traded over the counter; issues and enforces regulations to prevent fraud in securities markets and investigates securities frauds and violations; supervises operations of stock exchanges and activities of securities dealers, investment advisers, and investment companies.

Selective Service System, 1515 Wilson Blvd., Arlington, VA 22209-2425; (703) 605-4010. Fax (703) 605-4006, Web http://www.sss.gov. Shiela Haley, manager of personnel; Evelyn Townes, personnel management specialist.

Supplies the armed forces with personnel when authorized; registers male citizens of the United States ages 18 to 25.

Small Business Administration, 409 3rd St. S.W., #7000, Washington, DC 20416; (202) 205-6605. Fax (202) 205-6802, Web http://www.sba.gov, personnel office (202) 205-6780. Jose Mendez, recruitment officer.

Provides small businesses with financial and management assistance; offers loans to victims of floods, natural disasters, and other catastrophes; licenses, regulates, and guarantees some financing of small-business investment companies; conducts economic and statistical research on small businesses.

U.S. International Trade Commission, 500 E St. S.W., Washington, DC 20436; (202) 205-2000. Fax (202) 205-2104, Web http://www.usitc.gov, personnel office (202) 205-2651. Lynn M. Bragg, chair.

Provides Congress, the president, and government agencies with technical information and advice on trade and tariff matters. Determines the impact of imports on U.S. industries in anti-dumping and countervailing duty investigations. Directs actions against certain unfair trade practices, such as intellectual property infringement.

U.S. Postal Service, 475 L'Enfant Plaza S.W., Washington, DC 20260-0001; (202) 268-2000. Fax (202) 268-4860, Web http://www.usps.gov, personnel office (202) 268-3646. Deborah Brown, human resources specialist.

Offers postal service throughout the country as an independent establishment of the executive branch.

U.S. Trade and Development Agency, 1621 N. Kent St., #200, Arlington, VA 22209; (703) 875-4357. Fax (703) 875-4009, e-mail info@tda.gov, Web http://www.tda.gov. J. Joseph Grandmaison, director.

Assists U.S. companies exporting to developing and middle-income countries. Provides technical assistance and identifies commercial opportunities in these countries.

6

Working
in Washington:
Interest Groups and
Think Tanks

Washington interest groups and think tanks tackle the hottest social and political issues of the day, making them interesting and exciting places to work. Working for one also can help prepare you for a variety of career options.

Interest groups and think tanks have many similarities. The most notable is that both attempt to influence and shape public policy, whether it's by issuing a report, holding a press conference, sending experts to Capitol Hill to testify before Congress, writing an op-ed article for a newspaper's editorial page, supplying experts to debate on TV talk shows, or cultivating friendships with reporters. Yet interest groups and think tanks also have some differences—in style, in focus, and frequently in the precise nature of their attempts to influence the political process. The similarities make it logical to include interest groups and think tanks together in this chapter, but the differences make it prudent to discuss them separately.

The Basics of Interest Groups

Washington offers an astounding range of interest groups. They focus either on a single issue, like the Electronic Privacy Information Center, or a series of related issues, like the American Civil Liberties Union. It seems like every major political issue—and lots of minor ones as well—has an interest group, and some topics like the environment and foreign policy have numerous groups. Washington has interest groups devoted to women's rights, gun control, health care reform, smoking, Middle East policy, abortion, privacy and free speech on the Internet, minority rights, Africa policy, hunger, gay rights, children, Cuba policy, and virtually every other topic you can think of.

Some of the best-known groups include Action on Smoking and Health, American Association of Retired Persons, American Israel Public Affairs Committee, Bread for the World, Center for Science in the Public Interest, Children's Defense Fund, Common Cause, Greenpeace, Handgun Control, Human Rights Campaign, National Abortion and Reproductive Rights Action League, National Organization for Women, National Rifle Association, National Right to Life Committee, Public Citizen, TransAfrica, and Zero Population Growth.

Interest groups profess to represent the "public" interest, and many seek to counterbalance the influence that businesses and trade associations have in Washington. Most get their funding from a combination of foundation grants, membership fees, donations, and publication sales, and some also earn money through government contracts.

Interest groups differ from think tanks most markedly in how they try to influence public policy. Whereas think tanks traditionally stay slightly above the day-to-day political fray, interest groups dive right in. Some have lobbyists—either professionals or volunteers—who push the group's viewpoint on Capitol Hill, with the White House, and with federal agencies and departments.

One of the least known but most important jobs of many interest groups is responding to proposed federal rules. For example, when the Food and Drug Administration proposes a new food safety rule, the Center for Science in the Public Interest and other food-oriented interest groups study the rule and file formal comments either supporting or opposing it (food manufacturers and their trade associations do likewise). Some interest groups also propose new rules of their own in petitions to federal agencies.

Pluses and Minuses of Working for an Interest Group

Some of the advantages of working for an interest group include the following:

- The psychic rewards can be enormous. Working day in and day out on issues that you care about and where you're making a difference is extremely rewarding. Meaningful work can in turn impart meaning to your life.

- Interest groups need people with skills in a wide range of areas—marketing, public relations, computer systems, policy analysis, writing, editing, research, fundraising, desktop publishing, events management, and graphic design, just to name a few—so there are lots of opportunities.

- Age is not as big a barrier as it can be in regimented business and government offices. If you have skills, you'll have opportunities to flourish—and to quickly move up—no matter how young you are.

PROFILE: LUCY ALDERTON

Lucy Alderton's degree is in animal sciences. So what's she doing in Washington? Working for the Center for Science in the Public Interest (CSPI), where she's project coordinator for the food safety program. "I'm actually using my major—it's great," she said.

Alderton never expected to work in the political arena. Her training was in the hard sciences—not political science—and she intended to go into veterinary medicine. But after graduating from the University of Maryland, she decided that vet school wasn't for her. Alderton then started trying to decide what to do next.

She applied to graduate school and in the meantime attended a conference presented by one of Washington's major public interest groups. She grabbed a copy of the list of participants and started arranging informational interviews with groups on the list. One of them was CSPI, where she applied for an internship. Before CSPI could respond she saw its ad in the *Washington Post* listing the food safety opening. Her application packet included an unusual item: a paper she wrote about the impact of stress on cattle during shipment.

That was three years ago, and ever since Alderton has worked at CSPI drafting comments about proposed regulations, researching outbreaks of foodborne illnesses, studying mad cow disease, helping prepare for press conferences, and helping prepare factsheets and lobbying materials for presentations to the Food and Drug Administration, the U.S. Department of Agriculture, and the Department of Health and Human Services.

Her on-the-job training has taught her how science issues are lobbied and how scientific facts can be used to argue both sides of a political issue. "It's been very interesting for me to learn the political side of the job," she said.

Alderton definitely thinks she's making a difference. "I see how USDA and FDA and Congress respond to our issues," she said. "They really respond to what we say." In one recent example, Alderton helped write a petition to the FDA seeking limits on bacteria in raw oysters. In response to the petition, the FDA opened a formal inquiry and may eventually impose regulations.

Alderton enjoys working at CSPI because its key issues—food safety and nutrition—are hot. "People always ask me about my job and what's going on—it's always in the media," she said. "People are interested in the work we do here because everybody eats."

Asked if there's a downside to her job, Alderton said: "It can get crazy. A lot of times we are understaffed, so you're being pulled in five different directions and doing everything." She added, though, that she has learned a lot by having to tackle many different subjects. Her advice for others who might want to work at a public interest group? "I think a lot of it is networking," she said. "Try everything—volunteering, going to conferences, informational interviewing, just getting out there."

- Interest groups are chronically understaffed, so you'll likely get to wear many hats and find lots of outlets for your creativity.

- The narrow focus of most interest groups lets you zero in on a particular topic and develop expertise.

- You get to meet and work with some really interesting, committed people, both within your own organization and in other groups with which you may form coalitions. Your coworkers will likely be bright, idealistic, creative, hard working, and motivated.

- The working environment is often collegial, with people working together and supportive instead of battling one another for the next rung on the corporate ladder.

- Working at an interest group opens the door to a variety of career options. You can move up within your initial group, move to a similar interest group, or use your job as a springboard to opportunities in government and business.

There also are disadvantages, some of which include the following:

- The pay can be low, especially in smaller organizations and entry-level jobs. Frequently, you can expect to make 25 percent less than you would at a comparable job in business or government.

- Some interest groups suffer from poor administration and organization, which can lead to chaotic working conditions.

- You probably won't be using state-of-the-art equipment, and your working space may be cramped.

- Interest groups are chronically understaffed, so the hours can be long and you may have to juggle many responsibilities.

- The narrow focus of most interest groups can be constraining, limiting your ability to learn about other topics.

- The work can be disheartening. You may care about your issue from the bottom of your heart, know that your position is in the public interest, and even be on the side of the angels. Unfortunately, angels don't always put you over the top when it comes to counting votes in Congress or persuading a federal agency to take a certain action. Washington is a conservative town where change occurs slowly, so you'll frequently find yourself butting your head against the wall. Often, you'll need to take strength from small victories that push your issue and the debate in the right direction. Progress occurs in increments in Washington when it occurs at all, which can be discouraging.

- Sometimes interest groups can be torn apart by internal conflict. People who work in them tend to be opinionated, and although everyone may agree on the ultimate goal, there may be competing visions of how to achieve it.

How to Get a Job with an Interest Group

If you'd like to work at an interest group, you must be able to demonstrate your commitment—especially if you want to work at a group devoted to social change. One of the best ways to do this is to volunteer. You don't necessarily have to volunteer at the group where you'd like to work, although this is a great way to get your foot in the door. Instead, if you're still in school volunteer at anything from a soup kitchen to a political organization in your community. If you're in Washington for an internship and you're not already interning at a public interest group, see if you can spare a few hours a week to volunteer at one.

Besides showing your commitment, this volunteer work gains you experience—a critical factor in getting hired in Washington. Interest groups don't necessarily require paid job experience. In fact, volunteer experience may be even better. Remember to highlight your volunteer experiences on your resume, and you might want to mention them in your cover letter to a public interest group.

Another excellent way to get your foot in the door at an interest group is to intern. Virtually all interest groups embrace interns. And because the groups are usually understaffed, interns often get substantive assignments. An internship gives you a chance to demonstrate your skills and commitment, lets you network with people in your office and related organizations, and puts you in the right spot should a permanent job become available.

Interest groups typically advertise job openings in the *Washington Post,* on their own Web sites, and on some of the online directories listed at the end of this chapter. Responding to help-wanted ads is important, but should be only one part of your search if you want an interest group job.

Informational interviews and the networking that goes along with them can be critical to landing an interest group job. Pick out some of the groups that most appeal to you and try to arrange informational interviews. But one caution: Before you go on *any* interview—even an informational interview—make sure you research the organization. This is easier than ever before because nearly all groups have Web sites that offer their missions, publications, press releases, and other materials. You do *not* want to walk into an informational interview and say, "Gee, what do you folks do here?" People in Washington do not have time to entertain idiots. You should have at least a basic understanding of the group's background so you can ask substantive questions about its work and operations.

Don't assume that you know what the group does just because you know what subject it focuses on. For example, although both Greenpeace and the National Wildlife Federation are environmental groups, their exact focus, missions, cultures, and methods of operation are very different.

One big benefit of informational interviews is they get you in the office, where simply looking around can at least give you an impression of a particular group. How chaotic is the office? Are the computers up to date? Does the staff look like a group where you'd fit in?

The other benefit, of course, is that you get to ask questions about the group and how it operates. You also can get leads for other informational interviews. For example, you might ask, "Are there other interest groups that you recommend I talk to as I explore job opportunities?" There's about a 99 percent chance that your interviewer will say yes and rattle off the names of some groups. You then can ask, "Are there any particular individuals at those groups that I should contact?" Another useful question: "Are there any interest groups that I might want to avoid?"

These questions are especially useful because folks who work in Washington's interest group community are usually well connected to their counterparts throughout the city. You never know where a particular contact might lead.

A personal example: When I moved to Washington more than a decade ago, I interviewed several times for a reporting job at a magazine published by a leading public interest group. It looked like the job was mine. Then the editor called with bad news. The group's finances were a tad shaky, so it was cutting back and would not be filling the job for which I'd applied.

As I applied for other jobs, one day a second interest group called. Would I be interested in coauthoring a book with its executive director? You bet! But how had they heard of me, because I had not applied there and was new in town? It turned out they called the editor of the magazine where I'd been turned down to see if she knew of any available writers. She had given them my name. That initial book assignment launched my freelance writing career.

Here are a few final tips for getting a job with an interest group:

• When writing to an interest group about a job, tailor your cover letter and—where practical—your resume as much as possible to its issue. Show that you have a particular interest in the issue. Don't just send a standard cover letter to all interest groups.

- Before going for an actual job interview at an interest group, thoroughly research the organization. At a minimum, you should know what issue(s) it tackles and its positions, where its funding comes from, a little about its history (especially how long it has been in existence), and its size (because your job will be very different in a group with two employees than in one with two hundred).

- For the interview, dress professionally even if you think the group is relaxed about its dress code. Employees may wear jeans and sneakers around the office, but you shouldn't wear them to your interview.

The Basics of Think Tanks

As originally envisioned, think tanks were designed to hire some of the best thinkers of the day to research and report on significant public policy issues. Most important, the thinkers were supposed to develop ideas for making the world a better place. The think tanks themselves were to be objective and independent of political influence. They also were supposed to be nonpartisan, other than generally being known as liberal or conservative.

That original vision still holds true at some think tanks, whereas others have largely abandoned it to become more directly involved in politics. The latest trend involves creating think tanks that are overtly political. The Republicans have a think tank called the National Policy Forum, and the Democrats have the Democratic Leadership Council. Some politicians are even setting up their own think tanks.

The granddaddy of Washington think tanks is the Brookings Institution, which traces its beginnings to 1916. Some other well-known think tanks are the American Enterprise Institute, Cato Institute, Economic Policy Institute, Free Congress Foundation, Heritage Foundation, Progress and Freedom Foundation, Urban Institute, and Worldwatch Institute.

Think tanks may be best known for churning out a steady stream of reports, studies, books, issue papers, and other printed materials. Some recent titles from a variety of think tanks provide a flavor of their work:

- *Reforming Affirmative Action in Employment: How to Restore the Law of Equal Treatment* (Heritage Foundation, 1995)

- *The Crisis in Emerging Financial Markets* (Brookings Institution, 1999)

- *Troubled Times: U.S.-Japan Trade Relations in the 1990s* (Brookings Institution, 1999)

- *An Elusive Consensus: Nuclear Weapons and American Security after the Cold War* (Brookings Institution, 1999)

- *Four Steps to Improve the Prospects of Social Security Reform* (Heritage Foundation, 1999)

- *The Magic Mountain: A Guide to Defining and Using a Budget Surplus* (American Enterprise Institute, 1999)

- *Privatizing Subsidized Housing* (American Enterprise Institute, 1997)

- *Medicare in the 21st Century: Seeking Fair and Efficient Reform* (American Enterprise Institute, 1999)

- *Privacy as Censorship: A Skeptical View of Proposals to Regulate Privacy in the Private Sector* (Cato Institute, 1998)

- *Preventive Defense: A New Security Strategy for America* (Brookings Institution, 1999)

- *The Effects of Recent Tax Reforms on Labor Supply* (American Enterprise Institute, 1998)

- *Universal Service: Competition, Interconnection, and Monopoly in the Making of the American Telephone System* (American Enterprise Institute, 1997)

- *Income Redistribution and the Realignment of American Politics* (American Enterprise Institute, 1997)

- *An Agenda for Federal Regulatory Reform* (American Enterprise Institute, 1997)

As the titles make clear, think tanks are wonk heaven. Some are more wonkish than others, but all focus on making and implementing public policy. Some focus on a broad range of issues, although others are more narrowly focused on such topics as defense or foreign relations.

How much influence do think tanks have on public policy? That's subject to debate. In a newspaper article in the *Salt Lake Tribune,* Harvard education professor Carol Weiss described the role of think tanks like this: "They fill a vacuum. The political parties are bereft of ideas; distrust of government is growing more widespread; and there is the feeling that federal agencies are too old-fogeyish to be effective. There is a need for ideas" (Aug. 3, 1997).

Working at a Think Tank

Most jobs at think tanks involve supporting the fellows, scholars, researchers, or whatever the "thinkers" are called. The jobs can include helping with research, writing and producing publications, arranging meetings and press conferences, working with reporters to get publicity, raising funds from foundations and other sources, performing administrative functions, and similar types of work.

A JOB BANK FOR CONSERVATIVES

If you're politically conservative and looking for a job in Washington, make sure you register with the free Job Bank operated by the Heritage Foundation, one of Washington's leading conservative think tanks.

The Job Bank has existed since 1980, and a wide range of think tanks, lobbying groups, corporate offices, trade associations, interest groups, and Capitol Hill offices contact it when they're seeking job candidates. All the organizations are conservative, and they contact the Job Bank to find job candidates of like mind.

To register with the Job Bank, you must fill out a questionnaire (available on the Internet at http://www.heritage.org/jobs) and prepare a one-page resume. You should send the questionnaire and two copies of your resume by e-mail to jobbank@heritage.org. If you don't have e-mail, you can mail the documents to

Brad Bennett
Job Bank Coordinator
The Heritage Foundation
214 Massachusetts Ave., N.E.
Washington, DC 20002

You should submit your materials to the Job Bank no more than one to two months before you're available to start work in Washington. The Job Bank is not a placement office for the Heritage Foundation, although the foundation uses it, and it does not place interns.

The Job Bank sends you a letter of confirmation when it receives your materials. Then it sends your resume to any employers who contact it seeking job candidates who match your qualifications. The Job Bank does not post job openings, and it also will not tell you where it has sent your resume. Your file remains active for six months. If you haven't found a job after six months, you must send in a new resume and a cover letter if you want your file to remain open.

The biggest advantage—or disadvantage, depending on your perspective—of working at a think tank instead of an interest group is that think tanks tend to be a bit quieter and less chaotic. This isn't always true—if the think tank's issue becomes hot the atmosphere heats up. But generally, the pace is a bit slower.

Another advantage of think tanks is that they're often home to former and future officials in the executive branch of the government. If you have aspirations to eventually work in the executive branch, you can make some very useful contacts. Former think tankers in President Clinton's administration include Secretary of State Madeleine K. Albright, Health and Human Services Secretary Donna Shalala, and United Nations Ambassador Bill Richardson.

Just like with interest groups, the best way to get your foot in the door at a think tank is to intern. Think tanks use flocks of interns, so they're very receptive to applications. Just remember that think tanks are not all alike, so you need to study them before deciding where to apply. Most important, you need to determine whether the think tank is basically liberal (like the Brookings Institution) or conservative (like the Heritage Foundation) so you'll find one where you'll be comfortable. The best way to research think tanks is to check their Web sites, which are typically packed with position papers, studies, and all kinds of other revealing documents.

Informational interviews at think tanks also can be a great way to make contacts. Just keep in mind my earlier advice about informational or job interviews at interest groups: Always carefully research the organization beforehand so that you know what it does, can describe how your skills apply to its mission, and can ask intelligent questions.

Interest Group and Think Tank Contacts

ONLINE DIRECTORIES

When searching these job directories, keep in mind that some Washington-area interest groups and think tanks are located in the Virginia and Maryland suburbs instead of in Washington, D.C., itself. This means that in addition to checking the Washington listings, you also need to check the listings for Virginia and Maryland.

ACCESS
http://www.communityjobs.org
ACCESS, a national nonprofit employment clearinghouse, offers a small group of job listings at public interest organizations in Washington. The listings are updated every Thursday. They're especially helpful because basic background data is included for each employer: number of employees, year founded, and budget. ACCESS also publishes a newspaper that has additional job listings. A six-month subscription, which includes ten issues, costs $59.

EarthNet Jobs
http://envirocitizen.org/jobs
Jobs and internships at environmental and activist organizations are listed here. You can't search the listings, but Washington jobs are clearly marked so that you can quickly find them while browsing. The site typically lists opportunities with Washington organizations such as Defenders of Wildlife, National Environmental Trust, Project on Government Oversight, Wilderness Society, Greenwire, Alliance to Save Energy, National Family Farm Coalition, Nuclear Information and Resource Service, and the U.S. Geological Survey.

Feminist Career Center
http://www.feminist.org/911/911jobs.html
Depending on when you visit, this site can offer anywhere from just a few to a

couple dozen job openings at Washington feminist and progressive organizations. It lists many jobs at the Feminist Majority Foundation, which operates the site, and also frequently lists jobs at such organizations as the Hotel Employees and Restaurant Employees Union, AFL-CIO, National Abortion Federation, National Organization for Women, American Civil Liberties Union, Americans United for Separation of Church and State, Advocacy Institute, Planned Parenthood Federation of America, and the Center on Budget and Policy Priorities, among others. Feminists also can submit their resumes, which are posted online for searching by interested employers. Another nice feature is a directory of dozens of internships nationwide, although the listings are not separated by location.

Good Works Job Search
http://www.essential.org/goodworks/jobs

On the national map, simply click on a state (or the District of Columbia) to see job listings in public interest organizations. The listings tend to be few in number and somewhat out of date, but this site is still worth checking.

Green Dream Jobs
http://www.sustainablebusiness.com/jobs

Environmental jobs and internships are listed at this site. You can search the listings by state, job type, skill level, and keyword. There usually are listings for a couple dozen internships and jobs with Washington-area organizations such as the Union of Concerned Scientists, U.S. Environmental Protection Agency, Co-op America, World Resources Institute, National Wildlife Federation, Environmental Defense Fund, Investor Responsibility Research Center, American Oceans Campaign, and Biodiversity Action Network, among others.

Idealist Nonprofit Career Center
http://www.idealist.org/career.html

Idealist, which is operated by Action without Borders, offers the best online list of job and internship openings at nonprofit groups in the United States and overseas. The jobs and internships are listed separately, and there typically are dozens of Washington positions in each category. The positions are at such groups as Common Cause, Congressional Hunger Center, U.S. Committee for Refugees, Scenic America, Leadership Conference on Civil Rights, American Rivers, Benton Foundation, Environmental Defense Fund, Union of Concerned Scientists, Share Our Strength, U.S. Term Limits, Landmine Survivors Network, Gay and Lesbian Victory Fund, League of Women Voters of the United States, People for the American Way, and Public Citizen's Critical Mass Energy Project, among many others. You can search the job listings by category, keyword, country, state, city, type, area of focus, and language needed, and you also can browse them by state. You can search the internship listings by area of focus, keyword, country, state, city, skills needed, language needed, compensation (paid or unpaid), and dates of availability, and you also can browse them by state. Idealist also offers two free mailing lists that distribute new internship and job listings to subscribers.

National Opportunity NOCs
http://www.opportunitynocs.org/OpNOCS/home.html

This site lists job openings in nonprofit organizations throughout the United States. You can search the listings by keywords or region, and you also can browse them by state. The site, which is operated by the Management Center in San Francisco, Calif., typically lists a few dozen jobs in the Washington region.

Nonprofit Career Network
http://www.nonprofitcareer.com
Job openings at nonprofit organizations are listed by state. The site typically lists a couple dozen jobs in the Washington area. You also can post your resume online. Searching the job listings is free, but posting your resume costs $40 for one year.

INTEREST GROUPS

Accuracy in Media, 4455 Connecticut Ave. N.W., #330, Washington, DC 20008; (202) 364-4401. Fax (202) 364-4098, e-mail ar@aim.org, Web http://www.aim.org. Donald Irvine, executive secretary.
Analyzes print and electronic news media for bias, omissions, and errors; approaches media with complaints. Maintains speakers bureau.

Action on Smoking and Health, 2013 H St. N.W., Washington, DC 20006; (202) 659-4310. Fax (202) 833-3921, Web http://ash.org. Amor Haynes, development director.
Educational and legal organization that works to protect nonsmokers from cigarette smoking; provides information about smoking hazards and nonsmokers' rights.

Advocacy Institute, 1707 L St. N.W., #400, Washington, DC 20036; (202) 659-8475. Fax (202) 659-8484, e-mail info@advocacy.org, Web http://www.advocacy.org. Ron Mezoe, director of operations and intern coordinator.
Public interest organization that offers counseling and training in advocacy skills and strategies to nonprofit groups interested in such issues as civil and human rights, public health, arms control, and environmental and consumer affairs.

Africare, 440 R St. N.W., Washington, DC 20001; (202) 462-3614. Fax (202) 387-1034. Carolyn Llatt, director of personnel; Carla Wilson, secretary of international development.
Seeks to improve the quality of life in rural Africa through development of water resources, increased food production, and delivery of health services.

AIDS Action, 1875 Connecticut Ave. N.W., #700, Washington, DC 20009; (202) 530-8030. Fax (202) 986-1345, e-mail aidsaction@aidsaction.org, Web http://www.aidsaction.org. Daniel Zingale, executive director.
Promotes and monitors legislation on AIDS research and education and on related public policy issues.

Alliance for Justice, 2000 P St. N.W., #712, Washington, DC 20036; (202) 822-6070. Fax (202) 822-6068, e-mail alliance@afj.org, Web http://www.afj.org. Nan Aron, president.
Membership: public interest lawyers and advocacy, environmental, civil rights, and consumer organizations. Promotes reform of the legal system to ensure access to the courts; monitors selection of federal judges; works to preserve the rights of nonprofit organizations to advocate on behalf of their constituents.

Alliance to Save Energy, 1200 18th St. N.W., #900, Washington, DC 20036; (202) 857-0666. Fax (202) 331-9588, Web http://www.ase.org. Dianne Streat, director of administration; Siobhan Ford, resource associate.

Coalition of government, business, consumer, and labor leaders concerned with increasing the efficiency of energy use. Advocates efficient use of energy; conducts research, demonstration projects, and public education programs.

American-Arab Anti-Discrimination Committee, 4201 Connecticut Ave. N.W., #300, Washington, DC 20008-1158; (202) 244-2990. Fax (202) 244-3196, e-mail adc@adc.org, Web http://www.adc.org. Lamia Doumani, office manager; Marvin Wingfield, director of education and outreach.

Nonsectarian organization that seeks to protect the rights and heritage of Americans of Arab descent. Works to combat discrimination against Arab Americans in employment, education, and political life and to prevent stereotyping of Arabs in the media.

American Association of Retired Persons, 601 E St. N.W., Washington, DC 20049; (202) 434-2277. Fax (202) 434-2320, Web http://www.aarp.org. Horace B. Deets, executive director.

Membership organization for persons age 50 and older. Provides members with training, employment information, and volunteer programs; offers financial services, including insurance, investment programs, and consumer discounts; makes grants through AARP Andrus Foundation for research on aging. Monitors legislation and regulations on issues affecting older Americans, including age discrimination, Social Security, Medicaid and Medicare, pensions and retirement, and consumer protection.

American Civil Liberties Union (ACLU), 122 Maryland Ave. N.E., Washington, DC 20002; (202) 544-1681. Fax (202) 546-0738, Web http://www.aclu.org, human resources office located in New York (212) 549-2500. Laura W. Murphy, director, Washington Office.

Initiates test court cases and advocates legislation to guarantee constitutional rights and civil liberties. Focuses on First Amendment rights, minority and women's rights, gay and lesbian rights, and privacy; supports legalized abortion, opposes government-sponsored school prayer and legislative restrictions on television content. Washington office monitors legislative and regulatory activities and public policy. (Headquarters in New York maintains docket of cases.)

American Conservative Union, 1007 Cameron St., Alexandria, VA 22314; (703) 836-8602, toll-free (800) 228-7345. Fax (703) 836-8606, e-mail acu@conservative.org, Web http://www.conservative.org. Christian Jose, executive director; Mark Hendrekson, intern coordinator.

Legislative interest organization concerned with national defense policy, legislation related to nuclear weapons, U.S. strategic position vis-à-vis the former Soviet Union, missile defense programs, U.S. troops under U.N. command, and U.S. strategic alliance commitments.

American Farmland Trust, 1200 18th St. N.W., #800, Washington, DC 20036; (202) 331-7300. Fax (202) 659-8339, Web http://www.farmland.org. Ralph Grossi, president.

Works with farmers to promote farming practices that lead to a healthy environment. Interests include preservation of farmlands from urban development, establishment of safeguards against soil erosion, and agricultural resource conservation policy development at all government levels. Initiates local preservation efforts and assists individuals and organizations engaged in safeguarding agricultural properties.

American Forests, 910 17th St. N.W., #600, Washington, DC 20006 (mailing address: P.O. Box 2000, Washington, DC 20013-2000); (202) 955-4500. Fax (202) 955-4588, Web http://www.amfor.org. Lu Rose, personnel director.

Citizens' interest group that promotes protection and responsible management of forests and natural resources. Provides information on conservation, public land policy, urban forestry, and timber management. Runs an international tree planting campaign to help mitigate global warming.

American Israel Public Affairs Committee, 440 1st St. N.W., #600, Washington, DC 20001; (202) 639-5200. Fax (202) 347-4889, e-mail help@aipac.org, Web http://www.aipac.org. Howard Kohr, executive director.

Works to maintain and improve relations between the United States and Israel.

American Jewish Committee, 1156 15th St. N.W., #1201, Washington, DC 20005; (202) 785-4200. Fax (202) 785-4115, Web http://www.ajc.org. Jeffrey Weintraub, director, Belfer Center for American Pluralism.

Human relations agency devoted to protecting civil and religious rights for all people. Interests include church-state issues, research on human behavior, Israel and the Middle East, Jews in the former Soviet Union, immigration, social discrimination, civil and women's rights, employment, education, housing, and international cooperation for peace and human rights. (Headquarters in New York.)

American Rivers, 1025 Vermont Ave. N.W., #720, Washington, DC 20005; (202) 347-7550. Fax (202) 347-9240, Web http://www.amrivers.org. Rebecca Wodder, president.

Works to preserve and protect the nation's river systems.

Americans for Democratic Action, 1625 K St. N.W., #210, Washington, DC 20006; (202) 785-5980. Fax (202) 785-5969, e-mail adaction@ix.netcom.com, Web http://www.adaction.org. Amy F. Isaacs, director; Valerie Dulk, intern specialist.

Legislative interest organization that seeks to strengthen civil, constitutional, women's, family, workers', and human rights.

Americans for Tax Reform, 1320 18th St. N.W., #200, Washington, DC 20036; (202) 785-0266, toll-free (888) 785-0266. Fax (202) 785-0261, e-mail amtxreform@aol.com, Web http://www.atr.org. Damon Ansell, director of state projects.

Advocates reduction of federal and state taxes; encourages candidates for public office to pledge their opposition to income tax increases through a national pledge campaign.

Americans for the Arts, 1000 Vermont Ave. N.W., 12th Floor, Washington, DC 20005; (202) 371-2830. Fax (202) 371-0424, Web http://www.artsusa.org. Sandra Gibson, executive vice president; Melissa Palarea, assistant to the president.

Membership: groups and individuals dedicated to advancing the arts and culture in U.S. communities. Provides information on programs, activities, and administration of local arts agencies; on funding sources and guidelines; and on government policies and programs. Monitors legislation and regulations.

Americans United for Separation of Church and State, 1816 Jefferson Pl. N.W., Washington, DC 20036; (202) 466-3234. Fax (202) 466-2587, e-mail americansunited@au.org, Web http://www.au.org. Jason Hays, operations manager.

Citizens' interest group. Opposes federal and state aid to parochial schools; works to ensure religious neutrality in public schools; supports religious free exercise; initiates litigation; maintains speakers bureau. Monitors legislation and regulations.

Amnesty International USA, 600 Pennsylvania Ave. S.E., 5th Floor, Washington, DC 20003; (202) 544-0200. Fax (202) 546-7142, Web http://www.amnesty-usa.org, human resources office located in New York (212) 633-4200. Stephen Rickard, director, Washington Office.

International organization that works for the release of men and women imprisoned anywhere in the world for their beliefs, political affiliation, color, ethnic origin, sex, language, or religion, provided they have neither used nor advocated violence. Opposes torture and the death penalty; urges fair and prompt trials for all political prisoners. (U.S. headquarters in New York.)

Anti-Defamation League, 1100 Connecticut Ave. N.W., #1020, Washington, DC 20036; (202) 452-8320. Fax (202) 296-2371, e-mail adlwashdc@aol.com, Web http://www.adl.org. Tony Howell, office manager.

Jewish organization interested in civil rights and liberties. Seeks to combat anti-Semitism and other forms of bigotry. Interests include discrimination in employment, housing, voting, and education; U.S. foreign policy in the Middle East; and the treatment of Jews worldwide. Monitors legislation and regulations affecting Jewish interests and the civil rights of all Americans. (Headquarters in New York.)

Arab American Institute, 918 16th St. N.W., #601, Washington, DC 20006; (202) 429-9210. Fax (202) 429-9214, e-mail aai@arab-aai.org. Diane Davidson, office manager.

Advocacy group concerned with political issues affecting Arab Americans. Seeks to involve the Arab-American community in party politics and the electoral process.

Arms Control Association, 1726 M St. N.W., #201, Washington, DC 20036; (202) 463-8270. Fax (202) 463-8273, e-mail aca@armscontrol.org, Web http://www.armscontrol.org. Spurgeon M. Keeny Jr., executive director; Craig Cerniello, senior research analyst.

Nonpartisan organization interested in arms control. Seeks to broaden public interest in arms control, disarmament, and national security policy.

Association of Community Organizations for Reform Now (ACORN), 739 8th St. S.E., Washington, DC 20003; (202) 547-2500. Fax (202) 546-2483, e-mail dcnatacorn@igc.apc.org. Chris Leonard, head organizer.

Works to advance the interests of minority and low-income families through community organizing and action. Interests include jobs, living wages, housing, welfare reform, and community reinvestment. (Headquarters in New Orleans.)

Atlantic Council of the United States, 910 17th St. N.W., 10th Floor, Washington, DC 20006; (202) 463-7226. Fax (202) 463-7241, e-mail info@acus.org. David C. Acheson, president.

Conducts studies and makes policy recommendations on American foreign security and international economic policies in the Atlantic and Pacific communities; sponsors conferences and educational exchanges.

Aviation Consumer Action Project, 2001 S St. N.W., #410, Washington, DC 20009 (mailing address: P.O. Box 19029, Washington, DC 20036); (202) 638-4000. Fax (202) 638-0746, e-mail acap71@erols.com, Web http://www.acap1971. org. Paul S. Hudson, director.

Consumer advocacy organization that represents interests of airline passengers before the Federal Aviation Administration on safety issues and before the Transportation Dept. on economic and regulatory issues; testifies before Congress.

B'nai B'rith International, 1640 Rhode Island Ave. N.W., Washington, DC 20036; (202) 857-6500. Fax (202) 296-0638, Web http://www.bnaibrith.org. Michelle Prewitt, associate director.

Provides information and coordinates political action on public policy issues important to the international Jewish community. The B'nai B'rith Youth Organization offers educational and leadership training programs for teenagers and counseling and career guidance services. Other interests include community volunteer programs, senior citizen housing, and the security and development of Israel.

Bread for the World, 1100 Wayne Ave., #1000, Silver Spring, MD 20910; (301) 608-2400. Fax (301) 608-2401, e-mail bread@bread.org, Web http://www.bread. org. David Beckmann, president.

Christian citizens' movement that works to eradicate world hunger. Organizes and coordinates political action on issues and public policy affecting the causes of hunger. Interests include domestic food assistance programs, international famine, and hunger relief.

Business Roundtable, 1615 L St. N.W., #1100, Washington, DC 20036-5610; (202) 872-1260. Fax (202) 466-3509, Web http://www.brtable.org. Michael Diconti, director of administration.

Membership: chief executives of the nation's largest corporations. Examines issues of concern to business, including antitrust law.

Center for Auto Safety, 2001 S St. N.W., #410, Washington, DC 20009; (202) 328-7700. Web http://www.autosafety.org. Clarence M. Ditlow III, executive director.

Public interest organization that receives written consumer complaints against auto manufacturers; monitors federal agencies responsible for regulating and enforcing auto and highway safety rules.

Center for Community Change, 1000 Wisconsin Ave. N.W., Washington, DC 20007; (202) 342-0519. Fax (202) 342-1132. Myrna Peralta, director, administrative services.

Provides technical assistance to community-based organizations serving minorities and the economically disadvantaged. Areas of assistance include community development block grants, housing, economic and resource development, rural development projects, and program planning.

Center for Defense Information, 1779 Massachusetts Ave. N.W., #615, Washington, DC 20036; (202) 332-0600, toll-free (800) 234-3334. Fax (202) 462-4559, e-mail info@cdi.org, Web http://www.cdi.org. Dale Bumpers, director.

Educational organization that advocates a strong defense while opposing excessive expenditures for weapons and policies that increase the risk of war. Interests include the defense budget, weapons systems, and troop levels.

Center for Democracy and Technology, 1634 Eye St. N.W., #1100, Washington, DC 20006; (202) 637-9800. Fax (202) 637-0968, e-mail info@cdt.org, Web http://www.cdt.org. Jerry Berman, executive director.

Promotes civil liberties and democratic values in new computer and communications media. Interests include free speech, privacy, freedom of information, electronic commerce, and design of the information infrastructure. Monitors legislation and regulations.

Center for Marine Conservation, 1725 DeSales St. N.W., #600, Washington, DC 20036; (202) 429-5609. Fax (202) 872-0619, Web http://www.cmc-ocean.org. Denise Toliver, director of administration; Delores Proctor, executive assistant.

Works to prevent the over-exploitation of living marine resources, including fisheries, and to restore depleted marine wildlife populations.

Center for Media and Public Affairs, 2100 L St. N.W., #300, Washington, DC 20037-1525; (202) 223-2942. Fax (202) 872-4014, Web http://www.cmpa.com. Christine Messina-Boyer, managing director.

Nonpartisan research and educational organization that studies media coverage of social and political issues and campaigns. Conducts surveys; publishes materials and reports.

Center for National Security Studies, Gelman Library, 2130 H St. N.W., #701, Washington, DC 20037; (202) 994-7060. Fax (202) 994-1446, e-mail cnss@gwu.edu. Kate Martin, director.

A project of the Fund for Peace. Monitors and conducts research on extradition, intelligence, national security, and civil liberties.

Center for Public Integrity, 910 17th St. N.W., 7th Floor, Washington, DC 20006; (202) 466-1300. Fax (202) 466-1101, e-mail contact@publicintegrity.org, Web http://www.publicintegrity.org. Ann Ernst, office manager.

Educational foundation supported by corporations, labor unions, foundations, and individuals. Publishes comprehensive investigative reports concerning ethics-related issues.

Center for Responsive Politics, 1320 19th St. N.W., #620, Washington, DC 20036; (202) 857-0044. Fax (202) 857-7809, Web http://www.opensecrets.org. Cary Haney, internship coordinator.

Conducts research on Congress and related issues, with particular interest in campaign finance and congressional operations.

Center for Science in the Public Interest, 1875 Connecticut Ave. N.W., #400, Washington, DC 20009-5728; (202) 332-9110. Fax (202) 265-4954, e-mail cspi@cspinet.org, Web http://www.cspinet.org. Janet Caputo, human resources associate.

Conducts research on food and nutrition. Interests include eating habits, food safety regulations, food additives, organically produced foods, alcohol beverages, and links between diet and disease. Monitors U.S. and international policy.

Center for Strategic and International Studies, 1800 K St. N.W., Washington, DC 20006; (202) 887-0200. Fax (202) 775-3199, Web http://www.csis.org. Susan Heffner, manager of human resources and employment; Patricia Owens, internship coordinator.

Independent bipartisan research institute that studies international and domestic policy issues. Interests include science and technology, international business and economics, political-military affairs, arms control, international communications, fiscal policy, and health care reform.

Center for Study of Responsive Law, 1530 P St. N.W., Washington, DC (mailing address: P.O. Box 19367, Washington, DC 20036); (202) 387-8030. Fax (202) 234-5176, Web http://www.csrl.org. John Richard, administrator.

Consumer interest clearinghouse that conducts research and holds conferences on public interest law. Interests include white-collar crime, the environment, occupational health and safety, the postal system, banking deregulation, insurance, freedom of information policy, and broadcasting.

Center for the Study of Social Policy, 1250 Eye St. N.W., #503, Washington, DC 20005-3922; (202) 371-1565. Fax (202) 371-1472, Web http://www.cssp.org. Mary Swilley, office manager; Cheryl Rogers, senior associate.

Assists states and communities in organizing, financing, and delivering human services, with a focus on children and families. Helps build capacity for local decision making; helps communities use informal supports in the protection of children; promotes non-adversarial approach to class action litigation on behalf of dependent children.

Center on Budget and Policy Priorities, 820 1st St. N.E., #510, Washington, DC 20002; (202) 408-1080. Fax (202) 408-1056, Web http://www.cbpp.org. Bill Wallton, human resources director; Sarah Thom, legislative assistant.

Research group that analyzes federal, state, and local government policies affecting low- and moderate-income Americans.

Children's Defense Fund, 25 E St. N.W., Washington, DC 20001; (202) 628-8787. Fax (202) 662-3510, Web http://www.childrensdefense.org. Herman Piper, intern coordinator.

Advocacy group concerned with programs for children and youth. Promotes adequate prenatal care for adolescent and lower-income women; works to prevent adolescent pregnancy.

Christian Coalition, 227 Massachusetts Ave. N.E., #101, Washington, DC 20002; (202) 547-3600. Fax (202) 543-2978, Web http://www.cc.org. Jeff Taylor, director, government affairs.

Membership: individuals who support traditional, conservative Christian values. Represents members' views to all levels of government and to the media. (Headquarters in Chesapeake, Va.)

Citizens Committee for the Right to Keep and Bear Arms, 1090 Vermont Ave. N.W., #800, Washington, DC 20005; (202) 326-5259. Fax (202) 398-1939. John M. Snyder, director, publications and public affairs.

Concerned with rights of gun owners. Maintains National Advisory Council, comprising members of Congress and other distinguished Americans, which provides advice on issues concerning the right to keep and bear arms. (Headquarters in Bellevue, Wash.)

Citizens for a Sound Economy, 1250 H St. N.W., #700, Washington, DC 20005-3908; (202) 783-3870. Fax (202) 783-4687, Web http://www.cse.org/cse. Deborah Korte, vice president of administration; Lila Chan, executive assistant.

Citizens' advocacy group that promotes reduced taxes, free trade, and deregulation.

Citizens for Tax Justice, 1311 L St. N.W., #400, Washington, DC 20005; (202) 626-3780. Fax (202) 638-3486, Web http://www.ctj.org. Michael Ettlinger, director of tax policy; Coo Nguyen, intern coordinator.

Coalition that works for progressive taxes at the federal, state, and local levels.

Clean Water Action, 4455 Connecticut Ave. N.W., #A300, Washington, DC 20008; (202) 895-0420. Fax (202) 895-0438, e-mail cwa@essential.org, Web http://www.essential.org/cwa. David R. Zwick, president.

Citizens' organization interested in clean, safe, and affordable water. Works to influence public policy through education, technical assistance, and grassroots organizing. Interests include toxins and pollution, drinking water, water conservation, sewage treatment, pesticides, mass burn incineration, bay and estuary protection, and consumer water issues. Monitors legislation and regulations.

Coalition to Stop Gun Violence, 1000 16th St. N.W., #603, Washington, DC 20036; (202) 530-0340. Fax (202) 530-0331, e-mail noguns@aol.com, Web http://www.gunfree.org. Shannon Pete, intern coordinator.

Membership: organizations and individuals seeking to ban handguns. Provides national, state, and local groups operating handgun education programs with materials; engages in research and field work to support legislation to ban or control handguns.

College Republican National Committee, 600 Pennsylvania Ave. S.E., #301, Washington, DC 20003; (202) 608-1411. Fax (202) 608-1429, Web http://www.crnc.org. Laura Dove, executive director.

Membership: Republican college students. Promotes grassroots support for the Republican party and provides campaign assistance.

Committee for the Study of the American Electorate, 421 New Jersey Ave. S.E., Washington, DC 20003; (202) 546-3221. Fax (202) 546-3571. Curtis Gans, director.

Nonpartisan research group that studies issues involving low and declining American voter participation.

Common Cause, 1250 Connecticut Ave. N.W., #600, Washington, DC 20036; (202) 833-1200. Fax (202) 659-3716, Web http://www.commoncause.org. Coleen O' Day, director of human resources; Chad Ramsey, organizer.

Citizens' legislative interest group. Records and analyzes campaign contributions to congressional candidates and campaign committees, particularly those from political action committees, and soft money contributions to national political parties.

Competitive Enterprise Institute, 1001 Connecticut Ave. N.W., #1250, Washington, DC 20036; (202) 331-1010. Fax (202) 331-0640, Web http://www.cei.org. Craig Conko, intern coordinator.

Advocates free enterprise and limited government. Produces policy analyses on tax, budget, financial services, antitrust, biotechnological, and environmental issues. Monitors legislation and litigates against restrictive regulations through its Free Market Legal Program.

Concord Coalition, 1019 19th St. N.W., #810, Washington, DC 20036; (202) 467-6222. Fax (202) 467-6333, Web http://www.concordcoalition.org. Paula Price, acting executive director.

Nonpartisan, grassroots organization advocating fiscal responsibility and ensuring Social Security, Medicare, and Medicaid are secure for all generations.

Congressional Accountability Project, 1611 Connecticut Ave. N.W., #3A, Washington, DC 20009; (202) 296-2787. Fax (202) 833-2406, Web http://www.essential.org/orgs/CAP/CAP.html. Gary Ruskin, director.

Seeks to reform rules on campaign finance, gifts, pensions, and ethics for members of Congress; advocates free online access to congressional documents; files ethics complaints against individual members of Congress.

Conservative Caucus, 450 Maple Ave. East, #309, Vienna, VA 22180; (703) 938-9626. Fax (703) 281-4108, Web http://www.conservativeusa.org. Charles Orndorfs, administrative vice chairman.

Legislative interest organization that promotes grassroots activity on issues such as national defense and economic and tax policy. The Conservative Caucus Research, Analysis, and Education Foundation studies public issues including Central American affairs, defense policy, and federal funding of political advocacy groups.

Consumer Federation of America, 1424 16th St. N.W., #604, Washington, DC 20036; (202) 387-6121. Fax (202) 265-7989. Jackie Balser, director of administration.

Federation of national, regional, state, and local consumer organizations. Promotes consumer interests in banking, credit, and insurance; telecommunications; housing; food, drugs, and medical care; safety; energy and natural resources development; and indoor air quality.

Consumers Union of the United States, 1666 Connecticut Ave. N.W., #310, Washington, DC 20009-1039; (202) 462-6262. Fax (202) 265-9548. Adrian Hahn, legislative counsel.

Consumer advocacy group that represents consumer interests before Congress and regulatory agencies and litigates consumer affairs cases involving the government. Interests include consumer impact of world trade. Publishes *Consumer Reports* magazine. (Headquarters in Yonkers, N.Y.)

Co-op America, 1612 K St. N.W., #600, Washington, DC 20006; (202) 872-5307, toll-free (800) 584-7336. Fax (202) 331-8166, e-mail info@coopamerica.org, Web http://www.coopamerica.org. Alisa Gravitz, executive director; Rasael Solomon, intern coordinator.

Educates consumers and businesses about social and environmental responsibility. Publishes a directory of environmentally responsible businesses, a financial planning guide for investment, and boycott information.

Council for a Livable World, 110 Maryland Ave. N.E., #409, Washington, DC 20002; (202) 543-4100. Fax (202) 543-6297, e-mail clw@clw.org, Web http://www.clw.org. John Isaacs, president.

Citizens' interest group that supports arms control treaties, reduced military spending, peacekeeping, and tight restrictions on international arms sales.

Cuban American National Foundation, 1000 Thomas Jefferson St. N.W., #505, Washington, DC 20007; (202) 265-2822. Fax (202) 338-0308, e-mail canfnet@icanect.net, Web http://www.canfnet.org. Jose Cardenas, director, Washington Office.

Conducts research and provides information on Cuba; supports the establishment of a democratic government in Cuba. (Headquarters in Miami.)

Democracy 21, 1825 Eye St. N.W., #400, Washington, DC 20006; (202) 429-2008. Fax (202) 293-2660, e-mail fwertheimer@Democracy21.org. Jen Suson, administrative assistant for internships.

Focuses on using the communications revolution to strengthen democracy and on eliminating the influence of big money in American politics.

Democratic Congressional Campaign Committee, 430 S. Capitol St. S.E., Washington, DC 20003; (202) 863-1500. Fax (202) 485-3512, Web http://www.dccc.org. David Plouffe, executive director; Jaqui Vaughn, internship coordinator.

Provides Democratic House candidates with financial and other campaign services.

Democratic Leadership Council, 600 Pennsylvania Ave. S.E., #400, Washington, DC 20003; (202) 546-0007. Fax (202) 544-5002, Web http://www.dlcppi.org. Martina Childress, internship coordinator.

Organization of Democratic members of Congress, governors, state and local officials, and concerned citizens. Builds consensus within the Democratic party on public policy issues, including economic growth, national security, national service, and expansion of opportunity for all Americans.

Democratic National Committee, 430 S. Capitol St. S.E., Washington, DC 20003; (202) 863-8000. Fax (202) 863-8174, e-mail dnc@democrats.org, Web http://www.democrats.org. Veronica Hariston, human resources director.

Formulates and promotes Democratic party policies and positions; assists Democratic candidates for state and national office; organizes national political activities; works with state and local officials and organizations.

Democratic Senatorial Campaign Committee, 430 S. Capitol St. S.E., Washington, DC 20003; (202) 224-2447. Fax (202) 485-3120, Web http://www.dscc.org. Dan Freedberg, intern coordinator.

Provides Democratic senatorial candidates with financial, research, and consulting services.

Drug Policy Foundation, 4455 Connecticut Ave. N.W., #B500, Washington, DC 20008-2328; (202) 537-5005. Fax (202) 537-3007, e-mail dpf@dpf.org, Web http://www.dpf.org. Rob Stewart, communications director (internships).

Supports reform of current drug control policy. Advocates medical treatment to control drug abuse; opposes random drug testing. Sponsors the International Conference on Drug Policy Reform annually.

Electronic Privacy Information Center, 666 Pennsylvania Ave. S.E., #301, Washington, DC 20003; (202) 544-9240. Fax (202) 547-5482, e-mail info@epic.org, Web http://www.epic.org. Marc Rotenberg, director.

Conducts research and conferences on domestic and international civil liberties issues, including privacy, information access, computer security, and encryption; litigates cases. Monitors legislation and regulations.

Empower America, 1701 Pennsylvania Ave. N.W., #900, Washington, DC 20006; (202) 452-8200. Fax (202) 833-0388, e-mail empower1@empower.org, Web http://www.empower.org. Christian Pinkston, executive director; Christian Lowe, communications director.

Public policy research organization that seeks to encourage economic growth through lower taxes, less government spending, and regulatory reform. Interests include social policy and the moral impact of popular culture.

Environmental Defense Fund, 1875 Connecticut Ave. N.W., #1016, Washington, DC 20009; (202) 387-3500. Fax (202) 234-6049, Web http://www.edf.org. Cheryl Pickard, office manager, Washington Office.

Citizens' interest group staffed by lawyers, economists, and scientists. Conducts research and provides information on pollution prevention, environmental health, and protection of the Amazon rain forest and the ozone layer. (Headquarters in New York.)

Environmental Working Group, 1718 Connecticut Ave. N.W., #600, Washington, DC 20009; (202) 667-6982. Fax (202) 232-2592, e-mail info@ewg.org, Web http://www.ewg.org. Molly Evans, operations manager; Melissa Haynes, analyst for public affairs.

Research and advocacy organization that studies and reports on the presence of herbicides and pesticides in food and drinking water. Monitors legislation and regulations.

Families USA, 1334 G St. N.W., #300, Washington, DC 20005; (202) 737-6340. Fax (202) 347-2417, e-mail info@familiesusa.org, Web http://www.familiesusa.org. Nesretiri Cooley, intern coordinator.

Organization of American families whose interests include health care and long-term care, Social Security, Medicare, and Medicaid. Monitors legislation and regulations affecting the elderly.

Family Research Council, 801 G St. N.W., Washington, DC 20001; (202) 393-2100. Fax (202) 393-2134, Web http://www.frc.org. Carol Wood, director, human resources.

Legislative interest organization that analyzes issues affecting the family and seeks to ensure that the interests of the family are considered in the formulation of public policy.

Federation of American Scientists, 307 Massachusetts Ave. N.E., Washington, DC 20002; (202) 546-3300. Fax (202) 675-1010, e-mail fas@fas.org, Web http://www.fas.org. Christa Fanelli, office manager.

Conducts studies and monitors legislation on U.S. nuclear arms policy; provides the public with information on arms control and related issues. Interests include the Strategic Defense Initiative (SDI) and arms control compliance.

Food Research and Action Center, 1875 Connecticut Ave. N.W., #540, Washington, DC 20009-5728; (202) 986-2200. Fax (202) 986-2525, Web http://www.frac.org. James Weill, president.

Public interest advocacy, research, and legal center that works to end hunger and poverty in the United States; offers legal assistance, organizational aid, training, and information to groups seeking to improve or expand federal food programs, including food stamp, child nutrition, and WIC (women, infants, and children) programs; conducts studies relating to hunger and poverty; coordinates network of anti-hunger organizations. Monitors legislation and regulations.

Freedom Forum, 1101 Wilson Blvd., Arlington, VA 22209; (703) 528-0800. Fax (703) 284-3770, e-mail news@freedomforum.org, Web http://www.freedomforum.org. Nate Ruffin, vice president, human resources.

Sponsors conferences, educational activities, training, and research that promote free press, free speech, and freedom of information and that enhance the teaching and practice of journalism.

Friends of the Earth, 1025 Vermont Ave. N.W., #300, Washington, DC 20005-6303; (202) 783-7400. Fax (202) 783-0444, e-mail foe@foe.org, Web http://www.foe.org. Jill Diskan, operations director; Kevin Payne, intern coordinator.

Environmental advocacy group. Interests include conservation and renewable energy resources and air and water pollution, including international water projects. Specializes in federal budget and tax issues related to the environment; ozone layer and ground water protection; and World Bank and International Monetary Fund reform.

Fund for the Feminist Majority Foundation, 1600 Wilson Blvd., #801, Arlington, VA 22209; (703) 522-2214. Fax (703) 522-2219, e-mail femmaj@feminist.org, Web http://www.feminist.org. Jennifer Jackman, director of policy and research; Sylvia Henriquez, intern coordinator.

Legislative interest group that seeks to increase the number of feminists running for public office; promotes a national feminist agenda.

Government Accountability Project, 1612 K St. N.W., #400, Washington, DC 20006; (202) 408-0034. Fax (202) 408-9855, e-mail gap1@erols.com, Web http://www.whistleblower.org. Louis Clark, executive director.

Membership: federal employees, union members, professionals, and interested citizens. Provides legal and strategic counsel to public and private employees who seek to expose corporate and government actions that are illegal, wasteful, or repressive; aids such employees in personnel action taken against them; assists grassroots organizations investigating corporate wrongdoing, government inaction, or corruption.

Greenpeace USA, 1436 U St. N.W., Washington, DC 20009; (202) 462-1177. Fax (202) 462-4507, e-mail gp@sharewest.com, Web http://www.greenpeaceusa. org. Charles Dykes, human resource assistant.

Seeks to protect the environment through research, education, and grassroots organizing. Interests include chemical and nuclear waste dumping, solid and hazardous waste disposal, and protection of marine mammals and endangered species. Supports the establishment of Antarctica as a world park, free of industry, military presence, and nuclear power and weaponry. Monitors legislation and regulations.

Guatemala Human Rights Commission/USA, 3321 12th St. N.E., Washington, DC 20017-4008; (202) 529-6599. Fax (202) 526-4611, e-mail ghrc@igc.apc.org. Alice Zachmann, coordinator.

Provides information and collects and makes available reports on human rights violations in Guatemala; publishes a biweekly report of documented cases of specific abuses and a quarterly bulletin of human rights news and analysis. Takes on special projects to further sensitize the public and the international community to human rights abuses in Guatemala.

Handgun Control, 1225 Eye St. N.W., #1100, Washington, DC 20005; (202) 898-0792. Fax (202) 371-9615, Web http://www.handguncontrol.org. Karen Marks, acting director of human resources.

Public interest organization that works for handgun control legislation and serves as an information clearinghouse.

High Frontier, 2800 Shirlington Rd., #405, Arlington, VA 22206-3601; (703) 671-4111. Fax (703) 931-6432, e-mail hifront@erols.com, Web http://www.erols. com/hifront. Bernice Coakley, director.

Educational organization that provides information on missile defense programs and proliferation. Advocates development of a single-stage-to-orbit space vehicle and research of space solar power. Operates speakers bureau. Monitors defense legislation.

Human Rights Campaign, 919 18th St. N.W., #800, Washington, DC 20006; (202) 628-4160. Fax (202) 347-5323, e-mail hrc@hrc.org, Web http://www.hrc. org. Lisa Berot, associate director, human resources.

Promotes legislation affirming the rights of lesbians and gays. Interests include civil rights; funding for AIDS research; lesbian health issues; and discrimination in housing, immigration, employment, and the military.

Human Rights Watch, 1522 K St. N.W., #910, Washington, DC 20005; (202) 612-4321. Fax (202) 371-0124, e-mail hrwdc@hrw.org, Web http://www.hrw. org. Allyson Collins, associate director.

International, nonpartisan human rights organization that monitors human rights violations worldwide. Subdivided into five regional concentrations—Africa, Americas, Asia, Helsinki (Europe), and Middle East. Coordinates thematic projects on women's rights, arms sales, and prisons. Sponsors fact-finding missions to various countries; publicizes violations and encourages international protests; maintains file on human rights violations. (Headquarters in New York.)

Humane Society of the United States, 2100 L St. N.W., Washington, DC 20037; (202) 452-1100. Fax (202) 778-6132, Web http://www.hsus.org, job line (301) 548-7762. Bob Roop, director of human resources.

Works for the humane treatment and protection of animals. Interests include protecting endangered wildlife and marine mammals and their habitats and ending inhumane or cruel conditions in zoos.

Institute for Justice, 1717 Pennsylvania Ave. N.W., #200, Washington, DC 20006; (202) 955-1300. Fax (202) 955-1329, e-mail general@instituteforjustice.org, Web http://www.instituteforjustice.org. Amin Shaheen, director of accounting and administration; Dana Berliner, staff attorney.

Sponsors seminars to train law students, grassroots activists, and practicing lawyers in applying advocacy strategies in public interest litigation. Seeks to protect from arbitrary government interference in free speech, private property rights, parental school choice, and economic liberty. Litigates cases.

Interfaith Alliance, 1012 14th St. N.W., #700, Washington, DC 20005; (202) 639-6370. Fax (202) 639-6375, e-mail TIAlliance@tialliance.org, Web http://www.tialliance.org. Roy Speckhardt, director of finance.

Membership: Protestant, Catholic, Jewish, and Muslim clergy; laity; and others who favor a positive, nonpartisan role for religious faith in public life. Advocates mainstream religious values; promotes tolerance and social opportunity; opposes the use of religion to promote political extremism at national, state, and local levels. Monitors legislation and regulations.

International Food Policy Research Institute, 2033 K St. N.W., Washington, DC 20006; (202) 862-5600. Fax (202) 467-4439, e-mail ifpri@cgnet.com, Web http://www.cgiar.org/ifpri. Sandra Freeman, senior human resources coordinator.

Research organization that analyzes the world food situation and suggests ways of making food more available in developing countries. Provides various governments with information on national and international food policy. Sponsors conferences and seminars; publishes research reports.

Izaak Walton League of America, 707 Conservation Lane, Gaithersburg, MD 20878-2983; (301) 548-0150. Fax (301) 548-0146, e-mail general@iwla.org, Web http://www.iwla.org/iwla. Paul W. Hansen, executive director.

Grassroots organization that promotes conservation of natural resources and the environment. Interests include air and water pollution and wildlife habitat protection. Provides information on acid rain and stream cleanup efforts at the local level.

Leadership Conference on Civil Rights, 1629 K St. N.W., #1010, Washington, DC 20006; (202) 466-3311. Fax (202) 466-3435. Wade Henderson, executive director; Joy Paluska, research assistant.

Coalition of national organizations representing minorities, women, labor, older Americans, people with disabilities, and religious groups. Works for enactment and enforcement of civil rights and social welfare legislation; acts as clearinghouse for information on civil rights legislation and regulations.

League of Conservation Voters, 1707 L St. N.W., #750, Washington, DC 20036; (202) 785-8683. Fax (202) 835-0491, Web http://www.lcv.org. Debra J. Callahan, president.

Works to support the environmental movement by helping elect environmentally concerned candidates to public office.

League of United Latin American Citizens, 1133 20th St. N.W., #750, Washington, DC 20036; (202) 408-0060. Fax (202) 408-0064, e-mail lulac@aol.com, Web http://www.lulac.org. Brent Wilkes, executive director, National Educational Service Centers.

Seeks full social, political, economic, and educational rights for Hispanics in the United States. Programs include housing projects for the poor, employment and training for youth and women, and political advocacy on issues affecting Hispanics, including immigration. Operates National Educational Service Centers (NESCs) and awards scholarships. (Headquarters in El Paso, Texas.)

League of Women Voters of the United States, 1730 M St. N.W., #1000, Washington, DC 20036; (202) 429-1965. Fax (202) 429-0854, Web http://www.lwv. org. Maxine Griffin, director of administrative and human resources; Julie Lemri, intern coordinator.

Membership: women and men interested in nonpartisan political action and study. Works to increase participation in government; provides information on voter registration and balloting. Interests include social policy, natural resources, international relations, and representative government.

Log Cabin Republicans, 1633 Que St. N.W., #210, Washington, DC 20009; (202) 347-5306. Fax (202) 347-5224, e-mail info@lcr.org, Web http://www.lcr. org. Rich Tafel, executive director.

Membership: lesbian and gay Republicans. Educates conservative politicians and voters on gay and lesbian issues; disseminates information; conducts seminars for members. Monitors legislation and regulations.

Mexican American Legal Defense and Educational Fund, 1518 K St. N.W., #410, Washington, DC 20005; (202) 628-4074. Fax (202) 393-4206, Web http://www. maldef.org. Marisa Demeo, regional counsel, Washington Office.

Gives legal assistance to Mexican-Americans and other Hispanics in such areas as equal employment, voting rights, bilingual education, and immigration; awards scholarship funds to Hispanic law students. Monitors legislation and regulations. (Headquarters in Los Angeles.)

National Abortion and Reproductive Rights Action League (NARAL), 1156 15th St. N.W., 7th Floor, Washington, DC 20005; (202) 973-3000. Fax (202) 973-3099, Web http://www.naral.org. Michel Jackson, human resources manager.

Membership: persons favoring legalized abortion. Promotes grassroots support of political candidates in favor of legalized abortion.

National Alliance for the Mentally Ill, 200 N. Glebe Rd., #1015, Arlington, VA 22203-3754; (703) 524-7600. Fax (703) 524-9094, e-mail membership@nami. org, Web http://www.nami.org. Deborah Murray, human resources director.

Membership: mentally ill individuals and their families and friends. Works to eradicate mental illness and improve the lives of those affected by brain diseases; sponsors public education and research. Monitors legislation and regulations.

National Association for the Advancement of Colored People (NAACP), 1025 Vermont Ave. N.W., #1120, Washington, DC 20005; (202) 638-2269. Fax (202) 638-5936, Web http://www.naacp.org. Hilary O. Shelton, director.

Membership: persons interested in civil rights for all minorities. Works for the political, educational, social, and economic equality and empowerment of minorities through legal, legislative, and direct action. (Headquarters in Baltimore.)

National Association of Arab-Americans, 1212 New York Ave. N.W., #230, Washington, DC 20005-3987; (202) 842-1840. Fax (202) 842-1614, e-mail naaainc@erols.com, Web http://www.naaa.net. Khalil Jahshan, president; Margot Andrews, director of administration and finance.

Organization of Americans of Arab descent or heritage. Acts as a representative on political issues for its membership.

National Association of Manufacturers, 1331 Pennsylvania Ave. N.W., #600, Washington, DC 20004-1790; (202) 637-3000. Fax (202) 637-3182, Web http://www.nam.org. Carol Coldron, director of human resources.

Represents industry views (mainly of manufacturers) to government on national and international issues. Reviews legislation, administrative rulings, and judicial decisions affecting industry. Sponsors the Human Resources Forum; operates a Web site for members and the public that provides information on legislative and other news; conducts programs on labor relations, occupational safety and health, regulatory and consumer affairs, environmental trade and technology, and other business issues.

National Association of Railroad Passengers, 900 2nd St. N.E., #308, Washington, DC 20002-3557; (202) 408-8362. Fax (202) 408-8287, Web http://www.narprail.org. Ross Capon, executive director.

Consumer organization. Works to expand and improve U.S. intercity and commuter rail passenger service, increase federal funds for mass transit, ensure fair treatment for rail freight transportation, and address environmental concerns pertaining to mass transit. Opposes subsidies for inter-city trucking; works with Amtrak on scheduling, new services, fares, and advertising.

National Audubon Society, 1901 Pennsylvania Ave. N.W., #1100, Washington, DC 20006; (202) 861-2242. Fax (202) 861-4290, Web http://www.audubon.org. Gretchen Miller, intern coordinator.

Citizens' interest group that promotes environmental preservation. Provides information on water resources, public lands, rangelands, forests, parks, wildlife and marine conservation, and the national wildlife refuge system. (Headquarters in New York.)

National Center for Neighborhood Enterprise, 1424 16th St. N.W., #300, Washington, DC 20036; (202) 518-6500. Fax (202) 588-0314, Web http://www.ncne. com. Robert L. Woodson Sr., chair.

Seeks new approaches to the problems confronting the African American community. Interests include economic development, the encouragement of entrepreneurship, housing, family development, and education.

National Center for Tobacco-Free Kids, 1707 L St. N.W., #800, Washington, DC 20036; (202) 296-5469, toll-free (800) 284-5437. Fax (202) 296-5427, Web http://www.tobaccofreekids.org. Jackie Bolt, director of finance and administration.

Seeks to reduce tobacco use by children through public policy change and educational programs. Provides technical assistance to state and local programs.

National Citizens' Coalition for Nursing Home Reform, 1424 16th St. N.W., #202, Washington, DC 20036-2211; (202) 332-2275. Fax (202) 332-2949. Sarah Burger, executive director.

Seeks to improve the long-term care system and quality of life for residents in nursing homes and other facilities for the elderly; coordinates the Campaign for Quality Care. Promotes citizen participation in all aspects of nursing homes; acts as clearinghouse for nursing home advocacy.

National Coalition Against the Misuse of Pesticides, 701 E St. S.E., #200, Washington, DC 20003; (202) 543-5450. Fax (202) 543-4791, e-mail ncamp@igc. apc.org, Web http://www.csn.net/ncamp. Beth Fiteni, program coordinator.

Coalition of family farmers, farmworkers, consumers, home gardeners, physicians, lawyers, and others concerned about pesticide hazards and safety. Issues information to increase public awareness of environmental, public health, and economic problems caused by pesticide abuse; promotes alternatives to pesticide use, such as the integrated pest management program.

National Coalition for the Homeless, 1012 14th St. N.W., #600, Washington, DC 20005-3406; (202) 737-6444. Fax (202) 737-6445, e-mail nch@ari.net, Web http://nch.ari.net. Mary Ann Gleason, executive director.

Advocacy network of persons who are or have been homeless, state and local coalitions, other activists, service providers, housing developers, and others. Seeks to create the systemic and attitudinal changes necessary to end homelessness. Works to meet the needs of persons who are homeless or at risk of becoming homeless.

National Coalition to Abolish the Death Penalty, 1436 U St. N.W., #104, Washington, DC 20009; (202) 387-3890. Fax (202) 387-5590, e-mail info@ncadp.org, Web http://www.ncadp.org. Steven Hawkins, executive director; Brian Henninger, program coordinator.

Membership: organizations and individuals opposed to the death penalty. Maintains collection of death penalty research. Provides training, resources, and conferences. Works with families of murder victims; tracks execution dates. Monitors legislation and regulations.

National Committee to Preserve Social Security and Medicare, 10 G St. N.E., #600, Washington, DC 20002; (202) 216-0420. Fax (202) 216-0451, Web http://www.ncpssm.org. Crystal Jones, human resources generalist.

Educational and advocacy organization that focuses on Social Security and Medicare programs and on related income security and health issues. Interests include retirement income protection, health care reform, and the quality of life of seniors. Monitors legislation and regulations.

National Congress of American Indians, 1301 Connecticut Ave. N.W., #200, Washington, DC 20036; (202) 466-7767. Fax (202) 466-7797, Web http://www. ncai.org. JoAnn K. Chase, executive director; Jack Jackson, director of governmental affairs.

Membership: native American and Alaska native governments and individuals. Provides information and serves as general advocate for tribes. Monitors legislative and regulatory activities affecting native American affairs.

National Consumers League, 1701 K St. N.W., #1200, Washington, DC 20006; (202) 835-3323. Fax (202) 835-0747, Web http://www.nclnet.org. Linda F. Golodner, president.

Citizens' interest group that engages in research and educational activities related to consumer issues. Interests include health care; child labor; food, drug, and product safety; environment; telecommunications; and financial services.

National Council for Adoption, 1930 17th St. N.W., Washington, DC 20009; (202) 328-1200. Fax (202) 332-0935, e-mail ncfadc@ibm.net, Web http://www. ncfa-usa.org. Mara Duffy, intern coordinator.

Organization of individuals, agencies, and corporations interested in adoption. Supports adoption through legal, ethical agencies; advocates the right to confidentiality in adoption. Conducts research and holds conferences; provides information; supports pregnancy counseling, maternity services, and counseling for infertile couples.

National Council of La Raza, 1111 19th St. N.W., #1000, Washington, DC 20036; (202) 785-1670. Fax (202) 776-1792, Web http://www.nclr.org. Rosanna Toledo, office manager; Concepcion Romero, intern coordinator.

Offers technical assistance to Hispanic community organizations; operates policy analysis center with interests in education, employment and training, immigration, language issues, civil rights, and housing and community development. Special projects focus on the Hispanic elderly, teenage pregnancy, health, and AIDS. Monitors legislation and regulations.

National Council on the Aging, 409 3rd St. S.W., 2nd Floor, Washington, DC 20024; (202) 479-1200. Fax (202) 479-0735, e-mail info@ncoa.org, Web http:// www.ncoa.org. James Firman, president.

Serves as an information clearinghouse on training, technical assistance, advocacy, and research on every aspect of aging. Provides information on social services for older persons. Monitors legislation and regulations.

National Federation of Independent Business, 600 Maryland Ave. S.W., #700, Washington, DC 20024; (202) 554-9000. Fax (202) 554-0496, Web http://www. nfibonline.com. Chris Pitts, intern coordinator.

Membership: independent business and professional people. Monitors public policy issues and legislation affecting small and independent businesses, including taxation, government regulation, labor-management relations, and liability insurance.

National Federation of Republican Women, 124 N. Alfred St., Alexandria, VA 22314; (703) 548-9688. Fax (703) 548-9836, Web http://www.nfrw.org. Mary Jo Arndt, president.

Political education and volunteer arm of the Republican party. Organizes volunteers for support of Republican candidates for national, state, and local offices; encourages candidacy of Republican women; sponsors campaign management schools. Recruits Republican women candidates for office.

National Gay and Lesbian Task Force and Policy Institute, 2320 17th St. N.W., Washington, DC 20009-2702; (202) 332-6483. Fax (202) 332-0207, e-mail ngltf@ngltf.org, Web http://www.ngltf.org. Kerry Lobel, executive director.

Educates the media and the public on issues affecting the lesbian and gay community. Interests include grassroots organizations, civil rights, antigay violence, sodomy law reform, and gays on campus. Monitors legislation.

National Jewish Coalition, 415 2nd St. N.E., #100, Washington, DC 20002; (202) 547-7701. Fax (202) 544-2434, Web http://www.njchq.org. Nancy Schoenburg, office manager; Seth Leibsohn, director of policy.

Legislative interest group that works to build support among Republican party decision makers on issues of concern to the Jewish community; studies domestic and foreign policy issues affecting the Jewish community; supports a strong relationship between the United States and Israel.

National League of Families of American Prisoners and Missing in Southeast Asia, 1001 Connecticut Ave. N.W., #919, Washington, DC 20036-5504; (202) 223-6846. Fax (202) 785-9410, e-mail powmiafam@aol.com, Web http://www. pow-miafamilies.org. Ann Mills Griffiths, executive director.

Membership: family members of MIAs and POWs and returned POWs of the Vietnam War. Works for the release of all prisoners of war, an accounting of the missing, and repatriation of the remains of those who have died serving their country in Southeast Asia. Works to raise public awareness of these issues; maintains regional and state coordinators; sponsors an annual recognition day.

National Legal Center for the Public Interest, 1000 16th St. N.W., #500, Washington, DC 20036; (202) 296-1683. Fax (202) 293-2118. Ernest B. Hueter, president.

Public interest law center and information clearinghouse. Studies judicial issues and the impact of the legal system on the private sector; sponsors seminars; does not litigate cases.

National Library on Money and Politics, 1320 19th St. N.W., #620, Washington, DC 20036; (202) 857-0318. Fax (202) 857-7809, Web http://www.opensecrets. org. Geoff Thomas, office manager; Cary Haney, intern coordinator.

Conducts research and analysis of political money and provides the media and others with direct assistance on the subject. A project of the Center for Responsive Politics.

National Neighborhood Coalition, 1875 Connecticut Ave. N.W., #410, Washington, DC 20009; (202) 986-2096. Fax (202) 986-1941, Web http://www.comminfoexch.org/nnc.htm. Betty Weiss, executive director; Janice Clark, program coordinator.

Membership: national and regional organizations that have neighborhood-based affiliates. Provides technical assistance to neighborhood groups, conducts research on issues affecting neighborhoods, monitors national programs and policies that affect inner-city neighborhoods.

National Organization for the Reform of Marijuana Laws (NORML), 1001 Connecticut Ave. N.W., #710, Washington, DC 20036; (202) 483-5500. Fax (202) 483-0057, e-mail natlnorml@aol.com, Web http://www.norml.org. Allen St. Pierre, executive director.

Works to reform federal, state, and local marijuana laws and policies. Educates the public and conducts litigation on behalf of marijuana consumers. Monitors legislation and regulations.

National Organization for Women (NOW), 1000 16th St. N.W., #700, Washington, DC 20036; (202) 331-0066. Fax (202) 785-8576, e-mail now@now.org, Web http://www.now.org. Cindi Hanford, equality action fund manager; Anita Murano, intern coordinator.

Membership: women and men interested in feminist civil rights. Works to end discrimination against lesbians and gays. Promotes the development and enforcement of legislation prohibiting discrimination on the basis of sexual orientation.

National Organization on Disability, 910 16th St. N.W., #600, Washington, DC 20006-2988; (202) 293-5960, TDD (202) 293-5968. Fax (202) 293-7999, Web http://www.nod.org. Mary Dolan, vice president and director.

Administers the Community Partnership Program, a network of communities that works to remove barriers and address educational, employment, social, and transportation needs of people with disabilities. Provides members with information and technical assistance; sponsors annual community awards competition; makes referrals. Monitors legislation and regulations.

National Parks and Conservation Association, 1776 Massachusetts Ave. N.W., #200, Washington, DC 20036-6404; (202) 223-6722, toll-free (800) 628-7275. Fax (202) 659-0650, Web http://www.npca.org. Karen Allen, human resources consultant; Jerome Uher, communications manager.

Citizens' interest group that seeks to protect national parks and other park system areas.

National Republican Congressional Committee, 320 1st St. S.E., Washington, DC 20003; (202) 479-7000. Fax (202) 863-0693, Web http://www.nrcc.org. Josh Holly, director of special projects.

Provides Republican House candidates with campaign assistance, including financial, public relations, media, and direct mail services.

National Republican Senatorial Committee, 425 2nd St. N.E., Washington, DC 20002; (202) 675-6000. Fax (202) 675-6058, Web http://www.nrsc.org. Mike Kroeger, personnel coordinator; Tom Breene, intern coordinator.

Provides Republican senatorial candidates with financial and public relations services.

National Rifle Association of America, 11250 Waples Mill Rd., Fairfax, VA 22030; (703) 267-1000. Fax (703) 267-3976, Web http://www.nra.org. Neil Sawyer, human resource manager.

Membership: target shooters, hunters, gun collectors, gunsmiths, police officers, and others interested in firearms. Promotes shooting sports and recreational shooting and safety; studies and makes recommendations on firearms laws. Opposes gun control legislation.

National Right to Life Committee, 419 7th St. N.W., Washington, DC 20004; (202) 626-8800. Fax (202) 737-9189, e-mail nrlc@nrlc.org, Web http://www.nrlc.org. David N. O'Steen, executive director.

Association of fifty state right-to-life organizations. Opposes abortion, infanticide, and euthanasia; supports legislation prohibiting abortion except when the life of the mother is endangered. Operates an information clearinghouse and speakers bureau. Monitors legislation and regulations.

National Right to Work Committee, 8001 Braddock Rd., Springfield, VA 22160; (703) 321-9820, toll-free (800) 325-7892. Fax (703) 321-7342, e-mail info@nrtw.org, Web http://www.nrtw.org. Mary Finnin, human resources.

Citizens' organization opposed to compulsory union membership. Supports right-to-work legislation.

National Security Archive, Gelman Library, 2130 H St. N.W., #701, Washington, DC 20037; (202) 994-7000. Fax (202) 994-7005, e-mail nsarchiv@gwu.edu, Web http://www.seas.gwu.edu/nsarchive. Sue Bechtl, administrator.

Research institute and library that provides information on U.S. foreign policy and national security affairs. Maintains collection of declassified and unclassified national security documents.

National Taxpayers Union, 108 N. Alfred St., 3rd Floor, Alexandria, VA 22314; (703) 683-5700. Fax (703) 683-5722, Web http://www.ntu.org. Rita Smith, director of marketing; Jeff Dirckson, director of congressional analysis.

Citizens' interest group that promotes tax and spending reduction at all levels of government. Supports constitutional amendments to balance the federal budget and limit taxes.

National Urban League, 1111 14th St. N.W., #1001, Washington, DC 20005-5603; (202) 898-1604. Fax (202) 408-1965, Web http://www.nul.org. William Spriggs, director, research and public policy.

Federation of affiliates concerned with the social welfare of African Americans and other minorities. Seeks elimination of racial segregation and discrimination; monitors legislation, policies, and regulations to determine impact on minorities; interests include employment, health, welfare, education, housing, and community development. (Headquarters in New York.)

National Wildlife Federation, 8925 Leesburg Pike, Vienna, VA 22184; (703) 790-4000. Fax (703) 442-7332, Web http://www.nwf.org. Lori Rheubottom, director of human resources; Roy Geiger, director of education.

Promotes conservation of natural resources; provides information on the environment and resource management; takes legal action on environmental issues.

Laurel Ridge Conservation Education Center in Vienna, Va., provides educational materials and outdoor programs.

National Women's Law Center, 11 Dupont Circle N.W., #800, Washington, DC 20036; (202) 588-5180. Fax (202) 588-5185. Marcia D. Greenberger and Nancy Duff Campbell, co-presidents.

Works to expand and protect women's legal rights through advocacy and public education. Interests include reproductive rights, health, education, employment, women in prison, income security, and family support.

National Women's Political Caucus, 1630 Connecticut Ave. N.W., #201, Washington, DC 20009; (202) 785-1100. Fax (202) 785-3605, Web http://www.nwpc. org. Nita Nunez, membership coordinator.

Seeks to increase the number of women in policymaking positions in federal, state, and local government. Identifies, recruits, trains, and supports pro-choice women candidates for public office. Monitors agencies and provides names of qualified women for high- and midlevel appointments.

Natural Resources Defense Council, 1200 New York Ave. N.W., #400, Washington, DC 20005-4709; (202) 289-6868. Fax (202) 289-1060, Web http://www. nrdc.org. Donna Wilcox, office manager.

Environmental organization staffed by lawyers and scientists who undertake litigation and research. Interests include air, water, land use, forests, toxic materials, natural resources management and conservation, preservation of endangered plant species, and ozone pollution. (Headquarters in New York.)

Nature Conservancy, 4245 N. Fairfax Dr., Arlington, VA 22203; (703) 841-5300. Fax (703) 841-1283, Web http://www.tnc.org. Laura Jarrell, office recruitment.

Acquires land to protect endangered species and habitats; maintains international system of natural sanctuaries; operates the Heritage Program, a cooperative effort with state governments to identify and inventory threatened and endangered plants and animals.

Nuclear Information and Resource Service, 1424 16th St. N.W., #404, Washington, DC 20036; (202) 328-0002. Fax (202) 462-2183, e-mail nirsnet@igc.org, Web http://www.nirs.org. Michael Mariotte, executive director.

Membership: organizations and individuals concerned about nuclear energy and nuclear waste. Information clearinghouse on nuclear power plants, nuclear waste, and radiation effects.

OMB Watch, 1742 Connecticut Ave. N.W., Washington, DC 20009; (202) 234-8494. Fax (202) 234-8584, e-mail ombwatch@ombwatch.org, Web http:// www.ombwatch.org/ombwatch.html. Barb Western, assistant to the executive director.

Research and advocacy organization that monitors and interprets the policies and activities of the Office of Management and Budget. Sponsors conferences and teaches the governmental decision-making process concerning accountability.

Peace Action, 1819 H St. N.W., #420, Washington, DC 20006-3603; (202) 862-9740. Fax (202) 862-9762, e-mail pamembers@igc.apc.org, Web http://www.

peace-action.org. Sheila Dormody, organizing director; Jim Bridgman, research and resource coordinator.

Grassroots organization that supports a negotiated comprehensive test ban treaty. Seeks a reduction in the military budget and a transfer of those funds to nonmilitary programs. Works for an end to international arms trade. Formerly Sane/Freeze.

People for the American Way, 2000 M St. N.W., #400, Washington, DC 20036; (202) 467-4999. Fax (202) 293-2672, e-mail pfaw@pfaw.org, Web http://www.pfaw.org. Judy Green, director of personnel and administration.

Nonpartisan organization that promotes protection of First Amendment rights through a national grassroots network of members and volunteers. Conducts public education programs on constitutional issues. Provides radio, television, and newspaper advertisements; maintains speakers bureau.

Physicians for Social Responsibility, 1101 14th St. N.W., #700, Washington, DC 20005; (202) 898-0150. Fax (202) 898-0172, e-mail psrnatl@psr.org, Web http://www.psr.org. Robert Musil, executive director.

Membership: doctors, dentists, and other individuals. Works toward the elimination of nuclear and other weapons of mass destruction, the achievement of a sustainable environment, and the reduction of violence and its causes. Conducts public education programs, monitors policy decisions on arms control, and serves as a liaison with other concerned groups.

Planned Parenthood Federation of America, 1120 Connecticut Ave. N.W., #461, Washington, DC 20036; (202) 785-3351. Fax (202) 293-4349, Web http://www.plannedparenthood.org. Jacquelyn Lendsey, vice president, public policy.

Educational, research, and medical services organization. Washington office conducts research and monitors legislation on fertility-related health topics, including abortion, reproductive health, contraception, family planning, and international population control. (Headquarters in New York accredits affiliated local centers, which offer medical services, birth control, and family planning information.)

Population Reference Bureau, 1875 Connecticut Ave. N.W., #520, Washington, DC 20009; (202) 483-1100. Fax (202) 328-3937, Web http://www.prb.org. Judi Jackson, human resources; Donna Clifton, assistant coordinator for international programs.

Educational organization engaged in information dissemination, training, and policy analysis on U.S. population trends and issues. Interests include international development and family planning programs, the environment, and U.S. social and economic policy.

Product Liability Alliance, 1725 K St. N.W., Washington, DC 20006; (202) 872-0885. Fax (202) 785-0586. Joy Goldman, director of administration.

Membership: manufacturers, product sellers and their insurers, and trade associations. Promotes enactment of federal product liability tort reform legislation.

Public Campaign, 1320 19th St. N.W., #M1, Washington, DC 20036; (202) 293-0222. Fax (202) 293-0202, e-mail info@publicampaign.org, Web http://

www.publicampaign.org. Ellen Miller, executive director.

Grassroots organization interested in campaign finance reform. Supports the Clean Money Campaign, a voluntary program in which candidates receive a set amount of public financing for elections if they reject private money and limit spending.

Public Citizen, 1600 20th St. N.W., Washington, DC 20009; (202) 588-1000. Fax (202) 588-7798, Web http://www.citizen.org. Joe Zillo, chief financial officer.

Public interest consumer advocacy organization comprising the following projects: Buyers Up, Congress Watch, Critical Mass Energy Project, Health Research Group, Litigation Group, and Global Trade Watch.

Rainbow PUSH Coalition, 1002 Wisconsin Ave. N.W., Washington, DC 20007; (202) 333-5270. Fax (202) 728-1192, Web http://www.rainbowpush.org. Nadine Chatman, deputy director; Kenyatta Hobson, assistant to bureau chief.

Independent political organization concerned with U.S. domestic and foreign policy. Interests include DC statehood, civil rights, defense policy, agriculture, poverty, the economy, energy, and the environment.

Reporters Committee for Freedom of the Press, 1815 N. Fort Myer Dr., #900, Arlington, VA 22209; (703) 807-2100. Fax (703) 807-2109, e-mail rcfp@rcfp.org, Web http://www.rcfp.org. Jane E. Kirtley, executive director.

Membership: reporters, news editors, publishers, and lawyers from the print and broadcast media. Maintains a legal defense and research fund for members of the news media involved in freedom of the press court cases; interests include freedom of speech abroad.

Republican National Committee, 310 1st St. S.E., Washington, DC 20003; (202) 863-8500. Fax (202) 863-8820, Web http://www.rnc.org. Jim Nicholson, chair.

Develops and promotes Republican party policies and positions; assists Republican candidates for state and national office; sponsors workshops to recruit Republican candidates and provide instruction in campaign techniques; organizes national political activities; works with state and local officials and organizations.

Resources for the Future, 1616 P St. N.W., Washington, DC 20036; (202) 328-5000. Fax (202) 939-3460, e-mail info@rff.org, Web http://www.rff.org. Hellen-Marie Spreich, personnel manager.

Research organization that conducts studies on economic and policy aspects of energy, conservation, and development of natural resources, including effects on the environment. Interests include hazardous waste, the Superfund, and biodiversity.

Rural Coalition, 110 Maryland Ave. N.E., #101, Washington, DC 20002; (202) 628-7160. Fax (202) 544-9613, e-mail ruralco@aol.com, Web http://www2.cibola.net/~sinfront/rcpage/html. Alicia Taylor, personnel director; Deborah Livingston, program director.

Alliance of organizations that develop public policies benefiting rural communities. Collaborates with community-based groups on agriculture and rural development issues, including health and the environment, minority farmers, farmworkers, native Americans' rights, and rural community development. Provides rural groups with technical assistance.

Safe Energy Communication Council, 1717 Massachusetts Ave. N.W., #106, Washington, DC 20036; (202) 483-8491. Fax (202) 234-9194, e-mail seccgen@aol.com. Scott Denman, executive director.

Coalition of national energy, environmental, and public interest media groups that works to increase public awareness of the ability of energy efficiency and renewable energy sources to meet an increasing share of U.S. energy needs and of the economic and environmental liabilities of nuclear power. Provides local, state, and national organizations with technical assistance through media skills training and outreach strategies.

Save America's Forests, 4 Library Court S.E., Washington, DC 20003; (202) 544-9219. Fax (202) 544-7462, Web http://www.saveamericasforests.org. Carl Ross, executive director.

Coalition of environmental and public interest groups, businesses, and individuals. Advocates recycling and comprehensive nationwide laws to prevent deforestation and to protect forest ecosystems.

Sentencing Project, 918 F St. N.W., #501, Washington, DC 20004; (202) 628-0871. Fax (202) 628-1091, Web http://www.sentencingproject.org. Gayle Hebron, executive assistant.

Develops and promotes sentencing programs that reduce reliance on incarceration; provides technical assistance to sentencing programs; compares domestic and international rates of incarceration; publishes research and information on criminal justice policy.

Share Our Strength, 733 15th St. N.W., #640, Washington, DC 20005; (202) 393-2925, toll-free (800) 969-4767. Fax (202) 347-5868, e-mail sos@charitiesusa.com, Web http://www.strength.org. Julie Nicholson, staff accountant; Darnice Griffin, internship coordinator.

Works to alleviate and prevent hunger and poverty in the United States and around the world. Meets immediate demands for food by providing food assistance; treats malnutrition and other consequences of hunger; promotes economic independence among people in need, while seeking long-term solutions to hunger and poverty. Helps mobilize industries, organizations, and individuals to contribute their talents to antihunger efforts.

Sierra Club, 408 C St. N.E., Washington, DC 20002; (202) 547-1141. Fax (202) 547-6009, e-mail information@sierraclub.org, Web http://www.sierraclub.org. Annette Henkin, office manager.

Citizens' interest group that promotes protection and responsible use of the Earth's ecosystems and its natural resources. Focuses on combating global warming/greenhouse effect through energy conservation, efficient use of renewable energy resources, auto efficiency, and constraints on deforestation. Monitors federal, state, and local legislation relating to the environment and natural resources. (Headquarters in San Francisco.)

Student Press Law Center, 1815 N. Fort Myer Dr., #900, Arlington, VA 22209; (703) 807-1904. Fax (703) 807-2109, e-mail splc@splc.org, Web http://www.splc. org. Mark Goodman, executive director.

Collects, analyzes, and distributes information on free expression and freedom of information rights of student journalists (print and broadcast) and on violations of those rights in high schools and colleges. Provides free legal assistance to students and faculty advisers experiencing censorship.

Surface Transportation Policy Project, 1100 17th St. N.W., 10th Floor, Washington, DC 20036; (202) 466-2636. Fax (202) 466-2247, e-mail stpp@transact.org, Web http://www.transact.org/stpp.htm. Carmen Hunt, office manager.

Advocates transportation policy and investments that conserve energy, protect environmental and aesthetic quality, strengthen the economy, promote social equity, and make communities more livable.

TransAfrica, 1744 R St. N.W., Washington, DC 20009-2410; (202) 797-2301. Fax (202) 797-2382, e-mail transforum@igc.org, Web http://www.igc.org/ transafrica. Selena Mendey Singleton, senior policy advisor; Mwiza Munthali, information specialist.

Focuses on U.S. foreign policy toward African nations, the Caribbean, and peoples of African descent. Provides members with information on foreign policy issues; conducts educational training programs for minority students considering careers in international affairs.

Union of Concerned Scientists, 1616 P St. N.W., #310, Washington, DC 20036; (202) 332-0900. Fax (202) 332-0905, e-mail ucs@ucsusa.org, Web http://www. ucsusa.org. Cheryl Siebert, intern coordinator.

Independent group of scientists and others that advocates safe and sustainable international, national, and state energy policies. Conducts research, advocacy, and educational outreach focusing on market-based strategies for the development of renewable energy and alternative fuels, transportation policy, carbon reduction, global warming, and energy efficiency. (Headquarters in Cambridge, Mass.)

U.S.-Asia Institute, 232 E. Capitol St. N.E., Washington, DC 20003; (202) 544-3181. Fax (202) 543-1748. Joji Konoshima, president.

Organization of individuals interested in Asia. Encourages communication among political and business leaders in the United States and Asia. Interests include foreign policy, international trade, Asian and American cultures, education, and employment. Conducts research and sponsors conferences and workshops in cooperation with the State Dept. to promote greater understanding between the United States and Asian nations. Conducts programs that take congressional staff members to Singapore, Japan, Indonesia, Malaysia, and China.

U.S. Chamber of Commerce, 1615 H St. N.W., Washington, DC 20062-2000; (202) 659-6000. Fax (202) 463-5836, Web http://www.uschamber.org. Bobby Brown, human resources specialist.

Federation of businesses, trade, and professional associations; state and local chambers of commerce; and American chambers of commerce abroad. Develops policy on legislative issues important to American business; sponsors programs on management, business confidence, small business, consumer affairs, economic policy, minority business, and tax policy; maintains a business forecast and survey center and a trade negotiation information service. Monitors legislation and regulations.

U.S. English, 1747 Pennsylvania Ave. N.W., #1100, Washington, DC 20006; (202) 833-0100. Fax (202) 833-0108, Web http://www.us-english.org. Judy Edwards, office manager.

Advocates English as the official language of federal and state government.

U.S. Public Interest Research Group (USPIRG), 218 D St. S.E., Washington, DC 20003; (202) 546-9707. Fax (202) 546-2461, e-mail uspirg@pirg.org, Web http://www.pirg.org. Rick Trilsch, administrative director.

Conducts research and advocacy on consumer and environmental issues, including telephone rates, banking practices, insurance, campaign finance reform, product safety, toxic and solid waste, safe drinking water, and energy; monitors private and governmental actions affecting consumers; supports efforts to challenge consumer fraud and illegal business practices. Serves as national office for state groups.

U.S. Term Limits, 1125 15th St. N.W., #501, Washington, DC 20005; (202) 463-3200. Fax (202) 463-3210, Web http://www.termlimits.org. Pauline McHeard, office manager.

Works with state and local activists to place initiatives before voters; supports term limits at all levels of government; seeks limits of three terms in the House and two in the Senate. Monitors legislation and regulations.

Vietnam Veterans of America, 1224 M St. N.W., Washington, DC 20005-5183; (202) 628-2700, toll-free (800) 882-1316. Fax (202) 628-5880, e-mail 71154.702@compuserve.com, Web http://www.vva.org. George Duggins, president.

Membership organization that provides information on legislation that affects Vietnam era veterans and their families. Engages in legislative and judicial advocacy in areas relevant to Vietnam era veterans.

Washington Institute for Near East Policy, 1828 L St. N.W., #1050, Washington, DC 20036; (202) 452-0650. Fax (202) 223-5364, e-mail info@washingtoninstitute.org, Web http://www.washingtoninstitute.org. Patrick Clawson, director for research.

Research and educational organization that seeks to improve the effectiveness of American policy in the Near East by promoting debate among policymakers, journalists, and scholars.

Washington Legal Foundation, 2009 Massachusetts Ave. N.W., Washington, DC 20036; (202) 588-0302. Fax (202) 588-0371, Web http://www.wlf.org. Connie Lawcher, executive director.

Public interest law and policy center. Interests include constitutional law, government regulation, media law, and criminal justice. Litigates on behalf of small businesses, members of Congress, and victims of violent crimes who bring civil suits against their attackers.

Washington Office on Latin America, 1630 Connecticut Ave. N.W., #200, Washington, DC 20009; (202) 797-2171. Fax (202) 797-2172, e-mail wola@wola.org, Web http://www.wola.org. Sussanna Aulbach, internship coordinator.

Acts as a liaison between government policymakers and groups and individuals concerned with human rights and U.S. policy in Latin America. Serves as an information resource center; monitors legislation.

Wilderness Society, 900 17th St. N.W., Washington, DC 20006; (202) 833-2300. Fax (202) 429-3958, e-mail tws@tws.org, Web http://www.wilderness.org. Katie Hogan, human resources administrator.

Promotes preservation of wilderness and the responsible management of all federal lands, including national parks and forests, wilderness areas, wildlife refuges, and land administered by the Interior Dept.'s Bureau of Land Management.

World Resources Institute, 10 G St. N.E., #800, Washington, DC 20002; (202) 729-7600. Fax (202) 729-7610, e-mail http://www.wri.org. Jonathan Lash, president.

International organization that conducts research on environmental problems and studies the inter-relationships of natural resources, economic growth, and human needs. Interests include forestry and land use, renewable energy, fisheries, and sustainable agriculture. Assesses environmental policies of aid agencies.

World Wildlife Fund, 1250 24th St. N.W., #400, Washington, DC 20037; (202) 293-4800. Fax (202) 293-9211, Web http://www.wwf.org. Meg Carlan, administrative assistant, human resources.

Conducts scientific research and analyzes policy on environmental and conservation issues, including pollution reduction, land use, forestry and wetlands management, parks, soil conservation, and sustainable development. Supports projects to promote biological diversity and to save endangered species and their habitats, including tropical forests in Latin America, Asia, and Africa. Awards grants and provides technical assistance to local conservation groups.

Zero Population Growth, 1400 16th St. N.W., #320, Washington, DC 20036; (202) 332-2200. Fax (202) 332-2302, e-mail zpg@igc.apc.org, Web http://www.zpg.org. Patricia Parker, director of finance of administration; Jay Keller, national field director.

Membership: persons interested in sustainable world populations. Promotes the expansion of domestic and international family planning programs; supports a voluntary population stabilization policy and women's access to abortion and family planning services; works to protect the earth's resources and environment.

THINK TANKS

Alexis de Tocqueville Institution, 1611 N. Kent St., #901, Arlington, VA 22209; (703) 351-4969. Fax (703) 351-0090, Web http://www.adti.net. Jen Brown, senior vice president.

Public policy research organization that conducts, sponsors, and publishes research and analysis. Advocates individual political and economic freedom, limited government, and free markets.

American Enterprise Institute for Public Policy Research, 1150 17th St. N.W., Washington, DC 20036; (202) 862-5800. Fax (202) 862-7177, e-mail info@aei.org, Web http://www.aei.org. Christopher C. DeMuth, president.

Research and educational organization. Interests include fiscal and monetary policy, health policy, international trade and finance, regulation, telecommunications policy, defense and arms control, U.S. foreign policy, legal and constitutional issues, social and individual responsibility, and education, culture, and religion.

Brookings Institution, 1775 Massachusetts Ave. N.W., Washington, DC 20036; (202) 797-6000. Fax (202) 797-6004, e-mail brookinfo@brook.edu, Web http://www.brookings.org. Michael H. Armacost, president.

Public policy research organization that seeks to improve the performance of American institutions, the effectiveness of government programs, and the quality of public policy through research and analysis. Sponsors lectures, debates, and policy forums.

Capital Research Center, 1513 16th St. N.W., Washington, DC 20036-1480; (202) 483-6900. Fax (202) 483-6902, Web http://www.capitalresearch.org. Robert Huberty, vice president.

Researches funding sources of public interest and advocacy groups; analyzes the impact these groups have on public policy; publishes findings in newsletters and reports.

Cato Institute, 1000 Massachusetts Ave. N.W., Washington, DC 20001-5403; (202) 842-0200. Fax (202) 842-3490, e-mail cato@cato.org, Web http://www.cato.org. Edward H. Crane III, president.

Public policy research organization that advocates individual liberty and limited government. Interests include privatization and deregulation, low and simple taxes, and reduced government spending. Encourages voluntary solutions to social and economic problems.

Center for National Policy, 1 Massachusetts Ave. N.W., #333, Washington, DC 20001; (202) 682-1800. Fax (202) 682-1818, e-mail thecenter@cnponline.org, Web http://www.cnponline.org. Jill Hanauer, vice president.

Public policy research and educational organization that serves as a forum for development of national policy alternatives. Studies issues of national and international concern including problems of governance; sponsors conferences and symposia.

Center for Policy Alternatives, 1875 Connecticut Ave. N.W., #710, Washington, DC 20009-5728; (202) 387-6030. Fax (202) 986-2539, e-mail info@cfpa.org, Web http://www.cfpa.org. Delba Riddick, chief operating officer; Dailla Brooks, intern coordinator.

Clearinghouse and research center that assists state and local officials in developing policy initiatives. Interests include state and local economic development and tax reform, toxic chemicals and environmental problems, governmental reform, health policy, voter registration, and women's rights issues; provides technical assistance.

Economic Policy Institute, 1660 L St. N.W., #1200, Washington, DC 20036; (202) 775-8810. Fax (202) 775-0819, e-mail epi@epinet.org, Web http://www. epinet.org. Jeff Faux, president; Julie Leavitt, office manager.

Research and educational organization that publishes analyses on economics, economic development, competitiveness, income distribution, industrial competitiveness, and investment. Conducts public conferences and seminars.

Ethics and Public Policy Center, 1015 15th St. N.W., #900, Washington, DC 20005; (202) 682-1200. Fax (202) 408-0632, e-mail ethics@eppc.org, Web http://www.eppc.org. Ethan Reedy, administrative director.

Conducts research and holds conferences on the role of formal education and morality in teaching facts, ideas, attitudes, and values.

Free Congress Research and Education Foundation, 717 2nd St. N.E., Washington, DC 20002-4368; (202) 546-3004. Fax (202) 543-5605, e-mail net@fcref. org, Web http://www.freecongress.org. Rob Callahan, vice president of administration.

Public policy research and education foundation. Through the Krieble Institute, provides citizens of the former Soviet bloc with training in democratic processes and free enterprise.

Heritage Foundation, 214 Massachusetts Ave. N.E., Washington, DC 20002-4999; (202) 546-4400. Fax (202) 546-0904, Web http://www.heritage.org. Edwin J. Feulner Jr., president; Mellissa Naudin, intern coordinator.

Public policy research organization that conducts research and analysis and sponsors lectures, debates, and policy forums advocating individual freedom, limited government, the free market system, and a strong national defense.

Institute for Policy Studies, 733 15th St. N.W., #1020, Washington, DC 20005; (202) 234-9382. Fax (202) 387-7915, Web http://www.igc.org/ifps. John Cavanagh, director.

Research and educational organization. Interests include foreign policy, the U.S. military-industrial complex, international development, human rights, and national security.

Investor Responsibility Research Center, 1350 Connecticut Ave. N.W., #700, Washington, DC 20036-1702; (202) 833-0700. Fax (202) 833-3555, e-mail irrc@aol.com, Web http://www.irrc.org. Scott Fenn, executive director.

Research organization that reports on and analyzes business and public policy issues affecting corporations and investors.

Joint Center for Political and Economic Studies, 1090 Vermont Ave. N.W., #1100, Washington, DC 20005-4961; (202) 789-3500. Fax (202) 789-6390, Web http://www.jointctr.org. Eddie N. Williams, president; Luther Elliott, personnel manager.

Researches and analyzes issues of concern to African Americans, focusing on economic and social policy issues and African American political participation. Publishes a biannual profile of African American elected officials in federal, state, and local government; holds forums on public policy issues.

Progress and Freedom Foundation, 1301 K St. N.W., #550E, Washington, DC 20005; (202) 289-8928. Fax (202) 289-6079, e-mail mail@pff.org, Web http://www.pff.org. Jeffrey A. Eisenach, president.

Studies the impact of the digital revolution and its implications for public policy; sponsors seminars, conferences, and broadcasts.

Rand Corporation, 1333 H St. N.W., #800, Washington, DC 20005; (202) 296-5000. Fax (202) 296-7960, Web http://www.rand.org. Bruce Hoffman, director, Washington Office.

Research organization. Interests include energy, emerging technologies and critical systems, space and transportation, technology policies, international cooperative research, water resources, ocean and atmospheric sciences, and other technologies in defense and nondefense areas. (Headquarters in Santa Monica, Calif.)

Urban Institute, 2100 M St. N.W., Washington, DC 20037; (202) 833-7200. Fax (202) 429-0687, Web http://www.urban.org. William Gorham, president; Tammy Pratt, personnel recruiter; Deborah Hoover, codirector of personnel.

Nonpartisan, public policy research and education organization. Interests include states' use of federal funds; delivery of social services to specific groups, including children of mothers in welfare reform programs; retirement policy, income, and community-based services for the elderly; job placement and training programs for welfare recipients; health care cost containment and access; food stamps; child nutrition; the homeless; housing; immigration; and tax policy.

Worldwatch Institute, 1776 Massachusetts Ave. N.W., 8th Floor, Washington, DC 20036; (202) 452-1999. Fax (202) 296-7365, e-mail worldwatch@worldwatch.org, Web http://www.worldwatch.org. Lester R. Brown, president.

Research organization that studies the environmental origins of world population growth and health trends; interests include the food supply and malnutrition.

7

Working in Washington: Trade Associations and Labor Unions

When political wars erupt in Washington, trade associations and labor unions are usually in the thick of the battle. But they don't just wait for fights to flex their muscles: Day in and day out, they actively push their causes with lawmakers, congressional staff, executive branch officials, journalists, and anyone else who can help them.

Hundreds of trade associations and labor unions have their headquarters in Washington, and many others headquartered in other cities such as New York have a Washington office. Their wide-ranging involvement in every aspect of the political process makes trade associations and labor unions some of the biggest players in Washington, and also gives them tremendous influence. The days when certain associations and unions handed politicians envelopes stuffed with cash may be over, but the efforts to win friends and influence people certainly are not.

Among trade associations, some of the biggest players in Washington include the Association of Trial Lawyers of America, National Automobile Dealers Association, American Medical Association, National Association of Realtors, National Association of Home Builders, National Association of Chain Drug Stores, American Insurance Association, Chemical Manufacturers Association, and the Air Transport Association of America.

On the union side, some of the major players include the AFL-CIO, Communications Workers of America, American Federation of Teachers, Service Employees International Union, National Education Association, United Food & Commercial Workers International Union, International Brotherhood of Electrical Workers, and the American Federation of State, County, and Municipal Employees.

Between them, trade associations and labor unions employ thousands of people in Washington. Some individual offices have hundreds of employees. For example, the Association of American Railroads employs 650 people in Washington, and the National Education Association employs about 500.

Lobbying by Trade Associations and Labor Unions

Most trade associations and labor unions lobby on many issues, although a group's exact focus depends on its membership. Some of the major issues they commonly tackle include privatizing Social Security, health care, occupational safety and health, international trade, civil rights, economic policy, taxes, and the federal minimum wage. One of the biggest battles that trade associations and labor unions fought recently was over adopting the North American Free Trade Agreement. Trade associations favored NAFTA because they believed it would lower costs and open markets, but unions opposed it because they thought it would cost American jobs as businesses shifted work to countries that paid lower wages. The associations won, and NAFTA passed.

Trade associations and labor unions use many tools to influence policy. Some are the same tools that other groups use: issuing studies and other documents, holding press conferences, testifying before Congress, cultivating reporters, organizing members to support or oppose legislation or candidates, and submitting formal comments about proposed federal rules that affect their members. But most associations and unions go much further in lobbying and attempting to build personal relationships with lawmakers and their staffs.

Some of the lobbying is direct, such as when a lobbyist for an association or union meets with a member of Congress and some of her staff members to push the group's position about a specific bill. Often, though, the effort to build relationships and exert influence is more subtle.

For example, virtually every major trade association and labor union has a political action committee (PAC) that contributes money to candidates and political parties. Together, the association and labor PACs contribute tens of millions of dollars in each election. In the 1998 election cycle alone, the International Brotherhood of Teamsters gave $8.1 million to federal candidates, the National Education Association contributed $5.1 million, and the International Brotherhood of Electrical Workers gave $4.3 million. On the association side, the Association of Trial Lawyers of America gave $5.9 million, the American Medical Association gave $4.9 million, and the National Automobile Dealers Association gave $3.1 million. In nearly every case, unions give the bulk of their money to Democrats, and most associations give the bulk of their money to Republicans.

Trade associations and labor unions also attempt to make friends through free trips. According to an Associated Press story, in January

PROFILE: BESS KOZLOW

In her job at the American Bankers Association, a trade association for the banking industry, Bess Kozlow is learning about lobbying and the political process. The lessons will be particularly useful if she fulfills her dream of someday running for the House of Representatives, the Senate, or even the White House.

Like so many others in Washington, Kozlow got her start as an intern. After graduating from college with a psychology degree, she got her first internship with the House member who represents her home district in California. She next interned at the White House Office of Public Liaison. That internship primarily involved scheduling, answering the telephone, and other administrative duties.

For Kozlow, the biggest benefit of working at the White House likely was meeting the person who became her roommate. The roommate subsequently heard from a coworker about a job opening at the American Bankers Association, and passed word to Kozlow. Kozlow called the ABA to inquire about the job, sent in a resume and cover letter, and after several interviews was hired.

She works as a program assistant in the grassroots division of the ABA's government relations department. Her division works with bankers around the country to organize responses to proposed banking legislation. She'd only worked in the office three months when interviewed for this book, so her work primarily involved administrative duties and learning about banking and legislative issues. Soon, though, she expected to start working directly with bankers.

The focus on a single issue required of trade association employees is both a plus and a minus, Kozlow said. On the plus side, she's learning a great deal about banking—and that subject knowledge may be especially useful if she wants to work in a congressional office again. But on the minus side, she's confined to banking and misses the variety of issues she handled as a Hill intern.

Kozlow expects to stay at the ABA for two or three years. "I think it's a good vehicle for me to learn about lobbying and the political process," she said. "This is definitely a good place for me to learn, which is my basic goal right now." After that, she may work in a congressional office or she may return to California to work before launching her political career by running for city supervisor or the state legislature.

But for now, she's quite content living in Washington. Why does she stay? "The opportunities," Kozlow said. "There's no other place in the country where you could find the scope of opportunities to get involved in any kind of government at all. You've got associations, the federal government, even the city government if you want. You'd be hard pressed to find that kind of breadth in another city."

1999 three House members and eleven aides stayed in a resort hotel at Hapuna Beach in Hawaii while attending an aviation industry conference. Their airfare, hotel rooms, and meals were paid for by the American Association of Airport Executives, a trade association for airport managers.

Which Washington trade associations and labor unions are most powerful? That's open to debate. *Fortune* magazine took a stab at the question in late 1998 when it surveyed nearly 2,700 members of Congress, Hill staffers, senior White House aides, and lobbyists. The magazine asked which twenty-five trade associations, labor unions, and interest groups had the most lobbying clout.

The poll found that two unions and seventeen trade associations ranked among the twenty-five most powerful. The unions included the AFL-CIO, which ranked fifth, and the National Education Association, which ranked twenty-first. The trade associations in the top twenty-five included the National Federation of Independent Business (3), Association of Trial Lawyers of America (6), Credit Union National Association (8), American Medical Association (10), U.S. Chamber of Commerce (11), Independent Insurance Agents of America (12), National Association of Manufacturers (13), American Farm Bureau Federation (14), National Restaurant Association (15), National Association of Home Builders (16), National Association of Realtors (17), National Association of Broadcasters (18), Motion Picture Association of America (19), American Bankers Association (20), Health Insurance Association of America (22), American Council of Life Insurance (23), and the National Beer Wholesalers Association (24).

Working at a Trade Association or Labor Union

The staff of a typical Washington trade association or labor union is effectively split into two parts. One part works on political issues, and the other plans conventions, develops education programs, recruits or organizes members, administers the organization, and provides various nonpolitical services to members. Some staffers, such as writers and graphic artists, may perform work for both parts of the organization, but most do not.

On the political side, new staffers can do anything from stuffing envelopes to attending congressional hearings. Some common tasks include monitoring newspapers and magazines, researching legislative issues and votes, writing position papers, helping arrange press conferences, helping organize grassroots activities by members, writing articles for member newsletters, and providing support to political campaigns of candidates backed by the organization, among many others.

As with so many Washington institutions, the best way to get your foot in the door at a trade association or labor union is to intern. Nearly all associations and unions welcome interns, so finding a slot shouldn't be hard if you have good skills.

The best way to learn about job openings at trade associations and labor unions is to check their Web sites. Nearly all groups now have Web sites, and many list job vacancies online. Most groups also run job ads in the *Washington Post,* which you also can access online. And don't forget about networking and informational interviews, which are valuable in any type of Washington job search.

Whether you're applying for an internship or a full-time job, be sure to use any connection—no matter how tentative—that you might have to the association or union. If your dad is a car dealer, be sure to mention that fact if you apply at the National Automobile Dealers Association. Likewise, if your mom is a teacher and a member of the National Education Association, mentioning that connection might help you get an interview if you apply at the teachers' union.

Entry-level salaries at trade associations and labor unions vary based on numerous factors, including your background and the exact job for which you're hired. As a general rule, associations pay more than unions, and larger associations and unions pay more than smaller ones. However, after a few years of experience with either associations or unions, you should be able to command a very respectable salary.

Trade Association and Labor Union Contacts

ONLINE DIRECTORY

JOBSmart
http://www.gwsae.org/Applications/JobBank
    JOBSmart offers details about job openings at associations located in Washington, D.C. The site commonly lists 100 or more openings, and you can sign up to be notified by e-mail when new listings are added. Not all the jobs are with trade associations—some are with other types of associations such as philanthropic associations—but this is nonetheless an excellent place to learn about job openings. The job listings are separated into numerous categories: administrative assistant/receptionist, CEO/executive director, communications/publications, education/training, executive assistant, executive staff, finance/administration, foundation/development, government relations/public relations, marketing, meetings/conventions, meetings/hospitality business partners, membership, MIS/information technology, and sales. You can browse the listings, or you can search them by keyword, region, and category. JOBSmart is operated by the Greater Washington Society of Association Executives.

TRADE ASSOCIATIONS

Aerospace Industries Association of America, 1250 Eye St. N.W., #1200, Washington, DC 20005-3922; (202) 371-8400. Fax (202) 371-8470, Web http://www.aia-aerospace.org. Jane Weeden, director of human resources.

Represents U.S. manufacturers of commercial, military, and business aircraft; helicopters; aircraft engines; missiles; spacecraft; and related components and equipment. Interests include international standards and trade.

Air Transport Association of America, 1301 Pennsylvania Ave. N.W., #1100, Washington, DC 20004; (202) 626-4000. Fax (202) 626-4166, Web http://www.air-transport.org. Karen Evans, director of human resources.

Membership: U.S. scheduled air carriers. Promotes aviation safety and the facilitation of air transportation for passengers and cargo. Monitors legislation and regulations.

Aluminum Association, 900 19th St. N.W., #300, Washington, DC 20006; (202) 862-5100. Fax (202) 862-5164, Web http://www.aluminum.org. J. Stephen Larkin, president.

Represents the aluminum industry. Develops voluntary standards and technical data; compiles statistics concerning the industry.

American Academy of Pediatrics, 601 13th St. N.W., #400N, Washington, DC 20005; (202) 347-8600, toll-free (800) 336-5475. Fax (202) 393-6137, e-mail kids1st@aap.org, Web http://www.aap.org. Mary McGowan, administrative director.

Advocates for maternal and child health legislation and regulations. Interests include increased access and coverage for persons under age 21, immunizations, injury prevention, environmental hazards, child abuse, emergency medical services, biomedical research, Medicaid, disabilities, pediatric AIDS, substance abuse, and nutrition. (Headquarters in Elk Grove Village, Ill.)

American Association of Airport Executives, 4212 King St., Alexandria, VA 22302; (703) 824-0500. Fax (703) 820-1395, Web http://www.airportnet.org. Tyra Harpster, vice president of finance.

Membership: airport managers, superintendents, consultants, authorities, commissions, government officials, and others interested in the construction, management, and operation of airports.

American Association of Health Plans, 1129 20th St. N.W., #600, Washington, DC 20036; (202) 778-3200. Fax (202) 331-7487, Web http://www.aahp.org. Dave Keyman, director of human resources.

Membership: managed health care plans and organizations. Provides legal counsel and conducts educational programs. Conducts research and analysis of managed care issues; produces publications. Monitors legislation and regulations.

American Bankers Association, 1120 Connecticut Ave. N.W., Washington, DC 20036; (202) 663-5000. Fax (202) 663-7533, Web http://www.aba.com. Donald G. Ogilvie, executive vice president.

Membership: commercial banks. Operates schools to train banking personnel; conducts conferences; formulates government relations policies for the banking community.

American Bus Association, 1100 New York Ave. N.W., #1050, Washington, DC 20005-3934; (202) 842-1645. Fax (202) 842-0850, Web http://www.buses.org. Peter J. Pantuso, president.

Membership: intercity privately owned bus companies, state associations, travel/tourism businesses, bus manufacturers, and those interested in the bus industry. Monitors legislation and regulations.

American Chiropractic Association, 1701 Clarendon Blvd., Arlington, VA 22209; (703) 276-8800. Fax (703) 243-2593, Web http://www.amerchiro.org. John Wanda, vice president of finance and administration.

Promotes professional growth and recognition for chiropractors. Interests include health care coverage, sports injuries, physical fitness, internal disorders, and orthopedics. Supports foundation for chiropractic education and research. Monitors legislation and regulations.

American Council of Life Insurance, 1001 Pennsylvania Ave. N.W., #500S, Washington, DC 20004-2599; (202) 624-2000. Fax (202) 624-2319, Web http://www.acli.com. Laura Eideide, human resources.

Membership: life insurance companies authorized to do business in the United States. Conducts research and compiles statistics at state and federal levels. Monitors legislation and regulations.

American Counseling Association, 5999 Stevenson Ave., Alexandria, VA 22304; (703) 823-9800, toll-free (800) 347-6647. Fax (703) 823-0252, Web http://www.counseling.org. Richard Yep, executive director.

Membership: professional counselors and counselor educators. Provides members with leadership training, continuing education programs, and advocacy services; develops professional and ethical standards for the counseling profession; accredits counselor education programs. Monitors legislation and regulations.

American Crop Protection Association, 1156 15th St. N.W., #400, Washington, DC 20005; (202) 296-1585. Fax (202) 463-0474, Web http://www.acpa.org. Mary K. Hindle, human resources director.

Membership: pesticide manufacturers. Provides information on pesticide safety, development, and use. Monitors legislation and regulations.

American Dental Association, 1111 14th St. N.W., #1100, Washington, DC 20005; (202) 898-2400. Fax (202) 898-2437, Web http://www.ada.org. Cindy Simms, manager; Frank McLaughlin, director of political action committee.

Conducts research; provides dental education materials; compiles statistics on dentistry and dental care. Monitors legislation and regulations. (Headquarters in Chicago.)

American Electronics Association, 601 Pennsylvania Ave. N.W., North Bldg., #600, Washington, DC 20004; (202) 682-9110. Fax (202) 682-9111, Web http://www.aeanet.org. Laurie Brown, human resources.

Membership: companies in the software, electronics, telecommunications, and information technology industries. Interests include international trade and investment, export controls, and U.S. competitiveness internationally. Holds conferences. Monitors legislation and regulations.

American Farm Bureau Federation, 600 Maryland Ave. S.W., #800, Washington, DC 20024; (202) 484-3600. Fax (202) 484-3604, Web http://www.fb.com. Merry Tobin, director of legislative services.

Federation of state farm bureaus in fifty states and Puerto Rico. Promotes agricultural research. Interests include commodity programs, domestic production, marketing, education, research, financial assistance to farmers, foreign assistance programs, rural development, the world food shortage, and inspection and certification of food. (Headquarters in Park Ridge, Ill.)

American Forest and Paper Association, 1111 19th St. N.W., #800, Washington, DC 20036; (202) 463-2700. Fax (202) 463-2785, Web http://www.afandpa.org. Lorna Rolingson, manager of human resources.

Membership: manufacturers of wood and specialty products and related associations. Interests include tax, housing, environmental, international trade, natural resources, and land-use issues that affect the wood products industry.

American Gaming Association, 555 13th St. N.W., #1010E, Washington, DC 20004-1109; (202) 637-6501. Fax (202) 637-6507, Web http://www.americangaming.org. Frank J. Fahrenkopf Jr., president.

Membership: casinos, casino and gaming equipment manufacturers, and financial services companies. Compiles statistics and serves as an information clearinghouse on the gaming industry. Administers a task force to study gambling addiction, raise public awareness, and develop assistance programs. Monitors legislation and regulations.

American Gas Association, 400 N. Capitol St. N.W., Washington, DC 20001; (202) 824-7000. Fax (202) 824-7115, Web http://www.aga.org. Morretta Henderson, director of human resources; Deborah Estes, managing director.

Membership: natural gas utilities and pipeline companies. Interests include all technical and operational aspects of the gas industry. Publishes comprehensive statistical record of gas industry; conducts national standard testing for gas appliances. Monitors legislation and regulations.

American Health Care Association, 1201 L St. N.W., Washington, DC 20005; (202) 842-4444. Fax (202) 842-3860, Web http://www.ahca.org. Heather Berger, director of human resources.

Federation of associations representing assisted living nursing facilities and subacute care providers. Sponsors and provides educational programs and materials.

American Herbal Products Association, 8484 Georgia Ave., #370, Silver Spring, MD 20910; (202) 588-1171. Fax (202) 588-1174, Web http://www.ahpa.org. Greg Grey, acting president.

Membership: U.S. companies and individuals that grow, import, process, or market herbs and herbal products; and associates in education, law, media, and medicine. Supports research; promotes standardization, consumer protection, competition, and self-regulation in the industry. Monitors legislation and regulations.

American Hospital Association, 325 7th St. N.W., Washington, DC 20004; (202) 638-1100. Fax (202) 626-2345, Web http://www.aha.org. Mary Lou Fine, director of human resources.

Membership: hospitals, other inpatient care facilities, outpatient centers, Blue Cross plans, areawide planning agencies, regional medical programs, hospital schools of nursing, and individuals. Conducts research and education projects in such areas as provision of comprehensive care, hospital economics, hospital facilities and design, and community relations; participates with other health care associations in establishing hospital care standards. Monitors legislation and regulations.

American Hotel and Motel Association, 1201 New York Ave. N.W., #600, Washington, DC 20005-3931; (202) 289-3100. Fax (202) 289-3199, Web http://www.ahma.com. Daria Jankura, human resources director.

Provides operations, technical, educational, marketing, and communications services to members; focus includes international travel. Monitors legislation and regulations.

American Insurance Association, 1130 Connecticut Ave. N.W., #1000, Washington, DC 20036; (202) 828-7100. Fax (202) 293-1219, Web http://www.aiadc.org. Christine Cronan, human resources administrator.

Membership: companies providing property and casualty insurance. Conducts public relations and educational activities; provides information on issues related to property and casualty insurance.

American Iron and Steel Institute, 1101 17th St. N.W., 13th Floor, Washington, DC 20036-4700; (202) 452-7100. Fax (202) 463-6573, Web http://www.steel.org. David Bell, vice president of finance and administration.

Represents the iron and steel industry. Publishes statistics on iron and steel production; promotes the use of steel; conducts research. Monitors legislation and regulations.

American Meat Institute, 1700 N. Moore St., #1600, Arlington, VA (mailing address: P.O. Box 3556, Washington, DC 20007); (703) 841-2400. Fax (703) 527-0938, Web http://www.meatami.org. J. Patrick Boyle, president.

Membership: national and international meat and poultry packers, suppliers, and processors. Provides statistics on meat and poultry production and exports. Funds research projects and consumer education programs. Monitors legislation and regulations.

American Medical Association, 1101 Vermont Ave. N.W., 12th Floor, Washington, DC 20005; (202) 789-7400. Fax (202) 789-7485, Web http://www.ama-association.org, human resources department in Chicago, (312) 464-5000. Lee Stillwell, senior vice president, public and private sector advocacy.

Membership: physicians, residents, and medical students. Provides information on health care. Monitors legislation and regulations. (Headquarters in Chicago.)

American Moving and Storage Association, 1611 Duke St., Alexandria, VA 22314; (703) 683-7410. Fax (703) 683-7527, Web http://www.moving.org. Joseph Harrison, president.

Represents members' views before the Transportation Dept. and other government agencies. Conducts certification and training programs. Provides financial support for research on the moving and storage industry.

American Nursery and Landscape Association, 1250 Eye St. N.W., #500, Washington, DC 20005-3922; (202) 789-2900. Fax (202) 789-1893, Web http://www.anla.org. Warren Quinn, director of operations.

Membership: wholesale growers, garden center retailers, landscape firms, and suppliers to the horticultural community. Monitors legislation and regulations on agricultural, environmental, and small business issues; conducts educational seminars on business management for members.

American Nurses Association, 600 Maryland Ave. S.W., #100W, Washington, DC 20024-2571; (202) 651-7000. Fax (202) 651-7001, Web http://www.nursingworld.org. David Hennage, executive director.

Membership: registered nurses. Sponsors the American Nurses Foundation. Monitors legislation and regulations.

American Optometric Association, 1505 Prince St., Alexandria, VA 22314; (703) 739-9200. Fax (703) 739-9497, Web http://www.aoa.org. Jeffrey G. Mays, director, Washington Office.

Membership: optometrists and optometry students. Monitors legislation and regulations and acts as liaison with international optometric groups and government optometrists; conducts continuing education programs for optometrists and provides information on eye care. (Headquarters in St. Louis.)

American Petroleum Institute, 1220 L St. N.W., Washington, DC 20005; (202) 682-8100. Fax (202) 682-8110, Web http://www.api.org. Emily Fletcher, human resources manager.

Membership: producers, refiners, marketers, and transporters of oil, natural gas, and related products such as gasoline. Provides information on the industry, including data on exports and imports, taxation, transportation, weekly refinery operations, and drilling activity and costs; conducts research on petroleum; and publishes statistical and drilling reports.

American Plastics Council, 1801 K St. N.W., #701L, Washington, DC 20006; (202) 974-5400. Fax (202) 296-7119, Web http://www.plasticsresource.com. Ronald H. Yocum, president.

Seeks to increase plastics recycling; conducts research on disposal of plastic products; sponsors research on waste-handling methods, incineration, and degradation; supports programs that test alternative waste management technologies. Monitors legislation and regulations.

American Psychiatric Association, 1400 K St. N.W., Washington, DC 20005; (202) 682-6000. Fax (202) 682-6850, e-mail apa@psych.org, Web http://www.psych.org. Deborah Brown, assistant director.

Membership: psychiatrists. Promotes availability of high-quality psychiatric care; provides the public with information; assists state and local agencies; conducts educational programs for professionals and students in the field.

American Psychological Association, 750 1st St. N.E., Washington, DC 20002-4242; (202) 336-5500. Fax (202) 336-6069, Web http://www.apa.org. Raymond D. Fowler, executive vice president.

Membership: professional psychologists, educators, and behavioral research scientists. Supports research, training, and professional services; works toward improving the qualifications, training programs, and competence of psychologists; monitors international research and U.S. legislation on mental health.

American Public Power Association, 2301 M St. N.W., Washington, DC 20037; (202) 467-2900. Fax (202) 467-2910, Web http://www.appanet.org. Eileen Peerless, human resources director.

Membership: local, publicly owned electric utilities nationwide. Represents industry interests before Congress, federal agencies, and the courts; provides educational programs; collects and disseminates information; funds energy research and development projects.

American Public Transit Association, 1201 New York Ave. N.W., #400, Washington, DC 20005; (202) 898-4000. Fax (202) 898-4070, Web http://www.apta.com. Evelyn Lozano, human resources manager.

Membership: rapid rail and motor bus systems and manufacturers, suppliers, and consulting firms. Compiles data on the industry; promotes research. Monitors legislation and regulations.

American Pulpwood Association, 600 Jefferson Plaza, #350, Rockville, MD 20852; (301) 838-9385. Fax (301) 838-9481, Web http://www.apulpa.org. Linda Roseberg, director of finance and administration.

Membership: logging contractors, pulpwood dealers, suppliers, and consumers. Administers programs to improve the productivity, safety, and efficiency of pulpwood harvesting and transport; provides information on new equipment, tools, and methods; works to ensure continued access to the timberland base. Monitors legislation and regulations.

American Resort Development Association, 1220 L St. N.W., #500, Washington, DC 20005; (202) 371-6700. Fax (202) 289-8544, Web http://www.arda.org. Adrienne Riley, director of operations.

Membership: U.S. and international developers, builders, financiers, marketing companies, and others involved in resort, recreational, and community development. Serves as an information clearinghouse; monitors federal and state legislation affecting land, timeshare, and community development industries.

American Road and Transportation Builders Association, 1010 Massachusetts Ave. N.W., 6th Floor, Washington, DC 20001; (202) 289-4434. Fax (202) 289-4435, e-mail artba@artba.com, Web http://www.artba-hq.org. Matt Jeannert, director of communications.

Membership: highway and transportation contractors; federal, state, and local engineers and officials; construction equipment manufacturers and distributors; and others interested in the transportation construction industry. Serves as liaison with government; provides information on highway engineering and construction developments.

American Trucking Associations, 2200 Mill Rd., Alexandria, VA 22314-4677; (703) 838-1700, toll-free (800) 282-5463. Fax (703) 684-4326, e-mail membership@trucking.org, Web http://www.trucking.org. Kay Howard, director of human resources.

Membership: state trucking associations, individual trucking and motor carrier organizations, and related supply companies. Maintains departments on industrial relations, law, management systems, research, safety, traffic, state laws, taxation, communications, legislation, economics, and engineering.

American Waterways Operators, 1600 Wilson Blvd., #1000, Arlington, VA 22209; (703) 841-9300. Fax (703) 841-0389. Thomas Allegretti, president.

Membership: operators of barges, tugboats, and towboats on navigable coastal and inland waterways and commercial shipyard owners. Acts as liaison with Congress, the U.S. Coast Guard, the Army Corps of Engineers, and the Maritime Administration. Monitors legislation and regulations.

American Wind Energy Association, 122 C St. N.W., 4th Floor, Washington, DC 20001; (202) 383-2500. Fax (202) 383-2505, e-mail awea@awea.org, Web http://www.econet.org/awea. Joy Diggs, assistant finance director.

Membership: manufacturers, developers, operators, and distributors of wind machines; utility companies; and others interested in wind energy. Advocates wind energy as an alternative energy source; makes industry data available to the public and to federal and state legislators. Promotes export of wind energy technology.

America's Community Bankers, 900 19th St. N.W., #400, Washington, DC 20006; (202) 857-3100. Fax (202) 296-8716, e-mail info@acbankers.org, Web http://www.acbankers.org. Mary Mason, employment coordinator.

Membership: insured depository institutions involved in community finance. Provides information on issues that affect the industry. Monitors economic issues affecting savings institutions; publishes homebuyers survey. Monitors legislation and regulations.

Associated Builders and Contractors, 1300 N. 17th St., 8th Floor, Rosslyn, VA 22209; (703) 812-2000. Fax (703) 812-8202, Web http://www.abc.org. Krista Kirk, director of human services; Charlotte Herbert, executive vice president, government affairs.

Membership: construction contractors engaged primarily in nonresidential construction, subcontractors, and suppliers. Sponsors apprenticeship, safety, and training programs. Provides labor relations information; compiles statistics. Monitors legislation and regulations.

Associated General Contractors of America, 1957 E St. N.W., Washington, DC 20006-5194; (202) 393-2040. Fax (202) 347-4004, Web http://www.agc.org. Carolyn Mauk, senior human resources director.

Membership: general contractors engaged primarily in nonresidential construction; subcontractors; suppliers; accounting, insurance and bonding, and law firms. Conducts training programs, conferences, seminars, and market development activities for members. Produces position papers on construction issues. Monitors legislation and regulations.

Association of American Railroads, 50 F St. N.W., 4th Floor, Washington, DC 20001; (202) 639-2100. Fax (202) 639-2558, Web http://www.aar.org. Janice Kittrell, human resources specialist.

Provides information on freight railroad operations, safety and maintenance, economics and finance, management, and law and legislation; conducts research; issues statistical reports.

Association of Trial Lawyers of America, 1050 31st St. N.W., Washington, DC 20007-4499; (202) 965-3500. Fax (202) 342-5484, Web http://www.atlanet.org. Irene Cardon, manager of human resources.

Membership: attorneys, judges, law professors, and students. Interests include aspects of legal and legislative activity relating to the adversary system and trial by jury, including property and casualty insurance.

Automotive Parts and Accessories Association, 4600 East-West Hwy., #300, Bethesda, MD 20814; (301) 654-6664. Fax (301) 654-3299, Web http://www. apaa.org. Deidre Lancaster, manager of human resources.

Membership: domestic and international manufacturers, manufacturers' representatives, retailers, and distributors in the automotive aftermarket industry, which involves service of a vehicle after it leaves the dealership. Offers educational programs, conducts research, and provides members with technical and international trade services; acts as liaison with government; sponsors annual marketing conference and trade shows.

Beer Institute, 122 C St. N.W., #750, Washington, DC 20001; (202) 737-2337. Fax (202) 737-7004, Web http://www.beerinst.org. Ray McGrath, president.

Membership: domestic and international brewers and suppliers to the domestic brewing industry. Monitors legislation and regulations.

Biotechnology Industry Organization, 1625 K St. N.W., #1100, Washington, DC 20006-1604; (202) 857-0244. Fax (202) 857-0237, e-mail bio@bio.org, Web http://www.bio.org. Ellen Fernandes, director of human resources.

Membership: companies engaged in biotechnology. Monitors government activities at all levels; promotes educational activities; conducts workshops.

Blue Cross and Blue Shield Association, 1310 G St. N.W., Washington, DC 20005; (202) 626-4780. Fax (202) 626-4833, Web http://www.bluecares.com. John Green, human resources generalist.

Membership: Blue Cross and Blue Shield insurance plans, which operate autonomously at the local level. Certifies member plans; acts as consultant to plans in evaluating new medical technologies and contracting with doctors and hospitals. Operates a national telecommunications network to collect, analyze, and disseminate data. (Headquarters in Chicago.)

Cellular Telecommunications Industry Association, 1250 Connecticut Ave. N.W., #800, Washington, DC 20036; (202) 785-0081. Fax (202) 776-0540, Web http://www.wow-com.com. Roberta Catucci, director of administration.

Membership: system operators, equipment manufacturers, engineering firms, and others engaged in the cellular telephone and mobile communications industry. Provides information for consumers and persons with disabilities. Monitors legislation and regulations.

Chemical Manufacturers Association, 1300 Wilson Blvd., Arlington, VA 22209; (703) 741-5000. Fax (703) 741-6097, Web http://www.cmahq.com. Kelly Shoemaker, human resources.

Membership: manufacturers of basic industrial chemicals. Provides members with technical research, communications services, and legal affairs counseling. Interests include environmental safety and health, transportation, energy, and international trade. Monitors legislation and regulations.

Chemical Specialties Manufacturers Association, 1913 Eye St. N.W., Washington, DC 20006; (202) 872-8110. Fax (202) 872-8114, e-mail info@csma.org, Web http://www.csma.org. Ralph Engel, president.

Membership: manufacturers, marketers, packagers, and suppliers in the chemical specialties industry. Specialties include cleaning compounds and detergents, insecticides, disinfectants, automotive and industrial products, polishes and floor finishes, antimicrobials, and aerosol products. Monitors scientific developments; conducts surveys and research; provides chemical safety information and consumer education programs; sponsors National Poison Prevention Week and Aerosol Education Bureau. Monitors legislation and regulations.

Computer and Communications Industry Association, 666 11th St. N.W., #600, Washington, DC 20001; (202) 783-0070. Fax (202) 783-0534, Web http://www.ccianet.org. Edward J. Black, president.

Membership: manufacturers and suppliers of computer data processing and communications-related products and services. Interests include telecommunications policy, capital formation and tax policy, communications and computer industry standards, intellectual property policies, encryption, international trade, and antitrust reform.

Cosmetic, Toiletry, and Fragrance Association, 1101 17th St. N.W., #300, Washington, DC 20036; (202) 331-1770. Fax (202) 331-1969, Web http://www.ctfa.org. Cheryl Shiapa, director of administration.

Membership: manufacturers and distributors of finished personal care products. Represents the industry at the local, state, and national levels. Interests include scientific research, legal issues, legislation, and regulatory policy.

Direct Marketing Association, 1111 19th St. N.W., #1100, Washington, DC 20036; (202) 955-5030. Fax (202) 955-0085, Web http://www.the-dma.org. Jerry Cerasale, senior vice president, government affairs.

Membership: telemarketers; users, creators, and producers of direct mail; and suppliers to the industry. Evaluates direct marketing methods that make use of personal consumer information. (Headquarters in New York.)

Distilled Spirits Council of the United States, 1250 Eye St. N.W., #900, Washington, DC 20005; (202) 628-3544. Fax (202) 682-8888, Web http://www.discus.health.org. Jean Gooding, vice president.

Membership: manufacturers and marketers of distilled spirits sold in the United States. Provides consumer information on alcohol-related issues and topics. Monitors legislation and regulations.

Edison Electric Institute, 701 Pennsylvania Ave. N.W., Washington, DC 20004; (202) 508-5000. Fax (202) 508-5759, Web http://www.eei.org, job line (202) 508-5492. Thomas R. Kuhn, president.

Membership: investor-owned electric power companies and electric utility holding companies. Interests include electric utility operation and concerns, including conservation and energy management, energy analysis, resources and environment, cogeneration and renewable energy resources, nuclear power, and research. Provides information and statistics relating to electric energy; aids member companies in generating and selling electric energy; and conducts information forums.

Electronic Industries Association, 2500 Wilson Blvd., #400, Arlington, VA 22201-3834; (703) 907-7500. Fax (703) 907-7501, Web http://www.eia.org. Dave McCurdy, president.

Membership: manufacturers, dealers, installers, and distributors of consumer electronics products. Provides consumer information and data on industry trends; advocates an open market. Monitors legislation and regulations.

Environmental Industry Associations, 4301 Connecticut Ave. N.W., #300, Washington, DC 20008; (202) 244-4700. Fax (202) 966-4818, Web http://www. envasns.org. Jacques Gerard, director of administration.

Membership: trade associations from the waste services and environmental technology industries. Represents the National Solid Waste Management Association and the Waste Equipment Technology Association.

Federation of American Health Systems, 1111 19th St. N.W., #402, Washington, DC 20036; (202) 833-3090. Fax (202) 861-0063, Web http://www.fahs.com. Thomas A. Scully, president.

Membership: investor-owned, for-profit hospitals and health care systems. Interests include health care reform, cost containment, and Medicare and Medicaid reforms. Maintains speakers bureau; compiles statistics on investor-owned hospitals. Monitors legislation and regulations.

Fertilizer Institute, 501 2nd St. N.E., Washington, DC 20002; (202) 675-8250. Fax (202) 544-8123. Whitney Yelverton, vice president of administration.

Membership: manufacturers, dealers, and distributors of fertilizer. Provides statistical data and other information concerning the effects of fertilizer and its relationship to world food production, food supply, and the environment.

Food Marketing Institute, 800 Connecticut Ave. N.W., #500, Washington, DC 20006-2701; (202) 452-8444. Fax (202) 429-4549, Web http://www.fmi.org. Timothy Hammonds, president.

Trade association of food retailers and wholesalers. Conducts programs in research, education, industry relations, and public affairs.

Generic Pharmaceutical Industry Association, 1620 Eye St. N.W., #800, Washington, DC 20006; (202) 833-9070. Fax (202) 833-9612. Charlene Belha, executive assistant to president.

Represents the generic pharmaceutical industry in legislative, regulatory, scientific, and health care policy matters. Attempts to increase availability and public awareness of generic medicines.

Grocery Manufacturers of America, 1010 Wisconsin Ave. N.W., #900, Washington, DC 20007; (202) 337-9400. Fax (202) 337-4508, Web http://www. gmabrands.com. Brad Yin, manager of human resources.

Membership: manufacturers of products sold through the retail grocery trade. Monitors legislation and regulations.

Health Industry Manufacturers Association, 1200 G St. N.W., #400, Washington, DC 20005; (202) 783-8700. Fax (202) 783-8750, Web http://www.himanet. com. Betty Charles, office director.

Membership: manufacturers of medical devices, diagnostic products, and health care information systems. Interests include safe and effective medical devices; conducts educational seminars. Monitors legislation, regulations, and international issues.

Health Insurance Association of America, 555 13th St. N.W., #600E, Washington, DC 20004; (202) 824-1600. Fax (202) 824-1722, Web http://www.hiaa.org. Niki McFaden, director of human resources.

Membership: health insurance companies that write and sell health insurance policies. Promotes effective management of health care expenditures; provides statistical information on health insurance issues. Monitors legislation and regulations.

Independent Bankers Association of America, 1 Thomas Circle N.W., #400, Washington, DC 20005; (202) 659-8111, toll-free (800) 422-8439. Fax (202) 659-9216, e-mail info@ibaa.org. Sandra Delony, assistant to the vice president.

Membership: medium-sized and smaller community banks. Interests include farm credit, deregulation, interstate banking, deposit insurance, and financial industry standards.

Independent Insurance Agents of America, 127 S. Peytoñ St., Alexandria, VA 22314; (703) 683-4422. Fax (703) 683-7556, Web http://www.iiaa.org. Kathy Navarro, human resources director.

Provides educational and advisory services; researches issues pertaining to auto, home, business, life, and health insurance; offers cooperative advertising program to members. Political action committee monitors legislation and regulations.

Information Technology Association of America, 1616 N. Fort Myer Dr., #1300, Arlington, VA 22209; (703) 284-5300. Fax (703) 525-2279, Web http://www.itaa.org. Harris N. Miller, president.

Membership: organizations in the computer software and services industry. Conducts research; holds seminars and workshops. Interests include small business, government procurement, competitive practices, communications, software, trade, and international copyright issues. Monitors legislation and regulations.

Information Technology Industry Council, 1250 Eye St. N.W., #200, Washington, DC 20005; (202) 737-8888. Fax (202) 638-4922, Web http://www.itic.org. Rhett Dawson, president.

Membership: providers of information technology products and services. Promotes the global competitiveness of its members and advocates free trade. Seeks to protect intellectual property and encourages the use of voluntary standards.

Insurance Information Institute, 1730 Rhode Island Ave. N.W., #710, Washington, DC 20036; (202) 833-1580. Fax (202) 223-5779, Web http://www.iii.org. Carolyn Gorman, vice president.

Membership: property and casualty insurance companies. Monitors state and federal issues concerning insurance. (Headquarters in New York.)

Intelligent Transportation Society of America, 400 Virginia Ave. S.W., #800, Washington, DC 20024-2730; (202) 484-4847. Fax (202) 484-3483, Web http:// www.itsa.org. Bill Collier, human resources manager.

Advocates application of electronic, computer, and communications technology to make surface transportation more efficient and to save lives, time, and money. Coordinates research, development, and implementation of intelligent transportation systems by government, academia, and industry.

International Dairy Foods Association, 1250 H St. N.W., #900, Washington, DC 20005; (202) 737-4332. Fax (202) 331-7820, Web http://www.idfa.org. Connie Tipton, senior vice president.

Membership: processors, manufacturers, marketers, and distributors of dairy foods in the United States and abroad. Provides members with marketing, public relations, training, and management services. Monitors legislation and regulations.

International Food Information Council, 1100 Connecticut Ave. N.W., #430, Washington, DC 20036; (202) 296-6540. Fax (202) 296-6547, e-mail foodinfo@ ific.health.org, Web http://ificinfo.health.org. Geraldine Carbo, director of human resources.

Membership: food and beverage companies and manufacturers of food ingredients. Provides the media, health professionals, and consumers with scientific information about food safety, health, and nutrition. Interests include harmonization of international food safety standards.

Mortgage Bankers Association of America, 1125 15th St. N.W., Washington, DC 20005; (202) 861-6500. Fax (202) 861-0736. Paul Reid, executive vice president.

Membership: institutions involved in real estate finance. Maintains School of Mortgage Banking; collects statistics on the industry. Conducts seminars and workshops in specialized areas of mortgage finance. Monitors legislation and regulations.

Motion Picture Association, 1600 Eye St. N.W., Washington, DC 20006; (202) 293-1966. Fax (202) 293-7674, Web http://www.mpaa.org. Jack Valenti, president.

Membership: motion picture producers and distributors. Advises state and federal governments on copyrights, censorship, cable broadcasting, and other topics; administers voluntary rating system for motion pictures; works to prevent video piracy.

National Abortion Federation, 1755 Massachusetts Ave. N.W., #600, Washington, DC 20036; (202) 667-5881, toll-free (800) 772-9100. Fax (202) 667-5890, Web http://www.prochoice.org. Terri Scott, office manager.

Federation of facilities providing abortion services. Offers information on medical, legal, and social aspects of abortion; sets quality standards for abortion care. Conducts training workshops and seminars. Monitors legislation and regulations.

National Air Transportation Association, 4226 King St., Alexandria, VA 22302-1507; (703) 845-9000, toll-free (800) 808-6282. Fax (703) 845-8176, Web http://www.nata-online.org. James K. Coyne, president.

Membership: companies that provide on-demand air charter, aircraft sales, flight training, maintenance and repair, avionics, and other services. Manages education foundation; compiles statistics; provides business assistance programs. Monitors legislation and regulations.

National Association for Homecare, 228 7th St. S.E., Washington, DC 20003; (202) 547-7424. Fax (202) 547-3540, Web http://www.nahc.org. Val J. Hala-mandaris, president.

Promotes high-quality hospice, home care, and other community services for those with chronic health problems or life-threatening illness. Conducts research and provides information on related issues. Works to educate the public concerning health and social policy matters. Oversees the National HomeCaring Council, which provides training, education, accreditation, and certification in the field. Monitors legislation and regulations.

National Association of Broadcasters, 1771 N St. N.W., Washington, DC 20036-2891; (202) 429-5300. Fax (202) 429-5343, e-mail register@nab.org, Web http://www.nab.org. Rachel Sishkin, manager of recruitment and personnel.

Membership: radio and television broadcast stations and broadcast networks holding an FCC license or construction permit; associate members include producers of equipment and programs. Assists members in areas of management, engineering, and research; interprets laws and regulations governing the broadcast media. Publishes materials about broadcasting industry.

National Association of Convenience Stores, 1605 King St., Alexandria, VA 22314-2792; (703) 684-3600. Fax (703) 836-4564, Web http://www.cstorecentral.com. Arnold Harris, office manager.

Membership: convenience store retailers and industry suppliers. Advocates industry position on labor, tax, environment, alcohol, and food-related issues; conducts research and training programs. Monitors legislation and regulations.

National Association of Federal Credit Unions, 3138 N. 10th St., Arlington, VA 22201; (703) 522-4770. Fax (703) 524-1082, Web http://www.nafcunet.org. Diane Davidson, vice president of human resources.

Membership: federally chartered credit unions. Represents interests of federal credit unions before Congress and regulatory agencies and provides legislative alerts for its members. Sponsors educational meetings focusing on current financial trends, changes in legislation and regulations, and management techniques.

National Association of Home Builders, 1201 15th St. N.W., Washington, DC 20005; (202) 822-0200. Fax (202) 822-0559, Web http://www.nahb.com. Dawn Duyer, director of human resources.

Membership: contractors, builders, architects, engineers, mortgage lenders, and others interested in home building and commercial real estate construction. Participates in updating and developing building codes and standards; offers technical information.

National Association of Manufacturers, 1331 Pennsylvania Ave. N.W., #600, Washington, DC 20004-1790; (202) 637-3000. Fax (202) 637-3182, Web http://www.nam.org. Carol Coldron, director of human resources.

Represents industry views (mainly of manufacturers) to government on national and international issues. Reviews legislation, administrative rulings, and judicial decisions affecting industry. Sponsors the Human Resources Forum; operates a Web site for members and the public that provides information on legislative and other news; conducts programs on labor relations, occupational safety and health, regulatory and consumer affairs, environmental trade and technology, and other business issues.

National Association of Realtors, 700 11th St. N.W., Washington, DC 20001-4507; (202) 383-1238. Fax (202) 383-7850, Web http://www.realtor.com. Joyce Ferrell, human resources manager.

Sets standards of ethics for the real estate business; promotes education, research, and exchange of information. Monitors legislation and regulations. (Headquarters in Chicago.)

National Association of Securities Dealers, 1735 K St. N.W., Washington, DC 20006-1506; (202) 728-8000. Fax (202) 728-8075, http://www.nasd.com. Frank G. Zarb, president.

Membership: investment brokers and dealers authorized to conduct transactions of the investment banking and securities business under federal and state laws. Serves as the self-regulatory mechanism in the over-the-counter securities market.

National Automobile Dealers Association, 8400 Westpark Dr., McLean, VA 22102-3591; (703) 821-7000. Fax (703) 821-7075, e-mail nada@nada.org, Web http://www.nada.org. Cori Miyamoto, human resources manager.

Membership: franchised dealers of domestic and imported new cars and trucks. Publishes the *National Automobile Dealers Used Car Guide* (Blue Book).

National Cable Television Association, 1724 Massachusetts Ave. N.W., Washington, DC 20036-1969; (202) 775-3550. Fax (202) 775-1055. Decker Anstrom, president.

Membership: companies that operate cable television systems, cable television programmers, and manufacturers and suppliers of hardware and software for the industry. Represents the industry before federal regulatory agencies and Congress and in the courts; provides management and promotional aids and information on legal, legislative, and regulatory matters.

National Confectioners Association, 7900 Westpark Dr., #A320, McLean, VA 22102; (703) 790-5750. Fax (703) 790-5752, Web http://www.candyusa.org. Trish Riordan, office manager.

Membership: confectionery manufacturers and suppliers. Provides information on confectionery consumption and nutrition; sponsors educational programs and research on candy technology. Monitors legislation and regulations.

National Cooperative Business Association, 1401 New York Ave. N.W., #1100, Washington, DC 20005-2146; (202) 638-6222. Fax (202) 638-1374, e-mail ncba@ncba.org, Web http://www.cooperative.org. Peggy Spangler, human resources director.

Alliance of cooperatives, businesses, and state cooperative associations. Provides information about starting and managing agricultural cooperatives in the United States and in developing nations. Monitors legislation and regulations.

National Electrical Manufacturers Association, 1300 N. 17th St., #1847, Rosslyn, VA 22209; (703) 841-3200. Fax (703) 841-3300, Web http://www.nema.org. Mari Bernardini, human resources services.

Membership: manufacturers of electrical products. Develops and promotes use of electrical standards; compiles and analyzes industry statistics. Interests include efficient energy management, product safety and liability, occupational safety, and the environment. Monitors international trade activities, legislation, and regulations.

National Fisheries Institute, 1901 N. Fort Myer Dr., #700, Arlington, VA 22209; (703) 524-8880. Fax (703) 524-4619, e-mail office@nfi.org, Web http://www.nfi. org. Kelly Andrews, office manager.

Membership: vessel owners and distributors, processors, wholesalers, importers, traders, and brokers of fish and shellfish. Monitors legislation and regulations on fisheries.

National Food Processors Association, 1350 Eye St. N.W., #300, Washington, DC 20005; (202) 639-5900. Fax (202) 639-5932. John R. Cady, president.

Membership: manufacturers and suppliers of processed and packaged food, drinks, and juice. Promotes agricultural interests of food processors; provides research, technical services, education, communications, and crisis management for members. Monitors legislation and regulations.

National Hospice Organization, 1901 N. Moore St., #901, Arlington, VA 22209; (703) 243-5900. Fax (703) 525-5762, Web http://www.nho.org. Paul White, director of operations.

Membership: institutions and individuals providing hospice care and other interested organizations and individuals. Promotes supportive care for the terminally ill and their families; sets hospice program standards; provides information on hospices. Monitors legislation and regulations.

National Mining Association, 1130 17th St. N.W., Washington, DC 20036-4677; (202) 463-2625. Fax (202) 463-6152, e-mail nma@nma.org, Web http://www. nma.org. Martha Anderson, director of human resources.

Membership: coal producers, coal sales and transportation companies, equipment manufacturers, consulting firms, coal resource developers and exporters, coal-burning electric utility companies, and other energy companies. Collects, analyzes, and distributes industry statistics; conducts special studies of competitive fuels, coal markets, production and consumption forecasts, and industry planning. Interests include exports, coal leasing programs, coal transportation, environmental issues, health and safety, national energy policy, slurry pipelines, and research and development, including synthetic fuels.

National Petroleum Refiners Association, 1899 L St. N.W., #1000, Washington, DC 20036; (202) 457-0480. Fax (202) 457-0486, Web http://www.npradc.org. Urvan Sternfels, president.

Membership: petroleum, petrochemical, and refining companies. Interests include allocation, imports, refining technology, petrochemicals, and environmental regulations.

National Pharmaceutical Council, 1894 Preston White Dr., Reston, VA 20191-5433; (703) 620-6390. Fax (703) 476-0904, e-mail main@npcnow.com. Karen Williams, president.

Membership: pharmaceutical manufacturers that research and produce trade-name prescription medication and other pharmaceutical products. Provides information on the quality and cost-effectiveness of pharmaceutical products and the economics of drug programs.

National Restaurant Association, 1200 17th St. N.W., Washington, DC 20036-3097; (202) 331-5900. Fax (202) 331-2429, Web http://www.restaurant.org. Dawn Worthington, human resources assistant.

Membership: restaurants, cafeterias, clubs, contract feeders, caterers, institutional food services, and other members of the food industry. Supports food service education and research. Monitors legislation and regulations.

National Retail Federation, 325 7th St. N.W., #1000, Washington, DC 20004-2802; (202) 783-7971. Fax (202) 737-2849, e-mail nrf@mcimail.com, Web http://www.nrf.com. Bruce Lampron, vice president of human resources.

Membership: international, national, and state associations of retailers and major retail corporations. Concerned with federal regulatory activities and legislation that affect retailers, including tax, employment, trade, and credit issues. Provides information on retailing through seminars, conferences, and publications.

National Soft Drink Association, 1101 16th St. N.W., Washington, DC 20036-6396; (202) 463-6732. Fax (202) 463-8172, Web http://www.nsda.org. Marie Franee, human resources.

Membership: companies engaged in producing or distributing carbonated soft drinks. Acts as industry liaison with government and the public.

National Wholesale Druggists' Association, 1821 Michael Faraday Dr., #400, Reston, VA (mailing address: P.O. Box 2219, Reston, VA 20195-0219); (703) 787-0000. Fax (703) 787-6930, Web http://www.nwda.org. Linda Caporaletti, director of human resources and administration.

Membership: full-service drug wholesalers. Works to improve relations among supplier and customer industries; serves as a forum on major industry issues; researches and disseminates information on management practices for drug wholesalers. Monitors legislation and regulations.

Nonprescription Drug Manufacturers Association, 1150 Connecticut Ave. N.W., Washington, DC 20036; (202) 429-9260. Fax (202) 223-6835. Rita McLaughlin, office manager.

Membership: manufacturers and distributors of nonprescription medicines; associate members include suppliers, advertising agencies, and research and testing laboratories. Promotes the role of self-medication in health care. Monitors legislation and regulations.

Nuclear Energy Institute, 1776 Eye St. N.W., #400, Washington, DC 20006-3708; (202) 739-8000. Fax (202) 785-4019, Web http://www.nei.org. Beverly Chesler, human resources benefits specialist.

Membership: utilities; industries; labor, service, and research organizations; law firms; universities; and government agencies interested in peaceful uses of nuclear energy, including the generation of electricity. Acts as a spokesperson for the nuclear power industry; provides information on licensing and plant siting, research and development, safety and security, waste disposal, and legislative and policy issues.

Pharmaceutical Research and Manufacturers of America, 1100 15th St. N.W., #900, Washington, DC 20005; (202) 835-3400. Fax (202) 835-3414, Web http://www.phrma.org. Denise Jing, human resources director.

Membership: companies that discover, develop, and manufacture prescription drugs. Provides consumer information on drug abuse, the safe and effective use of prescription medicines, and developments in important areas, including AIDS. Provides pharmaceutical industry statistics.

Recording Industry Association of America, 1330 Connecticut Ave. N.W., #300, Washington, DC 20036; (202) 775-0101. Fax (202) 775-7253, Web http://www.riaa.com. Briggette Tenor, director.

Membership: creators, manufacturers, and marketers of sound recordings. Educates members about new technology in the music industry. Advocates copyright protection and opposes censorship. Works to prevent recording piracy, counterfeiting, bootlegging, and unauthorized record rental and imports. Certifies gold, platinum, and multiplatinum recordings. Publishes statistics on the recording industry.

Recreation Vehicle Industry Association, 1896 Preston White Dr., Reston, VA (mailing address: P.O. Box 2999, Reston, VA 20195-0999); (703) 620-6003. Fax (703) 620-5071, e-mail rvia@rvia.org, Web http://www.rvia.org. Janice Micka, director of human resources.

Membership: manufacturers of recreation vehicles and their suppliers. Compiles shipment statistics and other technical data; provides consumers and the media with information on the industry. Assists members' compliance with American National Standards Institute requirements for recreation vehicles. Monitors legislation and regulations.

Rubber Manufacturers Association, 1400 K St. N.W., #900, Washington, DC 20005; (202) 682-4800, toll-free (800) 220-7622. Fax (202) 682-4854, Web http://www.rma.org. Lisa Murphy, chief financial officer.

Membership: manufacturers of tires, tubes, roofing, sporting goods, and mechanical and industrial products. Interests include recycling.

Smokeless Tobacco Council, 1627 K St. N.W., #700, Washington, DC 20006; (202) 452-1252. Fax (202) 452-0118. Mary Mack, vice president.

Members: smokeless tobacco manufacturers. Monitors legislation and regulations.

Snack Food Association, 1711 King St., #1, Alexandria, VA 22314; (703) 836-4500. Fax (703) 836-8262, Web http://www.snax.com or http://www.sfa.org. Liz Wells, director of administration.

Membership: snack food manufacturers and suppliers. Promotes industry sales; compiles statistics; conducts research and surveys; assists members with training and education; provides consumers with industry information. Monitors legislation and regulations.

Society of the Plastics Industry, 1801 K St. N.W., #600K, Washington, DC 20006; (202) 974-5200. Fax (202) 296-7005, Web http://www.socplas.org. Ginger Lion, human resources director.
Promotes the plastics industry. Monitors legislation and regulations.

Software and Information Industry Association, 1730 M St. N.W., #700, Washington, DC 20036; (202) 452-1600. Fax (202) 223-8756, Web http://www.siia. net. Katrina Hunt, director of administration.
Membership: publishers of microcomputer software. Promotes the industry worldwide; conducts investigations and litigation to protect members' copyrights; collects data, including monthly sales information; offers contracts reference and credit information exchange services; sponsors conferences and seminars. Monitors legislation and regulations.

Steel Manufacturers Association, 1730 Rhode Island Ave. N.W., #907, Washington, DC 20036-3101; (202) 296-1515. Fax (202) 296-2506, Web http://www. steelnet.org. Thomas A. Danjczek, president; Chad Cumminf, director of political and legislative affairs.
Membership: steel producers in North America and abroad. Helps members exchange information on technical matters; provides information on the steel industry to the public and government. Monitors legislation and regulations.

Sugar Association, 1101 15th St. N.W., #600, Washington, DC 20005; (202) 785-1122. Fax (202) 785-5019, e-mail sugar@sugar.org. Alicia Overton, administrative manager.
Membership: sugar processors, growers, refiners, and planters. Provides nutritional information on sugar.

Synthetic Organic Chemical Manufacturers Association, 1850 M St. N.W., #700, Washington, DC 20036; (202) 296-8577. Fax (202) 296-8120, Web http://www. socma.com. Edmund Fording, president.
Membership: companies that manufacture, distribute, and market organic chemicals, and providers of custom chemical services. Interests include international trade, environmental and occupational safety, and health issues; conducts workshops and seminars. Promotes commercial opportunities for members. Monitors legislation and regulations.

United Fresh Fruit and Vegetable Association, 727 N. Washington St., Alexandria, VA 22314; (703) 836-3410. Fax (703) 836-7745. Thomas Stenzel, president.
Membership: growers, shippers, wholesalers, retailers, food service operators, importers, and exporters involved in producing and marketing fresh fruits and vegetables. Represents the industry before the government and the public sector.

U.S. Oil and Gas Association, 801 Pennsylvania Ave. N.W., #840, Washington, DC 20004-2615; (202) 638-4400. Fax (202) 638-5967. Wayne Gibbens, president.
Membership: major and independent petroleum companies. Monitors legislation and regulations affecting the petroleum industry.

LABOR UNIONS

AFL-CIO (American Federation of Labor–Congress of Industrial Organizations), 815 16th St. N.W., Washington, DC 20006; (202) 637-5000. Web http://www. aflcio.org. Karla Garla, director of human resources.

Voluntary federation of national and international labor unions in the United States. Represents members before Congress and other branches of government. Each member union conducts its own contract negotiations.

AFL-CIO Maritime Committee, 1150 17th St. N.W., #700, Washington, DC 20036; (202) 835-0404. Fax (202) 872-0912. Talmage E. Simpkins, executive director.

Membership: AFL-CIO maritime unions. Provides information on the maritime industry and unions. Interests include seamen's service contracts and pension plans, maritime safety, U.S. merchant marine, and the rights of Panama Canal residents. Monitors legislation and regulations.

Air Line Pilots Association International, 1625 Massachusetts Ave. N.W., Washington, DC 20036; (703) 689-2270. Fax (703) 689-4370, Web http://www.airspacemag.com/ALPA. Sherri Taylor, human resources administrator.

Membership: airline pilots in the United States and Canada. Promotes air travel safety; assists investigations of aviation accidents. Monitors legislation and regulations. (Affiliated with the AFL-CIO.)

Amalgamated Transit Union, 5025 Wisconsin Ave. N.W., 3rd Floor, Washington, DC 20016; (202) 537-1645. Fax (202) 244-7824, Web http://www.atu.org/atu. Gene Parker, office manager.

Membership: transit workers in the United States and Canada, including bus, van, subway, and light rail operators; clerks, baggage handlers, and maintenance employees in urban transit, over-the-road, and school bus industries; and municipal workers. Assists members with contract negotiations and grievances; conducts training programs and seminars. Monitors legislation and regulations. (Affiliated with the AFL-CIO.)

American Association of University Professors, 1012 14th St. N.W., #500, Washington, DC 20005; (202) 737-5900, toll-free (800) 424-2973. Fax (202) 737-5526, e-mail aaup@aaup.org, Web http://www.aaup.org. Howard Awrich, director of human resources.

Membership: college and university faculty members. Defends faculties' academic freedom and tenure; advocates collegial governance; assists in the development of policies ensuring due process. Conducts workshops and education programs. Monitors legislation and regulations.

American Federation of Government Employees, 80 F St. N.W., Washington, DC 20001; (202) 737-8700. Fax (202) 639-6490, Web http://www.afge.org. Bobby L. Harnage, president.

Membership: approximately 700,000 federal government employees. Provides legal services to members; assists members with contract negotiations and grievances. Monitors legislation and regulations. (Affiliated with the AFL-CIO.)

American Federation of Teachers, 555 New Jersey Ave. N.W., 10th Floor, Washington, DC 20001; (202) 879-4400. Fax (202) 879-4545, Web http://www.aft.org/index.htm. Gregory Humphrey, executive assistant to president.

Membership: public and private school teachers, higher education faculty, and school-related personnel. Assists members with contract negotiation and grievances; conducts training programs and workshops. Monitors legislation and regulations. (Affiliated with the AFL-CIO.)

American Postal Workers Union, 1300 L St. N.W., Washington, DC 20005; (202) 842-4200. Fax (202) 842-4297, Web http://www.apwu.org. Robert Tunstall, secretary treasurer.

Membership: approximately 366,000 postal employees, including clerks, motor vehicle operators, special delivery messengers, and other employees. Assists members with contract negotiation and grievances; conducts training programs and workshops. Monitors legislation and regulations. (Affiliated with the Postal, Telegraph, and Telephone International and the AFL-CIO.)

Association of Flight Attendants, 1275 K St. N.W., Washington, DC 20005-4006; (202) 712-9799. Fax (202) 712-9798, e-mail afatalk@afanet.org, Web http://www.afanet.org. Patricia A. Friend, president.

Membership: approximately 44,000 flight attendants. Helps members negotiate pay, benefits, and better working conditions; conducts training programs and workshops. Monitors legislation and regulations. (Affiliated with the AFL-CIO.)

Bakery, Confectionery, Tobacco Workers, and Grain Millers International Union, 10401 Connecticut Ave., Kensington, MD 20895; (301) 933-8600. Fax (301) 946-8452. Kurt Yeager, director of finance.

Membership: approximately 120,000 workers from the bakery and tobacco industries. Helps members negotiate pay, benefits, and better working conditions; conducts training programs and workshops. Monitors legislation and regulations. (Affliated with the AFL-CIO.)

Communications Workers of America, 501 3rd St. N.W., Washington, DC 20001; (202) 434-1100. Fax (202) 434-1279, Web http://www.cwa-union.org. Brenda Stewart, head of human resources.

Membership: approximately 600,000 workers in telecommunications, printing and news media, public service, cable television, electronics, and other fields. Assists members with contract negotiation and grievances; conducts training programs and workshops. Monitors legislation and regulations. (Affiliated with the AFL-CIO.)

Graphic Communications International Union, 1900 L St. N.W., Washington, DC 20036; (202) 462-1400. Fax (202) 721-0600, Web http://www.gciu.org. Gerald Deneau, secretary and treasurer of international union.

Membership: approximately 150,000 members of the print industry, including lithographers, photoengravers, and bookbinders. Assists members with contract negotiation and grievances; conducts training programs and workshops. Monitors legislation and regulations. (Affiliated with the AFL-CIO.)

Hotel Employees and Restaurant Employees International, 1219 28th St. N.W., Washington, DC 20007; (202) 393-4373. Fax (202) 333-0468, Web http://www.erols.com/hereiu. Matthew Walker, director of resources.

Membership: approximately 241,000 hotel and restaurant employees. Helps members negotiate pay, benefits, and better working conditions; conducts training programs and workshops. Monitors legislation and regulations. (Affiliated with the AFL-CIO.)

International Association of Bridge, Structural, Ornamental, and Reinforcing Iron Workers, 1750 New York Ave. N.W., #400, Washington, DC 20006; (202) 383-4800. Fax (202) 638-4856. Jan Howell, office manager.

Membership: approximately 82,000 iron workers. Helps members negotiate pay, benefits, and better working conditions; conducts training programs and workshops. Monitors legislation and regulations. (Affiliated with the AFL-CIO.)

International Association of Fire Fighters, 1750 New York Ave. N.W., 3rd Floor, Washington, DC 20006; (202) 737-8484. Fax (202) 737-8418, Web http://www.iaff.org. Fred Nesbitt, director, governmental affairs.

Membership: more than 225,000 professional fire fighters and emergency medical personnel. Assists members with contract negotiation and grievances; conducts training programs and workshops. Monitors legislation and regulations. (Affiliated with the AFL-CIO and the Canadian Labour Congress.)

International Association of Machinists and Aerospace Workers, 9000 Machinists Pl., Upper Marlboro, MD 20772-2687; (301) 967-4500. Fax (301) 967-4588, Web http://www.iamaw.org. Thomas Buffenbarger, president.

Membership: machinists in more than 200 industries. Helps members negotiate pay, benefits, and better working conditions; conducts training programs and workshops. Monitors legislation and regulations. (Affiliated with the AFL-CIO, the Canadian Labour Congress, the Railway Labor Executives Association, the International Metalworkers Federation, and the International Transport Workers' Federation.)

International Brotherhood of Boilermakers, Iron Ship Builders, Blacksmiths, Forgers, and Helpers, 2722 Merrilee Dr., #360, Fairfax, VA 22031; (703) 560-1493. Fax (703) 560-2584, Web http://www.boilermakers.org. Andy Abbott, director, legislative affairs.

Membership: approximately 80,000 workers in construction, repair, maintenance, manufacturing, and related industries in the United States and Canada. Helps members negotiate pay, benefits, and better working conditions; conducts training programs and workshops. Monitors legislation and regulations. (Headquarters in Kansas City, Kan.; affiliated with the AFL-CIO.)

International Brotherhood of Electrical Workers, 1125 15th St. N.W., Washington, DC 20005; (202) 833-7000. Fax (202) 467-6313, e-mail IBEWnet@compuserve.com, Web http://www.ibew.org. Peter Keenan, director of personnel.

Helps members negotiate pay, benefits, and better working conditions; conducts training programs and workshops. Monitors legislation and regulations. (Affiliated with the AFL-CIO.)

International Brotherhood of Painters and Allied Trades, 1750 New York Ave. N.W., 8th Floor, Washington, DC 20006; (202) 637-0700. Fax (202) 637-0771,

Web http://www.ibpat.net or http://www.ibpat.org. Michael E. Monroe, general president.

Membership: more than 130,000 painters, paint makers, drywall finishers, decorators, carpet and soft tile layers, scenic artists, and workers in allied trades. Helps members negotiate pay, benefits, and better working conditions; conducts training programs and workshops. Monitors legislation and regulations. (Affiliated with the AFL-CIO.)

International Brotherhood of Teamsters, 25 Louisiana Ave. N.W., Washington, DC 20001; (202) 624-6800. Fax (202) 624-8102, Web http://www.teamsters.org. Linda Sist, assistant director of human resources.

Membership: more than 1.4 million workers in the transportation and construction industries, factories, offices, hospitals, warehouses, and other workplaces. Helps members negotiate pay, benefits, and better working conditions; conducts training programs and workshops. Monitors legislation and regulations. (Affiliated with the AFL-CIO.)

International Longshore and Warehouse Union, 1775 K St. N.W., #200, Washington, DC 20006; (202) 463-6265. Fax (202) 467-4875. Lindsay McLaughlin, legislative director.

Membership: approximately 45,000 longshore and warehouse personnel. Helps members negotiate pay, benefits, and better working conditions; conducts training programs and workshops. Monitors legislation and regulations. (Headquarters in San Francisco; affiliated with the AFL-CIO.)

International Longshoremen's Association, 1101 17th St. N.W., #400, Washington, DC 20036; (202) 955-6304. Fax (202) 955-6048. John Bowers Jr., legislative director.

Membership: approximately 61,000 longshore personnel. Helps members negotiate pay, benefits, and better working conditions; conducts training programs and workshops. Monitors legislation and regulations. (Headquarters in New York; affiliated with the AFL-CIO.)

International Union of Bricklayers and Allied Craftworkers, 815 15th St. N.W., Washington, DC 20005; (202) 783-3788. Fax (202) 393-0219, Web http://www.bacweb.org. John T. Joyce, president.

Membership: bricklayers, stonemasons, and other skilled craftworkers in the building industry. Helps members negotiate pay, benefits, and better working conditions; conducts training programs and workshops. Monitors legislation and regulations. (Affiliated with the AFL-CIO and the International Masonry Institute.)

International Union of Electronic, Electrical, Salaried, Machine, and Furniture Workers, 1126 16th St. N.W., Washington, DC 20036; (202) 785-7200. Fax (202) 785-7441, Web http://www.iue.org. Richard Chapman, assistant to the president.

Membership: approximately 125,000 workers in the field of industrial electronics and furniture and general manufacturing. Helps members negotiate pay, benefits, and better working conditions; conducts training programs and workshops. (Affiliated with the AFL-CIO.)

International Union of Operating Engineers, 1125 17th St. N.W., Washington, DC 20036; (202) 429-9100. Fax (202) 778-2616, Web http://www.iuoe.org. Frank Hanley, president.

Membership: approximately 400,000 operating engineers, including heavy equipment operators, mechanics, and surveyors in the construction industry, and stationary engineers, including operations and building maintenance staff. Helps members negotiate pay, benefits, and better working conditions; conducts training programs and workshops. Monitors legislation and regulations. (Affiliated with the AFL-CIO.)

Laborers' International Union of North America, 905 16th St. N.W., Washington, DC 20006; (202) 737-8320. Fax (202) 737-2754, Web http://www.liuna. org. Arthur A. Coia, president.

Membership: approximately 750,000 construction workers; federal, state, and local government employees; health care professionals; mail handlers; custodial service personnel; shipbuilders; and hazardous waste handlers. Helps members negotiate pay, benefits, and better working conditions; conducts training programs and workshops. Monitors legislation and regulations. (Affiliated with the AFL-CIO.)

National Alliance of Postal and Federal Employees, 1628 11th St. N.W., Washington, DC 20001; (202) 939-6325. Fax (202) 939-6389, Web http://www.napfe. com. James M. McGee, president.

Membership: approximately 70,000 postal and federal employees. Helps members negotiate pay, benefits, and better working conditions; conducts training programs and workshops. Monitors legislation and regulations.

National Association of Government Employees, 317 S. Patrick St., Alexandria, VA 22314; (703) 519-0300. Fax (703) 519-0311, Web http://www.nage.org. Kenneth T. Lyons, national president; Chris Donnellan, legislative director.

Membership: approximately 200,000 federal government employees. Helps members negotiate pay, benefits, and better working conditions; conducts training programs and workshops. Monitors legislation and regulations. (Headquarters in Quincy, Mass.; affiliated with the AFL-CIO.)

National Association of Letter Carriers, 100 Indiana Ave. N.W., Washington, DC 20001; (202) 393-4695. Fax (202) 737-1540, e-mail nalinf@access.digex.net, Web http://www.nacl.org. Vincent R. Sombrotto, president.

Membership: approximately 315,000 city letter carriers working for, or retired from, the U.S. Postal Service. Assists members with contract negotiation and grievances; conducts training programs and workshops. Monitors legislation and regulations. (Affiliated with the AFL-CIO and the Postal, Telegraph, and Telephone International.)

National Education Association, 1201 16th St. N.W., Washington, DC 20036; (202) 833-4000. Fax (202) 822-7767, Web http://www.nea.org. Don Cameron, executive director.

Membership: more than 2.4 million educators from preschool to university graduate programs. Promotes the interest of the profession of teaching and the cause of education in the United States. Monitors legislation and regulations at state and national levels.

National Federation of Federal Employees, 1016 16th St. N.W., #300, Washington, DC 20036; (202) 862-4400. Fax (202) 862-4432. Steve Hantzis, executive director.

Membership: approximately 52,000 federal government employees. Helps members negotiate pay, benefits, and better working conditions; conducts training programs and workshops. Monitors legislation and regulations.

National Rural Letter Carriers' Association, 1630 Duke St., 4th Floor, Alexandria, VA 22314-5545; (703) 684-5545. Fax (703) 548-8735, Web http://www. nrlca.org. Steven R. Smith, president.

Membership: approximately 100,000 rural letter carriers working for, or retired from, the U.S. Postal Service. Seeks to improve rural mail delivery. Helps members negotiate pay, benefits, and better working conditions; conducts training programs and workshops. Monitors legislation and regulations.

National Treasury Employees Union, 901 E St. N.W., #600, Washington, DC 20004; (202) 783-4444. Fax (202) 783-4085, Web http://www.nteu.org. Robert M. Tobias, president.

Membership: approximately 150,000 employees from the Treasury Dept. and eighteen other federal agencies. Helps members negotiate pay, benefits, and better working conditions; conducts training programs and workshops. Monitors legislation and regulations.

Office and Professional Employees International Union, 1660 L St. N.W., #801, Washington, DC 20036; (202) 393-4464. Fax (202) 347-0649, Web http://www.opeiu.org. Juliette Fisher, manager.

Membership: 130,000 workers, including computer analysts, programmers, and data entry operators; copywriters; nurses and other health care personnel; attorneys; law enforcement officers and security guards; accountants; secretaries; bank employees; and insurance workers and agents. Helps members negotiate pay, benefits, and better working conditions; conducts training program and workshops. Monitors legislation and regulations. (Headquarters in New York; affiliated with the AFL-CIO and the Canadian Labour Congress.)

Operative Plasterers' and Cement Masons' International Association of the United States and Canada, 14405 Laurel Pl., #300, Laurel, MD 20707; (301) 470-4200. Fax (301) 470-2502, Web http://www.opcmia.org. Nick Scholz, office manager.

Membership: approximately 58,000 concrete masons and terrazzo workers. Helps members negotiate pay, benefits, and better working conditions; conducts training programs and workshops. Monitors legislation and regulations. (Affiliated with the AFL-CIO.)

Paper Allied-Industrial, Chemical, and Energy Workers International Union, 2722 Merrilee Dr., #250, Fairfax, VA 22031; (703) 876-9300. Fax (703) 876-8952. Paula R. Littles, legislative director.

Membership: approximately 90,000 workers in the energy, chemical, pharmaceutical, and allied industries. Assists members with contract negotiation and grievances; conducts training programs and workshops. Monitors legislation and regulations. (Headquarters in Lakewood, Colo.; affiliated with the AFL-CIO.)

Service Employees International Union, 1313 L St. N.W., Washington, DC 20005; (202) 898-3200. Fax (202) 898-3402, Web http://www.seiu.org. Jacqueline Brown, director of human resources.

Membership: more than one million service providers, including teachers; nurses, doctors, and other health care professionals; school bus drivers; janitors; and others. Helps members negotiate pay, benefits, and better working conditions; conducts training programs and workshops. Monitors legislation and regulations. (Affiliated with the AFL-CIO.)

Sheet Metal Workers' International Association, 1750 New York Ave. N.W., Washington, DC 20006; (202) 783-5880. Fax (202) 662-0895, Web http://smwia. org. Kathy Bishop, office manager.

Membership: more than 130,000 U.S. and Canadian workers in the building and construction trades, manufacturing, and the railroad and shipyard industries. Assists members with contract negotiation and grievances; conducts training programs and workshops. Monitors legislation and regulations. (Affiliated with the Sheet Metal and Air Conditioning Contractors' Association, the AFL-CIO, and the Canadian Labour Congress.)

Transportation Communications International Union, 3 Research Pl., Rockville, MD 20850; (301) 948-4910. Fax (301) 948-1369. Bonnie Gray, office manager.

Membership: approximately 120,000 railway workers. Assists members with contract negotiation and grievances; conducts training programs and workshops. Monitors legislation and regulations. (Affiliated with the AFL-CIO and Canadian Labour Congress.)

Union of Needletrades Industrial and Textile Employees (UNITE), 888 16th St. N.W., #303, Washington, DC 20006; (202) 347-7417. Fax (202) 347-0708, e-mail unite@bellatlantic.net, Web http://www.unite.org. Ann Hoffman, legislative director.

Membership: approximately 285,000 workers in basic apparel and textiles, millinery, shoe, laundry, retail, and related industries; and in auto parts and auto supply. Assists members with contract negotiation and grievances; conducts training programs and workshops. Monitors legislation and regulations. (Headquarters in New York; affiliated with the AFL-CIO.)

United Association of Journeymen and Apprentices of the Plumbing and Pipe Fitting Industry of the United States and Canada, 901 Massachusetts Ave. N.W., Washington, DC 20001; (202) 628-5823. Fax (202) 628-5024, Web http://www.ua.org. Thomas H. Patchell, general secretary treasurer.

Membership: approximately 290,000 workers who fabricate, install, and service piping systems. Assists members with contract negotiation and grievances; sponsors training programs, apprenticeships, and workshops. Monitors legislation and regulations. (Affiliated with the AFL-CIO and the Canadian Federation of Labour.)

United Auto Workers, 1757 N St. N.W., Washington, DC 20036; (202) 828-8500, toll-free (800) 243-8829. Fax (202) 293-3457, Web http://www.uaw.org, personnel office in Detroit (313) 926 5000. Stephen P. Yokich, president.

Membership: approximately 775,000 active and 500,000 retired North American workers in aerospace, automotive, defense, manufacturing, steel, technical, and other industries. Assists members with contract negotiation and grievances; conducts training programs and workshops. Monitors legislation and regulations. (Headquarters in Detroit; affiliated with the AFL-CIO.)

United Brotherhood of Carpenters and Joiners of America, 101 Constitution Ave. N.W., Washington, DC 20001; (202) 546-6206. Fax (202) 543-5724. Douglas J. McCarron, president.

Membership: approximately 500,000 carpenters and joiners. Helps members negotiate pay, benefits, and better working conditions; conducts training programs and workshops. Monitors legislation and regulations. (Affiliated with the AFL-CIO.)

United Farm Workers of America, c/o AFL-CIO, 815 16th St. N.W., Washington, DC 20006; (202) 637-5212. Fax (202) 637-5012, Web http://www.ufw.org. Giez Kashkooli, manager.

Membership: approximately 50,000 farm workers. Helps members negotiate pay, benefits, and better working conditions; conducts training programs and workshops. Interests includes immigration and migrant workers. Monitors legislation and regulations. (Affiliated with the AFL-CIO.)

United Food and Commercial Workers International Union, 1775 K St. N.W., Washington, DC 20006; (202) 223-3111. Fax (202) 466-1562, Web http://www. ufcw.org. Bette Mercer, director of human resources.

Membership: approximately 1.4 million workers in food-related industries, including supermarkets, department stores, insurance and finance, and packing houses and processing plants. Helps members negotiate pay, benefits, and better working conditions; conducts training programs and workshops. Monitors legislation and regulations. (Affiliated with the AFL-CIO and Canadian Labour Congress.)

United Mine Workers of America, 900 15th St. N.W., Washington, DC 20005; (202) 842-7200. Fax (202) 842-7227, Web http://www.umwa.org. Judy Medley, human resources.

Membership: coal miners and other mining workers. Represents members in collective bargaining with industry. Conducts educational, housing, and health and safety training programs; monitors federal coal mining safety programs.

United Steelworkers of America, 1150 17th St. N.W., #300, Washington, DC 20036; (202) 778-4384. Fax (202) 293-5308, Web http://www.uswa.org. William Klinefelter, legislative and political director.

Membership: more than 700,000 steelworkers in the United States and Canada. Helps members negotiate pay, benefits, and better working conditions; conducts training programs and workshops. Monitors legislation and regulations. (Headquarters in Pittsburgh; affiliated with the AFL-CIO.)

United Transportation Union, 304 Pennsylvania Ave. S.E., Washington, DC 20003; (202) 543-7714. Fax (202) 543-0015. James Brunkenhoefer, national legislative director.

Membership: approximately 150,000 workers in the transportation industry. Helps members negotiate pay, benefits, and better working conditions; conducts training programs and workshops. Monitors legislation and regulations. (Headquarters in Cleveland, Ohio; affiliated with the AFL-CIO.)

United Union of Roofers, Waterproofers, and Allied Workers, 1660 L St. N.W., #800, Washington, DC 20036; (202) 463-7663. Fax (202) 463-6906, Web http://www.unionroofers.com. Barbara Newell, executive assistant to the international president.

Membership: approximately 25,000 roofers, waterproofers, and allied workers. Helps members negotiate pay, benefits, and better working conditions; conducts training programs and workshops. Monitors legislation and regulations. (Affiliated with the AFL-CIO.)

Utility Workers Union of America, 815 16th St. N.W., Washington, DC 20006; (202) 347-8105. Fax (202) 347-4872, Web http://www.aflcio.org/uwua. Rosanna Sarley, office manager.

Membership: approximately 50,000 workers in utilities and related industries. Helps members negotiate pay, benefits, and better working conditions; conducts training programs and workshops. Monitors legislation and regulations. (Affiliated with the AFL-CIO).

8

Working
in Washington:
The News Media

It may seem strange in a book about public policy jobs in Washington to include a chapter about the news media. The media don't set public policy, do they?

Yes and no. Strictly speaking, the media do not establish public policy. However, news stories can have a tremendous influence on what happens in Washington. That makes the media key players in the policy process.

The media play such a key role that they are often referred to as the fourth branch of government, a characterization that places them on a par with the executive, legislative, and judicial branches. The label probably goes too far. It's likely more accurate, as some political scientists contend, to say that the media are more of an intermediary institution between the government and the people, placing them on the level of interest groups or political parties. Nonetheless, reporters' and editors' decisions about what subjects to cover and what facts to include in a particular story can help propel or kill proposed policies.

This is not a new phenomenon. Four decades ago political scientist Douglass Cater wrote in his classic book, *The Fourth Branch of Government* (1959), that the Washington reporter does not just record the actions of government. "He as much as anyone . . . helps to shape the course of government," Cater wrote. "He is the indispensable broker and middleman among the subgovernments of Washington. . . . He can illumine policy and notably assist in giving it sharpness and clarity; just as easily, he can prematurely expose policy and, as with an undeveloped film, cause its destruction."

On a few occasions, news stories have directly shaped momentous political events. In the late 1890s, two New York newspapers engaged in a circulation battle, the *World* and the *Journal,* dragged the United States into the Spanish-American War. More recently, in the early 1970s the Watergate investigation by *Washington Post* reporters Bob Woodward and Carl Bernstein helped topple the presidency of Richard Nixon.

Politicians, government officials, lobbyists, interest groups, and public relations practitioners are well aware of the media's influence. That's why virtually no policy proposal is fashioned in Washington without a carefully developed "media plan." The plan can include passing along tentative policy ideas to reporters to see how their resulting stories are received, leaking documents or information to a reporter, attempting to "spin" how reporters write a story, and many other similar tactics. All the efforts pay homage to an old saying: Whoever controls the flow of information controls the political agenda.

The Washington Press Corps

Thousands of journalists work in Washington. They labor for major local newspapers such as the *Washington Post,* smaller daily and weekly newspapers around Washington, bureaus of out-of-town newspapers, national wire services, regional news services, network television bureaus, local television stations, radio networks, local radio stations, Web sites, general circulation magazines, trade publications, newsletters, and specialized publications like the *National Journal* and Congressional Quarterly's *CQ Weekly.*

Whether Washington qualifies as a plum reporting assignment depends on your perspective. For most Washington reporters, the best part of the job is having a front-row seat to history. There's also an undeniable amount of glamour involved. In addition, a stint in Washington can significantly boost your journalism career, whether you're a new reporter or a veteran. And reporting from Washington can lead to lots of other job opportunities—some very lucrative, such as working in a high-level post at a trade association—if you eventually want to leave journalism.

However, Washington reporting also can have some downsides and risks. Here are a few:

- Washington reporters are under strong pressure to run with journalistic "packs" that can strangle initiative and creativity.

- For various reasons, much Washington reporting focuses on personalities, controversies, and political horse races, causing frustration for reporters who want to write about substantial issues.

- Polls repeatedly show that many Americans have little or no interest in Washington stories.

- Reporters—especially those from less prominent media outlets—can have trouble gaining regular access to key sources.

- Reporters are often barraged by interests that want to place their own "spin" on a story.

- Reporters risk developing an "inside the Beltway" mentality that causes them to lose touch with the concerns of people outside Washington.

- Reporters who become well known and powerful risk losing their objectivity as they develop into Washington insiders.

Getting a Job in the Washington Media

Like just about everyone else in Washington, media outlets—large and small alike—gobble up interns. If you want a Washington media internship, your chances of landing one are pretty good if you have decent credentials and are willing to be somewhat flexible about where you work.

Obtaining a full-time job, on the other hand, can be tricky. If you're fresh out of college and have little or no professional journalism experience, many of Washington's major media institutions won't hire you. They only hire people with experience. So forget your fantasy of waltzing into the *Washington Post* and snagging a job doing investigations with Bob Woodward.

But don't despair. Lots of less prominent Washington media outlets welcome applicants with minimal experience. They can serve as excellent entry points into Washington journalism and stepping stones into more prestigious jobs in the city's press corps.

Newsletters offer some of the best opportunities for newly minted journalists. Washington has hundreds of newsletters, most of which cover narrow topics in great depth. There are newsletters about regulation of the air transport industry, federal education issues, banking regulation, employment discrimination, and environmental laws and regulations, among many other subjects. To read an interview with a newsletter reporter, see the box titled "Profile: Neil Baumgardner."

The dozens of smaller, community newspapers published in the Washington region also offer many opportunities for journalism newcomers. They range from tiny weeklies to mid-sized dailies, and typically cover a section of the Washington suburbs or surrounding area. Most don't pay a lot—salaries from the mid-teens to the lower twenties are common— but they can offer a superb chance to gain experience, learn about the Washington area, and get your name noticed by larger media outlets. For information about the *Journal* chain of daily newspapers, see the box titled "Community Newspapers Can Be Stepping Stones."

If you absolutely have your heart set on working at one of Washington's media powerhouses and lack experience, you may be able to wiggle your way through the door with an internship. But be forewarned: competition for internships at the major players can be brutal.

PROFILE: NEIL BAUMGARDNER

On the day he was interviewed for this book, Neil Baumgardner was on his way to conduct an interview of his own with Poland's defense minister, who was in Washington for the NATO Summit. It was a long way from the University of South Carolina, where Baumgardner graduated only a year earlier with a degree in international studies.

Baumgardner is the international defense reporter at *Defense Daily,* a high-profile newsletter published in Washington. Washington is home to hundreds of newsletters, which are published by everyone from individuals to large publishing companies. Typically, newsletters cover a narrow topic in great detail, whether it's defense, taxes, airline regulation, or nuclear power, and have avid, highly placed readers.

Baumgardner, who never took a journalism course, ended up at *Defense Daily* in a roundabout way. While still in school he decided that he'd like to intern in Washington after graduation. He identified possible internships through research at the career center library and on the Internet. He had one major requirement: The internship had to pay because he otherwise lacked the money to support himself. He fired off some applications, and ended up with a ten-week paid internship at an organization called Business Executives for National Security.

He then set about finding a permanent job related to national affairs or defense issues, his primary interests. His method: sending resumes to every publication and think tank in Washington concerned with his issues. *Defense Daily* bit, initially hiring him as a combination Web and production editor in a job he largely created himself.

How did he slide from there into his job as international defense reporter? He just mentioned to the editor that it would be nice to have more coverage of international defense issues, the editor agreed, and Baumgardner added the reporting job to his other duties. Baumgardner said he likes writing for a newsletter because he can cover specific issues in more depth than television or newspaper reporters typically do.

Baumgardner believes that "saturation" is critical to landing a job in Washington. "Even if you don't hear about an opening, send a resume anyway because you might get lucky," he said. Baumgardner certainly did.

Interning at the *Washington Post*

The *Washington Post* offers one of the most coveted internship programs in Washington. The *Post* program is limited to the summer—the newspaper doesn't use interns in the fall or winter. Nonetheless, it typically draws 700 applications annually from some of the top journalism students in the nation, and selects eighteen to twenty-two students each

COMMUNITY NEWSPAPERS CAN BE STEPPING STONES

If you'd like to work in Washington's news media but have little or no job experience, you might want to consider starting out at one of the community newspapers published in the area.

Many weekly and daily community newspapers serve Washington's suburbs. Some require job applicants to have a small amount of work experience, although others will hire recent graduates.

The *Journal,* which publishes Sunday through Friday, is the largest daily community newspaper in the Washington area. Its six localized editions—the *Alexandria Journal, Arlington Journal, Fairfax Journal, Prince William Journal, Montgomery Journal,* and *Prince George's Journal*—have a combined circulation of 136,000 on weekdays and 386,000 on Sundays.

The *Journal* occupies a "unique niche between the real small community newspapers and the much larger *Washington Post* and *Washington Times,*" said Jane Touzalin, the *Journal's* senior editor. "We don't cover the kind of chicken dinner events that the small papers cover, but neither do we cover Congress and the war in Yugoslavia and the things the big papers cover."

Most *Journal* reporters come to the paper as their second job after getting their start on a weekly or smaller daily, Touzalin said. "Because we're small, we don't have a lot of editors with a lot of time to do basic journalism training," she said. "We expect reporters to come in and hit the ground running."

However, the paper does have a couple of entry-level positions that are suitable for college graduates with no experience. These jobs don't necessarily require journalism degrees, although applicants must have written for their school newspapers or interned at another newspaper. Reporters in these positions typically write obituaries, handle the police log, and cover basic general assignment stories for six months or so before switching to a regular beat.

Most *Journal* reporters "are on their way somewhere else, and we realize that," Touzalin said. "We're very happy when they leave for a better job or more money or both." Starting salaries range between about $21,000 and $23,000, depending on experience, and few reporters stay more than two years.

Many former *Journal* reporters and editors now work at the *Washington Times,* Touzalin said, and lots of former *Journal* editors work at the *Washington Post.* Other staffers have gone to the *Army Times,* America Online (which is headquartered in a Washington suburb), other Web-related jobs, or newsletters.

The *Journal* is a place for reporters to learn and get noticed, Touzalin said. "There's enough guidance here that they can learn from their assignment editors," she said, "but enough freedom so that they can learn how to make their own way, come up with their own ideas, develop their own beats, and just get a lot of experience on their own.

"It's also a very high visibility job. The other papers look at the *Journal* to see what we're covering, so our reporters' stories get read pretty widely. And I think *Journal* reporters who do well get noticed. They also make a lot of good contacts for jobs if they want to stay in this area."

If you want to apply to the *Journal,* send a cover letter, a resume, and five or six clips from a mix of news and feature stories to Touzalin, who hires for the Fairfax, Arlington, and Alexandria editions of the newspaper. She also shares resumes with editors of the other editions.

Jane Touzalin
Senior Editor
The Journal
6408 Edsall Rd.
Alexandria, VA 22312

Touzalin said what the *Journal* really needs is copy editors. "If you can edit copy, you can get a job," she said. Also in high demand: designers.

More information about the *Journal* is available at its Web site: http://www.jrnl.com.

---

summer. Most internships go to reporters, although the newspaper also typically chooses several copy editors, a photographer, and a graphic artist.

Applicants must be juniors, seniors, or graduate students by the annual deadline of November 1. Most of those who get chosen have worked at their college newspapers and interned for a couple of other major newspapers. To apply, you must submit an application form, a resume, two letters of recommendation, a 500-word autobiography, six to eight clips of articles you've written, and a college transcript.

How do you stand out? One key is submitting outstanding clips, according to Jana Long, a personnel administrator who runs the intern program. They don't have to be flashy—clips that show you can cover routine, daily stories are fine. Applicants who want to work in the paper's Style section should submit feature articles. Enterprise clips that display a new angle to a story also are "always interesting and stand out," Long said. In all stories, Long said, editors look for strong writing and whether the reporter has "a voice that rises from the story."

Editors also carefully review candidate autobiographies and letters of recommendation—especially recommendation letters from other newspapers indicating the applicant can handle daily deadlines, Long said. "Even though it is an internship, we are looking for those students who understand what it takes to put out a daily newspaper and have been exposed to daily deadlines," she said. "Even though they do get more attention than a new hire, it is important that they are able to hit the ground running."

Those selected for internships undergo a one-week orientation that includes everything from a bus tour of Washington to training about ethics issues. Reporters are then assigned to various sections of the newspaper and immediately start writing stories. Some may not like the stories they're assigned (this can be especially true of reporters assigned to suburban bureaus), but they do not perform clerical tasks. "Unless they're Xeroxing something that's pertinent to something they're working on, they're not running errands for editors or anything like that," Long said. "They're working as full-fledged reporters." All interns also are paid like full-fledged staffers, earning about $790 weekly in 1999.

The *Post* internship is especially coveted because it can lead to a full-time job at the newspaper. The newspaper usually offers full-time jobs to anywhere from one to five interns each year, Long said. About 80 current staff members started as interns, including executive editor Leonard Downie Jr. and managing editor Robert Kaiser. Full-time jobs normally require at least three to five years of professional experience, so for recent graduates the internship route is the only way into a full-time position.

You can get the application form for the *Post* internship from the Internet (http://www.washingtonpost.com/intern) or by writing to:

Summer News Program
Washington Post
1150 15th St., N.W.
Washington, D.C. 20071-5508

Application forms are available starting in August each year, and completed applications are due by November 1. The Internet site also has biographies of previous interns.

News Media Contacts

ABC News Washington Bureau, 1717 DeSales St. N.W., Washington, DC 20036; (202) 222-7777.

The Washington bureau serves ABC television and radio affiliates nationwide. (Headquarters in New York City.)

Army Times Publishing Co., 6883 Commercial Dr., Springfield, VA 22159; (703) 750-9000. Fax (703) 750-8622, Web http://www.armytimes.com. Sandy Roy, director of human resources.

Publishes seven weekly newspapers: *Air Force Times, Army Times, Defense News, Federal Times, Marine Corps Times, Navy Times,* and *Space News.*

Associated Press, 2021 K St. N.W., #600, Washington, DC 20006; (202) 776-9400. Fax (202) 776-9570. Sandy Johnson, bureau chief.

Wire service that serves print and broadcast media outlets. (Headquarters in New York City.)

Broadcasting and Cable, 1705 DeSales St. N.W., Washington, DC 20036; (202) 659-2340. Fax (202) 429-0651.

Weekly magazine serving the broadcast and cable industries.

Bureau of National Affairs, 1231 25th St. N.W., Washington, DC 20037; (202) 452-4200. Fax (202) 452-4226, Web http://www.bna.com. Tony Harris, director of employment and diversity.

Publishes more than 200 print and electronic news and information services about health care, business, labor relations, law, economics, taxation, environmental protection, safety, and other public policy and regulatory issues. Publications include the *Daily Report for Executives* and the *Daily Labor Report.*

Business Publishers, 8737 Colesville Rd., Suite 1100, Silver Spring, MD 20910-3925; (301) 589-5103. Fax (301) 589-4530, e-mail bpinews@bpinews.com, Web http://www.bpinews.com.

Publishes nearly fifty newsletters about the environment, construction, energy, health and safety, human services, education, and transportation. Titles include *Air/Water Pollution Report, Defense Cleanup, Emergency Preparedness News, Fair Employment Report, Federal Research Report, Hazardous Waste News, Mental Health Report,* and *Nuclear Waste News.*

C-SPAN, 400 North Capitol St. N.W., Suite 650, Washington, DC 20001; (202) 737-3220. Fax (202) 737-3323, e-mail human_resources@c-span.org, job line (202) 626-7963, Web http://www.cspan.org.

Provides live televised coverage of House and Senate proceedings. Other programs cover congressional hearings, speeches, conventions, and other public policy events.

Cable News Network Washington Bureau, 820 First St. N.E., 11th Floor, Washington, DC 20002; (202) 898-7900. Fax (202) 898-7923, Web http://www.cnn.com.

Produces Washington and international stories for CNN television and radio news programs. (Headquarters in Atlanta.)

Campaigns and Elections, 1414 22nd St. N.W., Washington, DC 20037; (202) 887-8530. Fax (202) 463-7085, e-mail campaignline@cq.com, Web http://www.campaignline.com. Ronald Faucheux, editor in chief; Mary-Clare Jalonick, associate editor.

Monthly magazine for the political industry published by Congressional Quarterly.

CBS News Washington Bureau, 2020 M St. N.W., Washington, DC 20036; (202) 457-4321. Fax (202) 659-2587. Jackie Dambron, intern coordinator.

Provides Washington stories for the CBS network and its affiliated radio and television stations nationwide. (Headquarters in New York City.)

Chronicle of Higher Education, 1255 23rd St. N.W., Washington, DC 20037; (202) 466-1000. Fax (202) 452-1033, Web http://chronicle.com.

Weekly newspaper for college and university faculty members and administrators.

Chronicle of Philanthropy, 1255 23rd St. N.W., Washington, DC 20037; (202) 466-1200. Web http://philanthropy.com. Scott Jaschik, managing editor.

Biweekly newspaper about the nonprofit world.

Congressional Quarterly, 1414 22nd St. N.W., Washington, DC 20037; (202) 887-8500. Fax (202) 728-1863, Web http://www.cq.com. Annette Billings, manager of human resources.

Publishes the *CQ Weekly,* a magazine about politics and government; online legislative tracking services; print and electronic news updates; abstracts and full text of the *Congressional Record;* the *Congressional Staff Directory;* and textbooks, reference books, and directories on government and politics.

Discovery Communications, 7700 Wisconsin Ave., Bethesda, MD 20814; (301) 986-0444. Fax (301) 771-4064, Web http://www.discovery.com.

Produces programming for numerous cable TV channels, including Discovery Channel, The Learning Channel, Animal Planet, Travel Channel, and Science Channel, among others.

Education Week, 6935 Arlington Rd., Suite 100, Bethesda, MD 20814-5233; (301) 280-3100. Fax (301) 280-3150, Web http://www.edweek.org. Steve Drummond, deputy managing editor.

Weekly newspaper about education issues.

Federal Computer Week, 3141 Fairview Park Dr., Suite 777, Falls Church, VA 22042; (703) 876-5100. Fax (703) 876-5126, Web http://www.fcw.com/pubs/fcw/fcwhome.htm. Jacqueline Dendieval, human resources director.

Weekly newspaper about federal government use of computers.

Federal Publications, 1120 20th St. N.W., Suite 500 South, Washington, DC 20036; (202) 337-7000. Fax (202) 659-2233, Web http://www.fedpub.com.

Produces print publications and electronic materials about government contracting, immigration law, personnel and employment, international law and buisness, and environmental law.

Gannett News Service, 1000 Wilson Blvd., Arlington, VA 22229; (703) 276-5800. Fax (703) 558-3813. Jeff Stinson, assignment editor; Dinah Eng, internship coordinator.

Wire service provides articles to Gannett newspapers nationwide.

Gazette Newspapers, 1200 Quince Orchard Blvd., Gaithersburg, MD 20878; (301) 948-3120. Web http://www.gazette.net. Donna Johnson, human resources director; Georgia MacDonald, managing editor.

Publishes chain of weekly newspapers serving Frederick, Montgomery, and Prince George's counties in Maryland.

Government Computer News, 8601 Georgia Ave., Suite 300, Silver Spring, MD 20910; (301) 650-2000. Fax (301) 650-2111, Web http://www.gcn.com.

Weekly newspaper for government computer managers.

The Hill, 733 15th St. N.W., Suite 1140, Washington, DC 20005; (202) 628-8500. Fax (202) 628-8503, Web http://www.hillnews.com. Jock Friedley, senior editor.

Weekly newspaper that covers Capitol Hill.

Jane's Information Group, 1340 Braddock Pl., Suite 300, Alexandria, VA 22314-1651; (703) 683-3700. Fax (703) 836-0297, Web http://www.janes.com. Karen Hines, human resources coordinator.

Produces print publications and electronic databases about defense, transportation, geopolitical issues, and law enforcement.

Journal Newspapers, 6408 Edsall Rd., Alexandria, VA 22312; (703) 846-8376. Fax (703) 846-8301, Web http://www.jrnl.com. Jane Touzalin, managing editor.

Daily newspaper that publishes six localized editions in the Washington area: the *Alexandria Journal, Arlington Journal, Fairfax Journal, Prince William Journal, Montgomery Journal,* and *Prince George's Journal.* For more information about the *Journal* newspapers, see the box titled "Community Newspapers Can Be Stepping Stones" (p. 178).

King Publishing Group, 627 National Press Bldg., 529 14th St. N.W., Washington, DC 20045; (202) 638-4260. Fax (202) 662-9719, Web http://www.king-publishing.com. Joan Cassady, president.

Publishes newsletters, including *Energy Daily, Defense Week, Navy News and Undersea Technology, Military Space,* and *White House Weekly,* among others.

Kiplinger Washington Editors, 1729 H St. N.W., Washington, DC 20006; (202) 887-6400. Fax (202) 778-8976, Web http://www.kiplinger.com. Cindy Gentilcore, director of personnel.

Publishes books, *Kiplinger's Personal Finance Magazine,* and newsletters, including *Kiplinger Letter, Kiplinger Tax Letter, Kiplinger California Letter,* and *Kiplinger Agriculture Letter.*

Knight Ridder Washington Bureau, 529 14th St. N.W., Suite 700, Washington, DC 20045; (202) 383-6000. Fax (202) 383-3951. Lee Matthews, office manager.

Supplies articles to Knight Ridder newspapers around the country and to other subscribers.

Legal Times, 1730 M St. N.W., Suite 802, Washington, DC 20036; (202) 457-0686. Fax (202) 457-0718, e-mail legaltimes@legaltimes.com. Carolyn Henderson, office manager.

Weekly newspaper that covers Washington's law and lobbying firms, interest groups, Congress, the Justice Department, courts, and regulatory agencies. Published by American Lawyer Media, Inc.

Los Angeles Times Washington Bureau, 1875 Eye St. N.W., Suite 1100, Washington, DC 20006; (202) 293-4650. Fax (202) 293-4650. Tom McCarthy, deputy national editor; Don Frederick, assistant to the national editor.

Washington office for the *Los Angeles Times.* (Headquarters in Los Angeles.)

McGraw-Hill, 1200 G St. N.W., Washington, DC 20006; (202) 383-2350. Web http://www.mcgraw-hill.com. Anna Schiefer, human resources director.

Publishes newsletters and other print and electronic products about aviation, electric power generation, nuclear power, natural gas, coal, federal energy policy, federal technology transfer policy, biotechnology, and other subjects.

National Journal Group, 1501 M St. N.W., #300, Washington, DC 20005; (202) 739-8400. Fax (202) 833-8069, Web http://www.nationaljournal.com. Mike Wright, executive editor.

Publishes magazines, newsletters, books, and directories about government and politics. Publications include *National Journal,* a weekly magazine about politics and government; *National Journal's Technology Daily,* a newsletter about technology policy; and a daily newsletter about events on Capitol Hill, among others.

National Public Radio, 635 Massachusetts Ave. N.W., Washington, DC 20001-3753; (202) 414-2000. Fax (202) 414-3329, e-mail nprlist@npr.org, Web http://www.npr.org. Denorah Howe, human resources associate.

Produces and distributes to public radio stations nationwide news and public affairs programming, congressional hearings, speeches, cultural and dramatic presentations, and programs for specialized audiences.

NBC News Washington Bureau, 4001 Nebraska Ave. N.W., Washington, DC 20016; (202) 885-4000. Fax (202) 362-2009. Jennifer Clayton, employee relations manager.

Supplies stories for the NBC network and its affiliated stations nationwide. (Headquarters in New York City.)

The New Republic, 1220 19th St. N.W., Washington, DC 20036; (202) 331-7494. Fax (202) 331-0275, Web http://www.thenewrepublic.com.

Weekly magazine about politics and the arts.

New York Times Washington Bureau, 1627 Eye St. N.W., Washington, DC 20006; (202) 862-0324. Fax (202) 862-0340, Web http://www.nytimes.com.

Produces articles for the *New York Times.* (Headquarters in New York City).

Newsweek Washington Bureau, 1750 Pennsylvania Ave. N.W., Suite 1220, Washington, DC 20006; (202) 626-2000. Fax (202) 626-2011, Web http://www.newsweek.com.

Washington bureau for the weekly national news magazine. (Headquarters in New York City.)

Newsworld Television, 500 N. Capitol St. N.W., Washington, DC 20001; (202) 783-8000. Marcia Wheatley, human resources director.

Independent television news bureau that serves clients around the world.

Phillips Publishing International, 7811 Montrose Rd., Potomac, MD 20854; (301) 340-2100. Web http://www.phillips.com. Debora Cohen, human resources.

Publishes newsletters, books, magazines, and directories. Publications include *Air Safety Week, Helicopter News, Airline Financial News, Defense Daily, Space Business News,* and *Electronic Commerce News,* among many others.

Potomac News, 14010 Smoketown Rd., Woodbridge, VA (mailing address P.O. Box 2470, Woodbridge, VA 22193); (703) 878-8000. Fax (703) 878-8099, Web http://www.potomacnews.com. Candy Johnson, human resources manager.

Daily newspaper serving Prince William and Stafford counties in Virginia. Also publishes the *Stafford Sun,* a weekly serving north Stafford County, and newspapers serving the Quantico Marine Corps base and Fort Belvoir. Owned by Media General.

Public Broadcasting Service, 1320 Braddock Pl., Alexandria, VA 22314; (703) 739-5000. Fax (703) 739-0775, e-mail www@pbs.org, Web http://www.pbs.org. Lanie Odlum, associate director of human resources.

Provides public television stations nationwide with educational, instructional, and cultural programming; also provides news and public affairs, science and nature, fundraising, and children's programming.

Reuters Washington Bureau, 1333 H St. N.W., Suite 410, Washington, DC 20005; (202) 898-8300.

Supplies articles to newspapers, radio stations, and television stations worldwide. (Headquarters in London.)

Roll Call, 50 F St. N.W., 7th Floor, Washington, DC 20001; (202) 824-6800. Fax (202) 824-0475, Web http://www.rollcall.com. David Meyers, copy editor.

Weekly newspaper that covers Capitol Hill.

Science, 1200 New York Ave. N.W., Washington, DC 20005; (202) 326-6500. Web http://www.sciencemag.org.

Weekly magazine published by the American Association for the Advancement of Science.

Science News, 1719 N St. N.W., Washington, DC 20036; (202) 785-2255. Fax (202) 659-0365, Web http://www.sciencenews.org.

Weekly magazine published by Science Service.

Scripps Howard News Service, 1090 Vermont Ave. N.W., Suite 1000, Washington, DC 20005; (202) 408-1484. Fax (202) 408-5950, Web http://www.shns.com. Al Thompson, copy editor.

Wire service that serves Scripps Howard newspapers in the United States and hundreds of other subscribing newspapers worldwide.

States News Service, 1333 F St. N.W., Washington, DC 20004; (202) 628-3100, ext. 211. Fax (202) 737-9818, e-mail editor@states.com, Web http://www.states.com.

Produces Washington articles for dozens of newspapers around the country.

Tax Analysts, 6830 N. Fairfax Dr., Arlington, VA 22213; (703) 533-4400. E-mail webmaster@tax.org, Web http://www.tax.org. Hazel Brutshe, human resources.

Produces a wide range of print and electronic products about tax policy.

Thompson Publishing Group, 1725 K St. N.W., Suite 700, Washington, DC 20006; (202) 872-4000. E-mail webmaster@thompson.com, Web http://www.thompson.com. Kathleen Dunten, vice president.

Publishes more than fifty handbooks, newsletters, and reference services about laws and regulations. Topics covered include energy, environment, food and drug law, health care, pension and benefits, personnel policy, state and local government programs, telecommunications, securities, and taxes.

Time Washington Bureau, 1050 Connecticut Ave. N.W., Suite 850, Washington, DC 20036; (202) 861-4000. Fax (202) 293-1085, Web http://cgi.pathfinder. com/time.

Washington bureau for the weekly national news magazine. (Headquarters in New York City.)

Times Community Newspapers, 1760 Reston Parkway, Suite 411, Reston, VA 20190; (703) 437-5400. Fax (703) 437-6019, Web http://timespapers.com.

Publishes more than a dozen weekly newspapers in Fauquier, Loudoun, and Fairfax counties in Northern Virginia.

United Communications Group, 11300 Rockville Pike, Suite 1100, Rockville, MD 20850; (301) 287-2700. E-mail webmaster@ucg.com, Web http://www. ucg.com.

Produces newsletters, magazines, books, directories, and electronic services. Some of the topics covered are computers, defense, mortgage banking, telecommunications, finance, health care, energy, government contracting, transportation, and securities.

United Press International, 1510 H St. N.W., #700, Washington, DC 20005; (202) 898-8000. Fax (202) 898-8057, Web http://www.upi.com. Tobin Beck, managing editor.

Wire service that serves print and broadcast media outlets.

U.S. News and World Report, 1050 Thomas Jefferson St. N.W., Washington, DC 20007; (202) 955-2000. Fax (202) 955-2049, Web http://www.usnews.com, human resources in New York City (212) 217-6362 (Ellen Weiss).

Weekly national news magazine.

USA TODAY, 1000 Wilson Blvd., Arlington, VA 22229; (703) 276-3400. Fax (703) 558-3840, Web http://www.usatoday.com.

Daily national newspaper published by Gannett.

Wall Street Journal Washington Bureau, 1025 Connecticut Ave. N.W., Suite 800, Washington, DC 20036; (202) 862-9200. Fax (202) 222-7891, human resources in New York City (212) 416-2000.

Provides articles for the *Wall Street Journal*. (Headquarters in New York City.)

WAMU-FM, American University, Washington, DC 20016-8082; (202) 885-1200. Web http://www.wamu.org. Cathy Nerritt, news director.

Radio station affiliated with National Public Radio and Public Radio International that provides news and public affairs programming.

Warren Publishing, 2115 Ward Ct. N.W., Washington, DC 20037; (202) 872-9200. Fax (202) 293-3435, e-mail info@telecommunications.com, Web http:// www.telecommunications.com.

Publishes numerous communications newsletters, including *Communications Daily, Audio Week, Consumer Multimedia Report, Television Digest, State Telephone Regulation Report, Mobile Communications Report, Satellite Week,* and *FCC Report,* among others.

Washington Business Journal, 1555 Wilson Blvd., Suite 400, Arlington, VA 22209; (703) 875-2200. Fax (703) 875-2231, e-mail washington@amcity.com,

Web http://www.amcity.com/washington. Ellen Duhamel, business manager; Betty Smith, special sections editor.

Weekly newspaper focused on Washington business. Owned by American City Business Journals.

Washington City Paper, 2390 Champlain St. N.W., Washington, DC 20009; (202) 332-2100. Fax (202) 462-8323, e-mail mail@washcp.com, Web http://www.washingtoncitypaper.com. Alisa Silverman, associate editor.

Weekly alternative newspaper.

Washington Monthly, 1611 Connecticut Ave. N.W., Washington, DC 20009; (202) 462-0128. Fax (202) 332-8413, Web http://www.washingtonmonthly.com. Megan Dominish, publisher.

Monthly magazine about politics and public policy.

Washington Post, 1150 15th St. N.W., Washington, DC 20071; (202) 334-6000. Web http://www.washingtonpost.com.

The largest daily newspaper published in Washington, DC

Washington Times, 3600 New York Ave. N.E., Washington, DC 20002; (202) 636-3000. Fax (202) 269-3419, e-mail wtnews@wt.infi.net, Web http://www.washtimes.com.

Daily newspaper, published by News World Communications.

Washingtonian, 1828 L St. N.W., Washington, DC 20036; (202) 296-3600. E-mail editorial@washingtonian.com, Web http://www.washingtonian.com. Alicia Abell, online editor.

Monthly magazine that covers the Washington region.

WETA-TV and **WETA-FM,** 2775 South Quincy St., Arlington, VA 22206; (703) 998-2600. Fax (703) 998-3401, Web http://www.weta.org.

Public television and radio stations serving the Washington area.

WJLA-TV, 3007 Tilden St. N.W., Washington, DC 20008; (202) 364-7777. Fax (202) 364-2481, Web http://www.wjla.com.

Channel 7, the Washington ABC affiliate.

WRC-TV, 4001 Nebraska Ave. N.W., Washington, DC 20016; (202) 885-4000. Fax (202) 885-4104, Web http://www.nbc4.com.

Channel 4, the Washington NBC affiliate.

WTOP-FM and **WTOP-AM,** 3400 Idaho Ave. N.W., Washington, DC 20016; (202) 895-5000. Fax (202) 895-5149, Web http://www.wtop.com.

An all-news radio station affiliated with CBS.

WTTG-TV, 5151 Wisconsin Ave. N.W., Washington, DC 20016; (202) 244-5151. Fax (202) 244-1745.

Channel 5, the Washington Fox affiliate.

WUSA-TV, 4100 Wisconsin Ave. N.W., Washington, DC 20016; (202) 895-5999. Fax (202) 966-7948, Web http://www.wusatv9.com.

Channel 9, the Washington CBS affiliate.

Appendixes

Appendix A:
Sample Resumes and
Cover Letters

Chronological Resume

HEATHER SMITH
1429 Front Street
Columbia, Missouri 55555
(555) 555-1212
E-mail: hsmith@columbia.net

EDUCATION

B.S., University of Missouri, 1999. Major in political science, minor in journalism. GPA: 3.7

EXPERIENCE

1997-99	Writer, University of Missouri Office of Information Services. Primary duties included researching and writing press releases about activities in the School of Journalism and the Departments of Drama and Music.
Summer 1998	Counselor, Camp Watochee, Gaylord, Michigan. Duties included coordinating all water sports for campers, supervising a cabin of eight girls ages 8-12, and designing and writing the camp newsletter.

ACTIVITIES

1997-99	Volunteer, Project Ruth Homeless Shelter
1995-99	Member, Delta Delta Delta Sorority; President 1998-99

SKILLS	Fluent in Spanish
	Familiar with PC and Mac platforms; MS Word, WordPerfect, PageMaker, Photoshop

Functional Resume

BRIAN TOMLINSON

E-mail: btom@esu.edu

School:
542 Halver Hall
Eastern State University
Novi, Michigan 55555
(517) 555-5555

Permanent:
1129 Third Ave.
Ossineke, Michigan 49766
(517) 555-1111

EDUCATION

• Undergraduate at Eastern State University, 1996-present. Major in public administration, minor in foreign relations. Board of Regents Scholar.

HIGHLIGHTS OF SKILLS

• Excellent researcher into public issues.
• Superior ability to assimilate large amounts of information.
• Strong ability to think on feet.
• Good presentation and speaking skills.

RELATED EXPERIENCE

• Member, Eastern State University debate team, 1996-present; captain, 1998-present. Won 75 percent of intercollegiate debates in freshman year, 95 percent in most recent year. As captain, mentor younger members of the team and help coach them.

• Volunteer, Kim Lee for Congress campaign, June-November 1998. Handled a variety of responsibilities, including distributing campaign literature, helping organize media events, and assisting in writing press releases, among others.

WORK EXPERIENCE

• Cashier at McDonald's, Ossineke, Michigan, 1995-96.

Cover Letter: In Response to Job Ad

123 Main St.
Spencer, Oregon 54321
(555) 555-1212
Nov. 1, 1999

Mr. Luis Gonzalez
The National Widget Association
1234 Pennsylvania Ave., N.W.
Washington, D.C. 20036

Dear Mr. Gonzalez:

Your ad in the *Post* states that you are seeking an administrative assistant who is energetic, is able to work under pressure with ease, and possesses strong writing skills. I believe that describes me perfectly, and I hope you will be kind enough to consider me for the position.

For the past four years, I have attended Central Oregon University full time, worked two part-time jobs to help put myself through school, and volunteered in the Big Brother program. All of these responsibilities have certainly placed me under pressure, but I have maintained a 3.8 grade point average. In addition, my writing skills were strong enough to get me hired as a tutor in the university's Writing Lab.

I believe that my energy, education, and enthusiasm make me a prime candidate for your position. I'm enclosing a resume to provide more information about my background.

I thank you for your consideration, and look forward to hearing from you.

Sincerely,

Paul Feldman

Cover Letter: Cold

423 Williams Hall
Central State University
Des Moines, Iowa 12345
(555) 555-5555
Dec. 19, 1999

Wenonah Hauter, Director
Critical Mass Energy Project
Public Citizen
215 Pennsylvania Ave., S.E.
Washington, D.C. 20003-1155

Dear Wenonah Hauter:

While attending Central State University in Iowa, I have been heavily involved in Citizens to Shut Down Smith. This antinuclear group seeks to shut down the Smith nuclear power plant because of a constant rash of operating and safety problems. I will be graduating in May, and would like to put my experience to work as a staff member for the Critical Mass Energy Project.

Through my work with Citizens to Shut Down Smith, I have learned how to read and evaluate Nuclear Regulatory Commission inspection reports, write news releases, and organize media events. Most important, I am very familiar with nuclear power issues, so I could quickly integrate into your staff.

I am enclosing a resume, and hope you will consider me when you have staff openings. I will call you in a few days to discuss job opportunities at the Critical Mass Energy Project.

Thank you very much.

Sincerely,

Sarah DiNardo

Appendix B:
Federal Jobs by
College Major

No matter what your college major and interests, there's a job for you in the federal government. The following list from the federal Office of Personnel Management names jobs that are frequently filled by candidates with specific majors. The jobs under each major are just examples, not an all-inclusive list of available positions.

ANY MAJOR
Administrative Officer
Air Traffic Controller
Civil Rights Analyst
Claims Examiner
Contact Representative
Contract Administration
Environmental Protection
General Investigator
Internal Revenue Officer
Logistics Management
Management Analyst
Paralegal Specialist
Personnel Occupations
Public Affairs
Supply Management
Writer and Editor

ACCOUNTING
Accountants
Auditors
Contract Specialists
Financial Administrators
Financial Institution Examiners
Financial Managers
GAO Evaluators
Intelligence Specialists
Internal Revenue Agents

AGRICULTURE
Agricultural Commodity Graders
Agricultural Engineers
Agricultural Management Specialist
Agricultural Market Reporters
Agricultural Marketing Specialist
Agricultural Program Specialist
Foreign Agriculture Affairs Specialists
Soil Conservationists
Soil Scientists

AGRONOMY
Agricultural Management Specialists
Agronomists
Soil Conservationists
Soil Scientists

ANTHROPOLOGY
Anthropologists
Management Analysts
Museum Curators
Museum Specialists
Program Analysts

ARCHEOLOGY
Archaeologists
Museum Curators
Museum Specialists

ARCHITECTURE
Architects
Construction Analysts
Construction Control Inspector
Landscape Architects
Naval Architects
Program Analysts

ARTS, FINE AND APPLIED
Arts Specialists
Audiovisual Production Specialists
Exhibits Specialists
General Arts and Information Specialists
Illustrators
Photographers
Recreation and Creative Arts Therapists
Visual Information Specialists

ASTRONOMY
Astronomers and Space Scientists
Geodesists

AVIATION
Aircraft Operators
Aircrew Technicians
Air Navigators
Air Safety Investigators
Air Traffic Controllers
Aviation Safety Inspectors

BIOLOGY
Entomologists
Fishery Biologists
GAO Evaluator
General Biological Scientists
Microbiologists
Range Conservationists
Wildlife Biologists
Zoologists

BOTANY
Agronomists
Botanists
Forestry Technicians
Geneticists
Horticulturists
Plant Pathologists
Plant Physiologists
Plant Protection and Quarantine Specialists
Range Conservationists

BUSINESS
Budget Analysts
Business and Industry Specialist
Commissary Store Managers
Contract Specialists
GAO Evaluators
Import Specialists
Internal Revenue Officers
Miscellaneous Administrative and Programs Specialists
Quality Assurance Specialists
Trade Specialists

CARTOGRAPHY
Cartographers
Cartographic Technicians
Geodetic Technicians

CHEMISTRY
Chemical Engineers
Chemists
Consumer Safety Officers
Environmental Engineers
Food Technologists
GAO Evaluators
Health Physicists
Intelligence Specialists
Toxicologists

COMMUNICATIONS
Communications Specialists
Public Affairs Specialists
Technical Writers and Editors
Telecommunications Managers
Writers and Editors

COMMUNITY OR CITY PLANNING
Community Planners
Realtors

COMPUTER SCIENCE
Computer Programmers
Computer Science Specialists
Computer Specialists
Management Analysts
Program Managers

CORRECTIONS
Correctional Institution Administrators
Correctional Officers
Program Analysts

COUNSELING
Chaplains
Educational Services Specialists
Educational and Vocational Training Specialists
Equal Opportunity Compliance Specialists
Personnel Specialists
Psychologists
Psychology Aides and Technicians

Social Service Aides and Assistants
Social Service Representatives
Vocational Rehab Specialist

CRIMINAL JUSTICE/LAW ENFORCEMENT
Border Patrol Agents
Criminal Investigators
Game Law Enforcement Agents
GAO Evaluators
Internal Revenue Officers
Police Officers
United States Marshals

DIETETICS AND NUTRITION
Dietitians
Food Technologists
Nutritionists

ECONOMICS
Actuaries
Budget Analysts
Contract Specialists
Economists
Financial Analysts
Financial Institution Examiners
GAO Evaluators
Loan Specialists
Trade Specialists
Transportation Industrial Analysts

EDUCATION
Education and Training Specialists
Educational Program Specialists
Educational Services Specialists
Educational and Vocational Training Specialists
Employee Development Specialists
Instructional Systems Specialists
Public Health Educators
Training Instructors
Vocational Rehabilitation Specialists

ELECTRONICS TECHNOLOGY
Communications Specialists
Electronics Mechanics
Electronics Technicians
Patent Examiners

EMPLOYEE/LABOR RELATIONS
Contractor Industrial Relations Specialists
Employee Relations Specialists
Hearing and Appeals Specialists
Labor Management Relations Examiners
Labor Relations Specialists
Mediators
Salary and Wage Administrator
Workers Compensation Claims Examiners

ENGINEERING (ANY SPECIALTY)
Aerospace Engineers
Biomedical Engineers
Civil Engineers
Computer Engineers
Electrical Engineers
Electronics Engineers
General Engineers
Industrial Engineers
Mechanical Engineers
Nuclear Engineers

ENGLISH AND LITERATURE
Editorial Assistants
Management Analysts
Miscellaneous Administration and Programs Specialists
Printing Specialists
Program Analysts
Program Managers
Public Affairs Specialists
Technical Writers and Editors
Writers and Editors

ENVIRONMENTAL STUDIES
Ecologists
Environmental Health Technicians
Environmental Protection Assistants
Environmental Protection Specialists
Fish and Wildlife Refuge Management
GAO Evaluators
General Fish and Wildlife Administrators
Miscellaneous Administration and Programs Specialists
Toxicologists

EPIDEMIOLOGY
Environmental Health Technicians
General Health Scientists

Industrial Hygienists
Microbiologists

FINANCE
Appraisers and Assessors
Budget Analysts
Financial Administrators
Financial Analysts
Financial Institution Examiners
Securities Compliance Examiners
Tax Examiners
Trade Specialists

FISH, GAME, AND WILDLIFE MANAGEMENT
Fish and Wildlife Refuge Management
Fishery Biologists
Game Law Enforcement Agents
General Biological Scientists
General Fish and Wildlife Administrators
Soil Conservationists
Wildlife Biologists
Wildlife Rescue Managers

FOOD TECHNOLOGY AND SAFETY
Consumer Safety Inspectors
Consumer Safety Officers
Dietitians and Nutritionists
Food Assistance Program Specialists
Food Technologists
Toxicologists

FOREIGN LANGUAGE
Air Safety Investigators
Border Patrol Agents
Customs Inspectors
Equal Employment Opportunity Specialists
Foreign Affairs Specialists
Foreign Agricultural Affairs Specialists
Intelligence Specialists
Language Specialists

FORESTRY
Fish and Wildlife Refuge Management
Foresters
General Fish and Wildlife Administrators
Management Analysts
Program Analysts
Soil Conservationists

GEOGRAPHY
Cartographers
Geographers

GEOLOGY
General Physical Scientists
Geodesists
Geologists
Hydrologists
Oceanographers

GEOPHYSICS
General Physical Scientists
Geophysicists

HEALTH
Environmental Health Technicians
General Health Scientists
Health Physicists
Health System Administrator
Health System Specialist
Industrial Hygienists
Public Health Programs Specialists
Safety and Occupational Health Management Specialists

HISTORY
Archives Technicians
Archivists
Exhibits Specialists
Historians
Intelligence Specialists
Management Analysts
Miscellaneous Administration and Programs Specialists
Museum Curators
Program Analysts

HOME ECONOMICS
Consumer Safety Officers
Food Technologists

HORTICULTURE
Agricultural Management Specialists
General Biological Scientists
Horticulturists
Plant Physiologists
Plant Protection and Quarantine Specialists

HOSPITAL ADMINISTRATION
Administrative Officers
General Health Scientists
Health System Administrators
Health System Specialists
Hospital Housekeepers
Miscellaneous Administration and Programs Specialists
Public Health Programs Specialists

HUMAN RESOURCE MANAGEMENT
Apprenticeship and Training Representatives
Employee Development Specialists
Equal Employment Opportunity Specialists
Military Personnel Management Specialist
Personnel Management Specialist
Personnel Staffing Specialist
Position Classification Specialists

HYDROLOGY
Environmental Engineers
Environmental Protection Specialists
Fish and Wildlife Refuge Management
General Fish and Wildlife Administrators
Hydrologists
Program Analysts

INDUSTRIAL MANAGEMENT
Business and Industrial Specialists
Equipment Specialists
Industrial Hygienists
Industrial Property Managers
Industrial Specialists
Management Analysts
Production Controllers
Program Analysts
Property Disposal Specialists
Quality Assurance Specialists

INSURANCE
Crop Insurance Administrators
Miscellaneous Administration and Programs Specialists
Program Analysts
Social Insurance Administrators
Social Insurance Claims Examiner
Unemployment Insurance Specialists

INTERNATIONAL RELATIONS
Foreign Affairs Specialists
Foreign Agricultural Affairs Specialists
Intelligence Specialists
International Relations Workers
Language Specialists
Public Affairs Specialists
Trade Specialists

JOURNALISM
Agricultural Market Reporters
Printing Specialists
Program Analysts
Public Affairs Specialists
Technical Writers and Editors
Writers and Editors

LAW
Administrative Law Judges
Attorneys
GAO Evaluators
Hearing and Appeals Specialists
Legal Instruments Examiners
Paralegal Specialists
Patent Attorneys
Tax Law Specialists

LAW ENFORCEMENT
Alcohol, Tobacco, and Firearms Inspectors
Border Patrol Agents
Criminal Investigators
Customs Inspectors
Game Law Enforcement Agents
Immigration Inspectors
Inspector, Investigator and Compliance Specialists
Police Officers
United States Marshals

LIBERAL ARTS/HUMANITIES
Contact Representatives
Customs Inspectors
Education Services Specialist
Equal Opportunity Compliance Specialist
Management Analysts
Personnel Management Specialist
Program Analysts
Social Insurance Claims Examiners
Veterans Claims Examiner

LIBRARY SCIENCE
Librarians
Library Technicians
Medical Record Librarians
Technical Information Services

MANAGEMENT
Administrative Officers
Logistics Management Specialists
Management Analysts
Manpower Development Specialists
Miscellaneous Administration and Program Specialists
Program Analysts
Support Services Administrators

MANAGEMENT, FACILITIES
Commissary Store Managers
Correctional Institution Administrators
Distribution Facility and Storage Managers
Equipment Specialists
Facility Managers
General Facilities and Equipment Managers
Housing Managers
Industrial Property Managers
Production Controllers

MANAGEMENT INFORMATION SYSTEMS
Computer Science Specialists
Computer Specialists
Financial Managers
Logistics Management Specialists
Management Analysts
Miscellaneous Administration and Programs Specialists
Operations Research Analysts
Program Analysts
Program Managers

MARKETING
Agriculture Marketing Specialists
Bond Sales Promotion Representatives
Business and Industry Specialists
Contract Specialists
Inventory Management Specialists
Packaging Specialists
Property Disposal Specialists
Supply Specialists
Trade Specialists

MATHEMATICS
Actuaries
Cartographers
Computer Science Specialists
Mathematical Statisticians
Mathematicians
Operations Research Analysts
Statisticians

MEDICAL SUPPORT
Diagnostic Radiological Technicians
Medical Instrument Technicians
Medical Record Technicians
Medical Technicians
Nuclear Medicine Technicians
Pathology Technicians
Therapeutic Radiological Technicians

METEOROLOGY
General Physical Scientists
Meteorologists

NATURAL RESOURCE MANAGEMENT
Fish and Wildlife Administrators
General Biological Scientists
Program Analysts
Wildlife Biologists
Wildlife Refuge Management

NURSING
Nurses
Physician's Assistants

PARK AND RECREATION MANAGEMENT
Foresters
Management Analysts
Outdoor Recreation Planners
Park Rangers
Recreation and Creative Arts Therapists
Recreation Specialists

PHARMACY
Consumer Safety Inspectors
Consumer Safety Officers
Pharmacists
Pharmacologists

PHYSICAL EDUCATION
Corrective Therapists
Outdoor Recreation Planners
Program Analysts
Recreation Aides and Assistants
Recreation and Creative Arts Therapists
Recreation Specialists
Sports Specialists

PHYSICAL SCIENCE
General Physical Scientists
Metallurgists
Physicists

PHYSICS
Astronomers and Space Scientists
General Physical Scientists
Geodesists
Geophysicists
Health Physicists
Hydrologists
Oceanographers
Patent Examiners
Physicists

POLITICAL SCIENCE/GOVERNMENT
Archivists
Budget Analysts
Foreign Affairs Specialists
GAO Evaluators
Historians
Miscellaneous Administration & Program Specialists
Program Analysts
Public Affairs Specialists
Social Scientists

PSYCHOLOGY
Educational Services Specialists
Employee Development Specialists
GAO Evaluators
Personnel Management Specialists
Personnel Staffing Specialists
Position Classification Specialists
Psychologists
Recreation and Creative Arts Therapists

PUBLIC ADMINISTRATION
Budget Analysts
Employee Development Specialists
Employee Relations Specialists
GAO Evaluators
Housing Managers
Management Analysts
Manpower Development Specialists
Miscellaneous Administrative and Programs Specialists
Program Analysts
Public Utilities Specialists

PUBLIC HEALTH
Environmental Health Technicians
Food Assistance Program Specialists
Food Inspectors
Health System Administrators
Health System Specialists
Industrial Hygienists
Public Health Educators
Public Health Programs Specialists
Social Insurance Administrators
Veterans Claims Examiners

PUBLIC RELATIONS
Contact Representatives
Foreign Affairs Specialists
Foreign Agriculture Affairs Specialists
Public Affairs Specialists

PURCHASING
Business and Industry Specialists
Commissary Store Managers
Contract Specialists
Purchasing Specialists

REAL ESTATE
Building Managers
Business and Industry Specialists
Contract Specialists
Housing Managers
Realtors

REHABILITATION THERAPY
Corrective Therapists
Manual Arts Therapists
Occupational Therapists

Physical Therapists
Prosthetic Representatives
Rehabilitation Therapy Assistants

SOCIAL WORK

Food Assistance Program Specialists
Psychology Aides and Technicians
Recreation Specialists
Social Science Aides and Technicians
Social Scientists
Social Service Aides and Assistants
Social Service Representatives
Social Workers

SOCIOLOGY

GAO Evaluators
Program Analysts
Social Science Aids and Technicians
Social Scientists
Social Service Aids and Assistants
Social Service Representatives
Sociologists

STATISTICS

Actuaries
Computer Science Specialists
Mathematical Statisticians
Operations Research Analysts
Program Analysts
Statisticians
Transportation Industry Analysts

SURVEYING

Geodesists
Land Surveyors

SYSTEMS ANALYSIS

Computer Science Specialists
Computer Specialists
Management Analysts
Miscellaneous Administration and Program Specialists
Program Analysts

THEOLOGY

Chaplains
Program Analysts
Social Workers

TRANSPORTATION
Cargo Schedulers
Highway Safety Specialists
Marine Cargo Specialists
Traffic Management Specialists
Transportation Industry Analysts
Transportation Loss/Damage Claims Examiners
Transportation Operators
Transportation Specialists
Travel Assistants

ZOOLOGY
Animal Scientists
Physiologists
Zoologists

Appendix C:
Federal Government
Vacancy Announcements

Federal Government Vacancy Announcements

The two vacancy announcements reproduced in this appendix—from the Federal Election Commission and the Environmental Protection Agency—are typical of those issued by federal government agencies and departments. All such announcements follow the same basic format, so these examples should give you a good idea of how federal agencies and departments announce jobs and what they require of job applicants.

The announcements were downloaded from the USAJOBS Web site (http://www.usajobs.opm.gov), which is operated by the U.S. Office of Personnel Management. USAJOBS is the main source for federal vacancy announcements. Chapter 5 describes how to read federal vacancy announcements, and also lists other sources of announcements besides USAJOBS.

AUDITOR: FEDERAL ELECTION COMMISSION

AUDITOR

OPEN PERIOD 04/27/1999 - 05/22/1999

SERIES/GRADE: GS-0511-07/11

SALARY: $ 28,901.00 TO $ 40,714.00 ANNUAL

PROMOTION POTENTIAL: GS-13

ANNOUNCEMENT NUMBER: #99-020

HIRING AGENCY: FEDERAL ELECTION COMMISSION

DUTY LOCATIONS: 0008 WASHINGTON, DC

REMARKS: APPLICATIONS MUST BE RECEIVED BY 5/22/99 TO BE CON-
SIDERED IN THE FIRST ROUND OF COMPETITION. ALL FEDERAL
APPLICANTS MUST SUBMIT THE MOST RECENT SF-50 AND PERFOR-
MANCE APPRAISAL. FAXED, E-MAILED OR INCOMPLETE APPLICA-
TIONS WILL NOT BE CONSIDERED AND WILL BE RETURNED. APPLI-
CANTS MUST ADDRESS KSA'S TO RECEIVE FULL CONSIDERATION
FOR THE POSITION. RECRUITMENT IS BEING HELD AT THE
GS-7/9/OR 11 LEVEL. MAX POTENTIAL: GS-13

CONTACT: KACY PHILLIPS

PHONE: (202) 694-1080

INTERNET ADDRESS: WWW.FEC.GOV

FEDERAL ELECTION COMMISSION

999 E STREET, NW

PERSONNEL

ROOM 236

WASHINGTON, DC 20463-0001

Full vacancy announcement follows. Please be sure to review for complete qualification and "How to Apply" information.

FEDERAL ELECTION COMMISSION

VACANCY ANNOUNCEMENT

POSITION: AUDITOR, GS-511-7/9/11, PROMOTION POTENTIAL: GS-13

THIS IS A PERMANENT, FULL-TIME BARGAINING UNIT POSITION

ANNOUNCEMENT NUMBER: #99-020

OPENING DATE: 4-27-99
CLOSING DATE: WHEN CLOSED
FIRST CUT OFF DATE: 5-22-99

AREA OF CONSIDERATION: ALL SOURCES

ORGANIZATION LOCATION: AUDIT DIVISION

THE FEDERAL ELECTION COMMISSION IS AN EXCEPTED SERVICE
AGENCY

*ALL APPLICATIONS MUST BE RECEIVED BY THE FIRST CUT OFF
DATE OF 5/22/99 IN ORDER TO BE CONSIDERED FOR THE FIRST
ROUND OF COMPETITION.

*ALL FEDERAL APPLICANTS MUST SUBMIT THE MOST RECENT SF-50
AND PERFORMANCE APPRAISAL.

*FAXED, E-MAILED OR INCOMPLETE APPLICATIONS WILL NOT BE
CONSIDERED AND WILL BE RETURNED.

DUTIES: Participates in comprehensive audits of campaign finance organizations consisting of the systematic examination and appraisal of complex financial records, financial and management reports, management controls, and policies and practices affecting or reflecting the financial condition and operating
results of an assigned issue area. Performs assigned financial examinations and
evaluations. Provides audit assistance to higher level auditors, as a member of

an audit team, conducts audits in financial and operational areas during regular and special audits.

QUALIFICATION REQUIREMENTS

All applicants must meet the basic requirements outlined below:

A. Degree—a degree in accounting or a degree in a related field such as business administration, finance, or public administration that includes or was supplemented by 24 semester hours in accounting. The 24 semester hours may include up to 6 hours of credit in business law; OR

B. Combination of education and experience—at least 4 years of experience in accounting, or an equivalent combination of accounting experience, college-level education, and training that provided professional accounting knowledge. Applicant's background must also include at least one of the following: 1) 24 semester hours in accounting or auditing courses (up to 6 semester hours may be in business law) of appropriate type and quality; OR 2) A certificate of Certified Public Accountant or Certified Internal Auditor, obtained through written examination.

In addition to meeting the above basic requirements, applicants must meet the requirements below for specific grade levels.

GS-7—In addition to meeting the basic requirements as described above, applicants must meet one of the following requirements:

A. Have successfully completed one year of graduate level education directly related to the work of the position; OR

B. Possess one year of specialized accounting/auditing experience equivalent to the GS-5 level that included performing a variety of tasks designed to provide experience in the practical application of accounting and auditing principles, procedures and techniques; OR

C. Meet Superior Academic Achievement Criteria. To be eligible for Superior Academic Achievement applicants must have one of the following: Ranked in the upper 1/3 of the graduating class in the college/university at time of application; OR A "B" or better average (GPA) of 2.95 or higher out of a possible 4.0 based on the average of all completed undergraduate courses, or all undergraduate classes completed during final 2 years; OR A "B+" or better average (GPA) of 3.45 or higher out of a possible 4.0 based on the average of all completed undergraduate courses in the major field of study, or all undergraduate courses in your major field of study completed in final 2 years; OR Election to a national scholastic honor society that meets the requirements of the Association of College Honor Societies other than freshman honor societies. Note: Grade point averages are to be rounded to one decimal place. For example, 2.95 will round to 3.0 and 2.94 will round to 2.9. Courses currently being taken will be considered in meeting GPA requirements.

GS-9—In addition to meeting the basic requirements as described above, applicants must meet one of the following requirements:

A. Two years of progressively higher level graduate education leading to a master's degree or equivalent graduate degree in accounting or a related degree; OR

B. One year of accounting/auditing experience equivalent to the GS-7 level. In order to be considered qualifying, specialized experience must demonstrate that the applicant has participated in the carrying out of portions of audits that involved the use and understanding of professional accounting and auditing theory, concepts, and practices.

GS-11—In addition to meeting the basic requirements as described above, applicants must have one year of programs and operation through several phases of the auditing cycle (i.e., planning, executing and reporting).

BASIS OF RATING: Qualified applicants will be evaluated on the basis of the quality and extent of their total accomplishments, experience, and/or education and the extent to which they possess the desired Knowledge, Skills and Abilities (KSAs). This evaluation will consider the following: GPA in applicable college course work; any additional accounting, auditing and related work experience, education or training beyond the basic qualifications; the possession of a CPA or CIA certificate; performance appraisals in the applicant's current position; any awards in the last three years and knowledge of spreadsheet and data base computer software. Therefore, it is important that applicants submit relevant information on these areas.

A narrative completed by the applicant, addressing each of the KSAs listed below for the grade level for which you wish to be considered must be submitted with the application in order to receive full credit. Completion of a narrative is not mandatory; however, failure to do so will reflect in the rating you receive in the evaluation of your application for this position.

KNOWLEDGE, SKILLS AND ABILITIES (KSAs): Candidates will be rated on the extent to which they possess the following knowledge, skills and abilities (KSAs):

For the GS-7/9 Level: 1) Ability to learn and apply Federal Election Commission law and related regulations, rulings and procedures. 2) Ability to apply auditing procedures to financial investigations. 3) Ability to plan and complete segments of audit examinations. 4) Ability to write clear, comprehensive report segments and complete reports covering non-complex examinations. 5) Ability to meet and deal tactfully with other professionals.

For the GS-11 Level: 1) Demonstrated ability to perform audits and/or financial investigations related to enforcement of Federal laws, regulations, rulings and procedures. 2) Knowledge of generally accepted accounting principles and ability to apply advanced auditing procedures and investigative techniques to complex audits and financial investigations. 3) Ability to plan and coordinate financial investigations that may involve multiple business entities and/or individuals. 4) Ability to orally articulate audit findings and procedures to lay persons and demonstrated ability to prepare audit reports that are clear, concise, objective and meet prescribed standards. 5) Ability to meet and deal effectively with other professionals.

EVALUATION METHODS: Based upon Qualification Standards and results achieved when the Element Crediting Plan is applied.
MAXIMUM POTENTIAL: GS-13

SIGNIFICANT WORKING CONDITIONS: Travel by plane and car is required approximately 30% of the time.

Personnel Office Contact: Kacy Phillips—(202) 694-1080

HOW TO APPLY: Applicants should submit an OF612, SF171, resume and/or any application that will give in-depth information on background. Background must include work history dating from the present back five years with references that may be contacted and phone numbers. Educational background must include courses completed, diplomas received and degrees awarded. RESUMES AND APPLICATIONS WITHOUT DETAILED EMPLOYMENT AND EDUCATIONAL INFORMATION WILL NOT BE CONSIDERED FOR THE POSITION. Please forward all information to the Federal Election Commission, 999 E St. NW/Rm. 236, Washington, DC 20463. Relocation expenses will not be paid by the FEC. FEC work areas are smoke free. FEC is EOE.

PROGRAM/MANAGEMENT ANALYST: ENVIRONMENTAL PROTECTION AGENCY

PROGRAM / MANAGEMENT ANALYST

OPEN PERIOD 04/12/1999 - 09/30/1999

SERIES/GRADE: GS-0343-07/07

SALARY: $ 27,508 TO $ 35,760, ANNUAL

PROMOTION POTENTIAL: GS-13

ANNOUNCEMENT NUMBER: LV-OS16-99

HIRING AGENCY: ENVIRONMENTAL PROTECTION AGENCY

DUTY LOCATIONS: MANY WASHINGTON, DC

REMARKS: APPLICANTS MUST VIEW THE FULL-TEXT ANNOUNCE-MENT FOR COMPLETE INSTRUCTIONS ON HOW TO APPLY. THE ANNOUNCEMENT IS AVAILABLE ON THE INTERNET AT WWW.USAJOBS.OPM.GOV OR CAN BE REQUESTED BY CALLING USAJOBS-BY-PHONE AT 912-757-3000. PREVIOUS APPLICANTS MUST REAPPLY.

CONTACT: TEAM VEGAS JOBLINE

PHONE: (702) 798-2418

U.S. ENVIRONMENTAL PROT AGCY

HUMAN RESOURCES OFFICE

P.O. BOX 98516

LAS VEGAS, NV 89193 8516

Full vacancy announcement follows. Please be sure to review for complete qual-ification and "How to Apply" information.

U.S. ENVIRONMENTAL PROTECTION AGENCY

WASHINGTON, D.C.

OUTSTANDING SCHOLAR ANNOUNCEMENT

ANNOUNCEMENT NUMBER: LV-OS16-99

OPENING DATE: April 12, 1999

CLOSING DATE: September 30, 1999*

* Positions will be filled as vacancies occur throughout the duration of this announcement. This announcement may be amended to suspend receipt of additional applications prior to the posted closing date whenever a sufficient number of applications are received.

Applicants under Outstanding Scholar Announcements 8-LV-8898 or LV-08-98(DH) must reapply.

The U.S. Environmental Protection Agency (EPA) is accepting applications to establish an inventory of applicants who meet the Office of Personnel Management's (OPM) Outstanding Scholar qualifications for administrative positions at the GS-07 grade level. These positions are located in the Washington, D.C., metropolitan area.

To qualify for consideration under these provisions, applicants must be U.S. citizens, college graduates and have an undergraduate grade-point average (GPA) of 3.45 or better on a 4.0 scale for all undergraduate course work, or have graduated in the upper 10 percent of their undergraduate class or major university subdivision. A major university subdivision is defined as a college/school within your university (e.g. College/School of Business). In addition, your total number of credits (including transferred classes) must have less than 10 percent of the total taken on a pass/fail basis. You may apply up to nine months before graduation, but you must have the GPA or class standing at the time you are offered a job. Any college major is qualifying for the listed occupations.

Applications will be accepted for the following positions:

GS-0028 Environmental Protection Specialist

GS-0343 Program/Management Analyst

GS-0501 Financial Specialist

GS-0560 Budget Analyst

GS-1035 Public Affairs Specialist

GS-1101 Grants Specialist

GS-1102 Contract Specialist

Starting 1999 salary range for GS-7 is $27,508 to $35,760 per year. All of these positions have promotion potential to either the GS-12 or GS-13 level. You will be considered for positions with either promotion potential.

DESCRIPTION OF DUTIES:

Environmental Protection Specialists—provide advice and assistance to state and local government agencies on matters relating to environmental protection plans and programs.

Program Analysts—analyze and evaluate the actual or potential effectiveness of current or projected operating programs in achieving their objectives.

Management Analysts—provide advice and service to management in such areas as planning, policy development, work methods and procedures, management utilization, etc., with the objective of improving management effectiveness.

Financial Specialists—perform work associated with the management and control of resources or funds.

Budget Analysts—examine the relative costs and benefits of alternate courses of budget and program action, check the propriety of obligations and expenditures, or develop budgetary policy and regulatory guidance.

Public Affairs Specialists—administer, oversee or perform work involved in establishing and maintaining mutual communication between Federal agencies and the general public and various internal or external foreign or domestic audiences.

Grant Specialists—review grant applications and negotiate grant agreements, make distinctions in rules, regulations, policies and practices between State and local governments, and profit and non-profit organizations.

Contract Specialists—obtain contract agreements through negotiation, assure compliance with the terms of contracts and analyze negotiations, and settle contractor claims and proposals in contract termination actions.

HOW TO APPLY

You must submit a complete application package that includes the attached interest form indicating each position. Determinations of eligibility will be based only on the information you supply in your application and supplemental attachments. Please do not send copies of previous job descriptions, manuscripts, personal endorsements, or other unsolicited materials. Because applications will not be returned, original documents should not be submitted.

All forms must be submitted at the same time. Application material submitted separately are incomplete and will not receive consideration. FAILURE TO SUBMIT ALL REQUIRED FORMS AT THE TIME OF APPLICATION WILL RESULT IN AN INELIGIBLE RATING FOR THIS POSITION.

APPLICATION PACKAGE: A complete application must include:

1. Your resume or the Optional Application for Federal Employment (OF-612) (the obsolete Application for Federal Employment (SF-171) will also be accepted). Your resume or application must contain the following:

- The attached interest form showing announcement number, title and series of the position(s). Previous editions of this form are not acceptable.

- Your full name, mailing address, day and evening phone number

- Country of citizenship

- Work experience (include job title, duties, employer's name and address, starting and ending dates, salary, and hours worked per week. Also indicate if we may contact your current supervisor).

- Education (include high school, colleges or universities, majors, type and year of any degrees, and a copy of all college transcript(s) [official or unofficial], or a complete list of college courses that includes grades, overall grade point average for all undergraduate courses (including courses you transferred), and semester/quarter hours earned. Do not submit your application unless you are including all of your transcripts). Applicants qualifying based on graduating in the upper 10 percent of their undergraduate class or major university subdivision must provide official documentation from their college or university. A major university subdivision is defined as a college/school within your university (e.g. College/School of Business). Applicants with degrees from foreign educational institutions must also include an education evaluation letter. If we cannot determine that you meet the Outstanding Scholar requirements, you will be determined ineligible.

- OPM Form 1386B, Applicant Race and National Origin form (submission of this form is optional, and it will be separated from your application upon receipt)

2. Displaced employees must provide all required proof of eligibility including a copy of their last Notification of Personnel Action (SF-50) which indicates tenure group, grade level and/or date of separation (see Special Notice section for eligibility requirements).

SEND YOUR APPLICATION PACKAGE TO:

MAILING ADDRESS
U.S. EPA
Human Resources Staff: Team Vegas
P.O. Box 98516
Las Vegas, NV 89193-8516

EXPRESS MAIL ADDRESS
U.S. EPA
Human Resources Staff: Team Vegas
4220 S. Maryland Parkway, Building C, Room 503
Las Vegas, NV 89119

In order to receive consideration, you must submit your application to the Las Vegas, NV, address listed above. Receipt of applications in any office other than Las Vegas will not be considered.

Applications will be accepted if received in person or postmarked by the closing/suspense date of this announcement. No extensions will be given. NOTE:

Applications sent in U.S. Government postage paid envelopes will not be considered.

Applicants who qualify for the Outstanding Scholar Program will be maintained in an applicant supply file by the Human Resources Staff: Team Vegas for Outstanding Scholar positions in the Washington, DC, metro area. All applicants will receive in the mail a Notice of Results showing either an eligible or ineligible rating. You will not receive notification if your application is referred for consideration. When this announcement/series is closed/suspended, the announcement will be removed from the OPM USAJOBS web site and that will serve as your notification.

All applicants for federal employment receive consideration without regard to race, religion, color, national origin, sex, sexual orientation, political affiliation, age (with authorized exemption), or any other non-meritorious factors. U.S. citizenship is required.

To request copies of this vacancy announcement:

Call the Office of Personnel Management's USA Jobs by Phone at (912) 757-3000, or download the full-text announcement from the Internet at www.usajobs.opm.gov

SPECIAL NOTICE:

DISPLACED EMPLOYEES REQUESTING SPECIAL SELECTION PRIORITY CONSIDERATION UNDER EPA's CAREER TRANSITION ASSISTANCE PROGRAM (CTAP) OR THE INTERAGENCY CAREER TRANSITION ASSISTANCE PROGRAM (ICTAP)

Individuals who have special priority selection rights under EPA's Career Transition Assistance Program (CTAP) or the Interagency Career Transition Assistance Program (ICTAP) must be well qualified for the position to receive consideration for special priority selection. CTAP and ICTAP eligibles will be considered well qualified if they have an undergraduate bachelor's degree in a subject directly related to the position of interest or 3 years of progressively responsible experience which demonstrates ability in all major aspects of the position.

Federal employees seeking CTAP/ICTAP eligibility must submit proof that they meet the requirements of 5 CFR 330.605(a) for CTAP and 5 CFR 330.704 for ICTAP. This includes a copy of the agency notice, documentation of promotion potential, a copy of their most recent Performance Rating and a copy of their most recent SF-50 noting current position, grade level and duty location. Please annotate your application to reflect that you are applying as a CTAP or ICTAP eligible.

WE ARE AN EQUAL OPPORTUNITY EMPLOYER

U.S. EPA OUTSTANDING SCHOLAR INTEREST FORM
ANNOUNCEMENT #LV-OS16-99

NOTE: AS DESCRIBED ON THE VACANCY ANNOUNCEMENT, YOU MUST INCLUDE THIS INTEREST FORM AS PART OF YOUR APPLICATION PACKAGE.

NAME:

PERMANENT ADDRESS:

PHONE #:   E-MAIL:

UNIVERSITY:

UNDERGRADUATE DEGREE AND MAJOR:

DATE OF GRADUATION:

Please answer the following:

1. Do you have a cumulative undergraduate GPA of 3.45 or above for all courses: YES NO GPA: _____

 - Please compute your GPA if you have transferred courses. Your computation must include all courses taken as an undergraduate. This will be verified prior to a job offer.

2. Did you rank in the top 10% of your graduating class or major university subdivision? YES NO

 - A major university subdivision is defined as a college/school within your university (e.g. College/School of Business)

 - Must provide official documentation from your university.

3. Total number of credits taken as an undergraduate student:

 - include transferred credits, CLEP, pass/fail, advanced placement etc.

4. Total number of credits taken on a pass/fail basis:

Is this greater than 10% of the total stated in #3: YES NO

5. Did you apply before under Outstanding Scholar Announcement 8-LV-8898 or LV-08-98? YES NO

NOTE: To qualify for consideration as an Outstanding Scholar, applicants must be U.S. citizens, college graduates and have an undergraduate grade-point average (GPA) of 3.45 or better on a 4.0 scale for all undergraduate course work (including transferred courses), or have graduated in the upper 10 percent of their undergraduate class or major university subdivision. You may apply up to nine months before graduation, but you must have the GPA or class standing at the time you are offered a job. Applicants must attach all of their college transcripts, or a complete list of college courses which includes overall grade point average for all undergraduate courses. Applicants qualifying based on graduating in the upper 10 percent of their undergraduate class or major university subdivision must provide official documentation from their college or university. In addition, your total number of credits (including transferred classes) must have less than 10 percent of the total taken on a pass/fail basis. Applicants with degrees from foreign educational institutions must also include an education evaluation form. If we cannot determine that you meet the educational requirements, you will be determined ineligible. See vacancy announcement for more information.

I am interested in the following position(s) in Washington, DC:

Environmental Protection Specialist, GS-028-7

Program/Management Analyst, GS-343-7

Financial Specialist, GS-501-7

Budget Analyst, GS-560-7

Public Affairs Specialist, GS-1035-7

Grants Specialist, GS-1101-7

Contract Specialist, GS-1102-7

I learned about the position(s) from: Job Fair   Internet   Friend   Other

PLEASE RETURN YOUR APPLICATION PACKAGE AND THIS INTEREST FORM TO:

MAILING ADDRESS

U.S. EPA

Human Resources Staff: Team Vegas

P.O. Box 98516

Las Vegas, NV 89193-8516

EXPRESS MAIL ADDRESS

U.S. EPA

Human Resources Staff: Team Vegas

4220 S. Maryland Parkway Building C, Room 503

Las Vegas, NV 89119

APPLICANT RACE AND NATIONAL ORIGIN

The United States District Court for the District of Columbia, in a Decree approved in a lawsuit entitled Luevano v. Lachance, Civil Action no. 79-0271, has ordered that Federal Government agencies provide data on the race and national origin of applicants for certain Federal occupations. The position for which you are applying is one of those occupations.

You are requested to complete this information. The data you supply will be used for statistical analysis pursuant to the requirements of the lawsuit. Submission of this information is voluntary. Your failure to do so will have no effect on the processing of your application for Federal employment.

The collection of this information is authorized by the Office of Personnel Management ONLY for the purposes of complying with the requirements of the Luevano v. Lachance Decree.

The categories below provide descriptions of race and national origins. Read the definition of category descriptions and then circle the category with which you identify yourself. If you are of mixed race and/or national origin, circle the category with which you most closely identify yourself. Please select only one.

A = American Indian or Alaskan Native—A person having origins in any of the original peoples of North America, and who maintains cultural identification through community recognition or tribal affiliation.

B = Asian or Pacific Islander—A person having origins in any of the original peoples of the Far East, Southeast Asia, the Indian subcontinent, or the Pacific Islands. For example, this area includes China, India, Japan, Korea, the Philippine Islands, and Samoa.

C = Black, not of Hispanic origin—A person having origins in any of the black racial groups of Africa. This does not include persons of Mexican, Puerto Rican, Cuban, Central or South American, or other Spanish cultures or origins.

D = Hispanic—A person of Mexican, Puerto Rican, Cuban, Central or South American, or other Spanish cultures or origins.

E = White, not of Hispanic origin—A person having origins in any of the original peoples of Europe, North America, or the Middle East. This does not include persons of Mexican, Puerto Rican, Cuban, Central or South American, or other Spanish cultures or origins.

F = Other

Appendix D:
Optional Application for Federal Employment

Form Approved
OMB No. 3206-0219

OPTIONAL APPLICATION FOR FEDERAL EMPLOYMENT - OF 612

You may apply for most jobs with a resume, this form, or other written format. If your resume or application does not provide all th e information requested on this form and in the job vacancy announcement, you may lose consideration for a job.

1 Job title in announcement	**2** Grade(s) applying for	**3** Announcement number

4 Last name	First and middle names	**5** Social Security Number

6 Mailing Address	**7** Phone Numbers (incl area code) Day ( )
City · State · Zip Code	Eve ( )

WORK EXPERIENCE

8 Describe your paid and nonpaid work experience related to the job for which you are applying. Do not attach jo b descriptions.

1) Job Title (if Federal, include series and grade)

From (MM/YY)	To (MM/YY)	Salary per $	Hours per week
Employer's name and address			Supervisor's name and phone number ( )

Describe your duties and accomplishments

2) Job Title (if Federal, include series and grade)

From (MM/YY)	To (MM/YY)	Salary per $	Hours per week
Employer's name and address			Supervisor's name and phone number ( )

Describe your duties and accomplishments

9 May we contact your current supervisor?
   YES [ ]   NO [ ] if we need to contact your current supervisor before making an offer, we will contact you first.

EDUCATION

10 Mark highest level completed. **Some HS** [ ] **HS/GED** [ ] **Associate** [ ] **Bachelor** [ ] **Master** [ ] **Doctoral** [ ]

11 Last high school (HS) or GED school. Give the school's name, city, State, ZIP Code (if known), and year diploma or GED received.

12 Colleges and universities attended. Do **not** attach a copy of your transcript unless requested.

1) Name			Total Credits Earned		Major(s)	Degree - Year
			Semester	Quarter		(if any) Received
City	State	Zip Code				
2)						
3)						

OTHER QUALIFICATIONS

13 **Job-related** training courses (give title and year). **Job-related** skills (other langu ages, computer software/hardware, tools, machinery, typing speed, etc.). **Job-related** certificates and lic enses (current only). **Job-related** honors, awards, and special accompl ishments (publications, memberships in professional/honor societies, leadership activities, public speaking, an d performance awards). Give dates, but do **not** send documents unless requested.

GENERAL

14 Are you a U.S. citizen?   YES [ ]   NO [ ]♦ Give the country of your citizenship. _____

15 Do you claim veterans' preference?   NO [ ]   YES [ ]♦ Mark your claim of 5 or 10 points below.
   5 points [   ]♦ Attach your DD 214 or other proof. 10 points [   ]♦ Attach an *Application for 10-Point Veterans' Preference* (SF 15) and proof required.

16 Were you ever a federal civilian employee?
                    NO [ ]   YES [ ]♦ For highest civilian grade give: Series   Grade   From   To

17 Are you eligible for reinstatement based on career or career-conditional Federal status?
                    NO [ ]   YES [ ]♦ **if requested, attach SF 50 proof.**

APPLICANT CERTIFICATION

18 **I certify** that, to the best of my knowledge and belief, all of the information on and attached to this application is true, correct, complete and made in good faith. **I understand** that false or fraudulent information on or attached to this application may be grounds for not hiring me or for firing me after I begin work, and may be punishable by fine or imprisonment. **understand** that any information I give may be investigated.

SIGNATURE   **DATE SIGNED**

Appendix E:
Some of the Best General Job Hunting Sites on the Internet

Need help writing the perfect resume? Researching an employer? Preparing for a job interview? Or maybe even choosing a career? Thousands of Internet sites offer useful tips, advice, and other resources for job seekers. Here are some of the best:

The Riley Guide: Employment Opportunities and Job Resources on the Internet http://www.dbm.com/jobguide

This huge directory is one of the premier job sites on the Internet. It has thousands of links divided by hundreds of subjects. A brief list of some of the subjects gives an idea of the site's breadth: airline industry, apparel industry, apprenticeships, articles on salary negotiations, best employers to work for, biotech engineering, broadcasting and journalism, choosing a career, city guides, college rankings, considering a job offer, cover letters, directories of nonprofit organizations, entertainment industry, finding funding for your new business, general recruiters and major job banks, guides to moving and relocation, hiring trends, hospitality, how to research employers, industry-specific job resources, information on international employment, interviewing, job banks online, labor unions, legal service jobs, natural sciences, outdoor jobs, posting your resume online, resort jobs, retail industry jobs, sales and marketing, searching for work online, summer work, teaching jobs, and working abroad.

Job Search Sites on the World Wide Web http://www.cco.purdue.edu/Student/jobsites.htm

This great site from Purdue University's Center for Career Opportunities offers links to hundreds of job-related Internet sites. The annotated links are divided into the following categories: general job searching sites, job searching sites by job field, job listings by specific geographic areas, federal government job listings, international job listings, classifieds, news groups, resume services, researching employers, reference and resource material, professional recruiters, sites maintained by offices at Purdue University, and other university placement and career services.

Librarians' Index to the Internet
http://sunsite.berkeley.edu/cgi-bin/searchindex?query=jobs&searchtype= subjects

Librarians created this excellent site, which has carefully annotated links to more than sixty of the best job-related sites on the Internet.

JobHunt
http://www.job-hunt.org/index.html

Job Hunt is a metadirectory of online job search resources and services. It has links to online job listings, sites that offer reference material, resume banks, university career resource centers, and more.

JobHuntersBible.com: Job Hunting Online
http://www.jobhuntersbible.com

Richard Bolles, the author of *What Color Is Your Parachute?* created this great site to complement the book. It offers useful articles about job listings online, resumes, counseling, contacts, and research, in addition to links to more than 100 selected job-related Internet sites.

WorkSearch
http://www.golden.net/~archeus/worksrch.htm

This site has annotated links to dozens of the best Internet articles about writing resumes and cover letters, interviewing, networking, and related topics.

Monster Campus
http://campus.monster.com

Monster Campus is aimed at those looking for their first job after college. It has a huge collection of articles, tips, and advice about everything from networking to applying for a job online. It also has sample resumes, cover letters, and thank you letters.

Kaplan Career Center
http://www.kaplan.com/career

Kaplan offers tips for selecting a career, a mock job interview game, advice for creating resumes and cover letters, and details about how to succeed on the job.

JobStar: California Job Search Guide
http://www.jobstar.org

Through original information and links to other sites, this site operated by a regional library agency in California provides sample cover letters, resume tips, career guides, salary listings, details about how to find hidden jobs, job listings, and much more. Although the job listings are limited to California positions, the site offers lots of helpful information for job seekers anywhere.

Career Education Center
http://careerweb.georgetown.edu/main1.html

The Career Education Center at Georgetown University in Washington, D.C., operates this excellent site. Through original materials and selected links, it covers such topics as choosing a career, creating resumes and cover letters, searching for a job or internship, developing interviewing skills, and evaluating and negotiating job offers.

Resume Tutor!
http://www1.umn.edu/ohr/ecep/resume

This superb interactive workbook from the University of Minnesota holds your hand through the resume writing process, providing lots of good advice along the way. One of the highlights is the resume critique form, which you can use to evaluate your resume.

The Damn Good Resume
http://www.damngood.com

This site's primary purpose is to sell resume books and software. However, it also offers dozens of tips for writing a resume, answers to common job seeker questions, advice on how to create a scannable resume, sample resumes, and more.

Careerlab: 200 Cover Letters for Job Hunters
http://www.careerlab.com/letters/default.htm

As this site's title promises, it provides 200 sample cover letters to go with your resume. Some of the letters leave a bit to be desired, but they may provide some good ideas for writing your own perfect letter.

America's Career InfoNet
http://www.acinet.org/acinet

This site from the Public Employment Service offers detailed outlooks of the U.S. job market, data about wages and trends in specific occupations and states, profiles of every state in the nation and links to sites about each state, and links to lots of other job-related Internet sites.

CareerCity Salaries
http://www.careercity.com/content/salaries/links.asp

How much can you expect to make at various jobs? The dozens of links at this site provide some answers.

Selected Bibliography

Artise, John A. "The Networker's Guide."
http://server1.pa.hodes.com/cm/cm28.html (Jan. 9, 1999).

Associated Press. "Lobbyists Court Lawmakers with Trips" (June 1, 1999).
http://www.nytimes.com/aponline/AP-Congress-Free-Trips.html (June 1, 1999).

Bardwell, Chris B. "How to Evaluate a Job Offer."
http://www.black-collegian.com/Feb97/Joboffer.html (Feb. 8, 1999).

Besson, Taunee. "Ten Common Interviewing Mistakes and How to Avoid Them."
http://www.cweb.com/dimensions/Career_Dimensions4.html#Network (Jan. 9, 1999).

Birnbaum, Jeffrey H. "The Power 25: The Influence Merchants." *Fortune* (Dec. 7, 1998). http://www.pathfinder.com/fortune/1998/981207/the.html (June 2, 1999).

Cater, Douglass. *The Fourth Branch of Government.* Boston: Houghton Mifflin, 1959.

Colvin, Donna, ed. *Good Works: A Guide to Careers in Social Change.* 5th ed. New York: Barricade Books, 1994.

Congressional Management Foundation. *Working in Congress: The Staff Perspective.* Washington, D.C.: Congressional Management Foundation, 1995.

Cook, Timothy E. *Governing with the News: The News Media as a Political Institution.* Chicago: University of Chicago Press, 1998.

Coxford, Lola M. "How to Write a Resume."
http://www.studentcenter.com/brief/resume/coxford.htm (Jan. 9, 1999).

Curzan, Mary H., Michael Brintnall, Mary A. Hepburn, Joseph LaPalombara, Alan Rosenthal, Robert H. Salisbury, and Candice J. Nelson. *Careers and the Study of Political Science: A Guide for Undergraduates.* 5th ed. Washington, D.C.: American Political Science Association, 1994.

Davidson, Roger H., and Walter J. Oleszek. *Congress and Its Members.* Washington, D.C.: CQ Press, 1981.

Davidson, Roger H., and Walter J. Oleszek. *Congress and Its Members.* 6th ed. Washington, D.C.: CQ Press, 1998.

Dey, Anita. "Seize the Internship Opportunity." *CollegePost* (March 6, 1997).
http://www.washingtonpost.com/wp-srv/scoop/interns/work.htm (Jan. 5, 1999).

Dixon, Pam. *Job Searching Online for Dummies.* Forest City, Calif.: IDG Books Worldwide, 1998.

Foundation for Public Affairs. *Public Interest Profiles 1998–99.* Washington, D.C.: Congressional Quarterly, 1998.

Frantzich, Stephen E. *Storming Washington: An Intern's Guide to National Government.* 4th ed. Washington, D.C.: American Political Science Association, 1994.

Graber, Doris, Denis McQuail, and Pippa Norris, eds. *The Politics of News: The News of Politics.* Washington, D.C.: CQ Press, 1998.

Graber, Steven, ed. *The Metropolitan Washington DC JobBank.* Holbrook, Mass.: Adams Media, 1997.

Grabowski, Sue. *Congressional Intern Handbook: A Guide for Interns and Newcomers to Capitol Hill.* Washington, D.C.: Congressional Management Foundation, 1996.

Haddad, Janet. "Landing the Perfect Non-Profit Job: A Personnel Manager's Top 10 Tips." http://www.communityjobs.org/10tips.html (May 26, 1999).

Hamilton, Leslie, and Robert Tragert. *100 Best Nonprofits to Work For.* New York: Macmillan, 1998.

Hess, Stephen. *The Washington Reporters.* Washington, D.C.: Brookings Institution, 1981.

Hillson, Barbara. "Internships and Fellowships: Congressional, Federal, and Other Work Experience Opportunities" (Congressional Research Service, Congressional Reference Division, June 2, 1997). http://www.senate.gov/~dpc/crs/reports/pdf/97-583.pdf (April 21, 1999).

Huch, Scott E., J. Marc Wheat, and Carie Stephens. *The Young Conservative Job Seeker's Guide to Washington, D.C.* Washington, D.C.: Heritage Foundation, August 1997. (Posted at http://www.heritage.org/jobs/guide.html, Jan. 5, 1999.)

The Insider's Guide to Washington Internships. 8th ed. Washington, D.C.: National Internships, 1994.

"Intern Opportunities Within the Federal Government." http://www.house.gov/watt/intern98.htm (March 2, 1999).

Keare, Bradley S. *1998 House Staff Employment Study.* Washington, D.C.: Congressional Management Foundation, 1998.

Kerwin, Cornelius M. *Rulemaking: How Government Agencies Write Law and Make Policy.* 2d ed. Washington, D.C.: CQ Press, 1999.

Klouda, Thomas J., Craig Schultz, and Richard Shapiro. *1997 Senate Staff Employment: Salary, Tenure, Demographics, and Benefits.* Washington, D.C.: Congressional Management Foundation, 1997.

Kraemer, Kathryn. "Federal Vacancy Announcement Analysis." http://www.resume-place.com/frames/federal/analsis.html (May 1, 1999).

Krannich, Ron, and Caryl Krannich. *Find a Federal Job Fast: How to Cut the Red Tape and Get Hired.* 4th ed. Manassas Park, Va.: Impact Publications, 1999.

Kushner, David. "Internship in Politics."
    http://www.tripod.com/explore/jobs_career/intern_visa/article2.html (Jan.
    9, 1999).

Malbin, Michael J. *Unelected Representatives: Congressional Staff and the
    Future of Representative Government.* New York: Basic Books, 1980.

McMahon, Mary. *Washington Job Source.* 4th ed. Washington, D.C.: Benjamin
    Scott, 1997.

Messmer, Max. "How to Write a Winner: Resumes and Cover Letters."
    http://interactive.wsj.com/public/current/articles/SB868470789506693000
    .htm (Feb. 10, 1999).

Minnesota Department of Economic Security. *Creative Job Search On-line
    Guide.* http://www.des.state.mn.us/cjs/cjs_site (Jan. 10, 1999).

"Mission Possible: Finding an Internship" (May 10, 1998).
    http://www.washingtonpost.com/wp-srv/scoop/interns/intern.htm#resume
    (Jan. 5, 1999).

Morin, William J. "How to Use, and Not Abuse, Your Network."
    http://server1.pa.hodes.com/cm/cm30.html (Jan. 9, 1999).

Omicinski, John. "Changing Role of Think Tanks Spurs Question." *Salt Lake
    Tribune* (Aug. 3, 1997).
    http://www.sltrib.com/97/aug/080397/nation_w/30158.htm (May 26,
    1999).

Richardson, Douglas. "Writing a Resume for Susie the Screener."
    http://www.gsia.cmu.edu/afs/andrew/gsia/coc/student/screener.html (Jan.
    9, 1999).

Rowh, Mark. *Great Jobs for Political Science Majors.* Chicago: VGM Career
    Horizons, 1999.

Savageau, David, and Geoffrey Loftus. *Places Rated Almanac.* 5th ed. New
    York: Macmillan, 1997.

"Surviving in Washington." http://loki.stockton.edu/~yeagerc/survive.htm (Jan.
    10, 1999).

Thomas Jefferson University. "The Handbook for Negotiating and Evaluating a
    Job Offer." http://jeffline.tju.edu/CWIS/CHP/cdc/html/joindex.html (Feb.
    8, 1999).

Tooley, Jo Ann. "Working for Credit: How to Make the Most Out of a Semes-
    ter-Long Internship." http://www.usnews.com/usnews/edu/student/dwin-
    tern.htm (March 2, 1999).

Troutman, Kathryn. "11 Steps to Successfully Apply for a Federal Job."
    http://www2.ari.net/jobs/secrets.html (Jan. 15, 1999).

U.S. Department of Labor, Bureau of Labor Statistics. *1998–99 Occupational
    Outlook Handbook.* http://stats.bls.gov/ocohome.htm (Jan. 5, 1999).

U.S. Department of Labor, Bureau of Labor Statistics. "Resumes, Application
    Forms, Cover Letters, and Interviews" (Spring 1987).
    http://www.pueblo.gsa.gov/cic_text/employ/resumes/resumes.txt (Dec. 7,
    1998).

U.S. Department of Labor, Bureau of Labor Statistics. "Working for US in the 1990s" (Summer 1993). http://www.pueblo.gsa.gov/cic_text/employ/workus/workus.txt (Dec. 7, 1998).

U.S. Department of Labor, Employment and Training Administration. "Tips For Finding the Right Job" (1996). http://www.pueblo.gsa.gov/cic_text/employ/tips4job/tipjob.txt (Feb. 5, 1999).

U.S. Office of Personnel Management. "Employment and Trends" (March 1999). http://www.opm.gov/feddata/etjan99.pdf (April 21, 1999).

U.S. Office of Personnel Management, "The Fact Book: Federal Civilian Workforce Statistics" (September 1998). http://www.opm.gov/feddata/factbook/index.htm (April 21, 1999).

U.S. Office of Personnel Management. "Occupations of Federal White-Collar and Blue-Collar Workers" (September 1998). http://www.opm.gov/feddata/ocwcbc97.pdf (April 21, 1999).

U.S. Office of Personnel Management. "Pay Structure of the Federal Civil Service" (September 1998). http://www.opm.gov/feddata/98paystr.pdf (April 21, 1999).

U.S. Office of Personnel Management, Employment Service. "Federal Employment Information Sources" (March 2, 1998). http://www.usajobs.opm.gov/ei42.htm (April 21, 1999).

U.S. Office of Personnel Management, Employment Service. "Federal Job Scams" (Feb. 15, 1997). http://www.usajobs.opm.gov/b8.htm (April 21, 1999).

U.S. Office of Personnel Management, Employment Service. "The Federal Job Search: A 3-Step Process" (Feb. 15, 1997). http://www.usajobs.opm.gov/b1a.htm (April 21, 1999).

U.S. Office of Personnel Management, Employment Service. "Federal Jobs by College Major" (Nov. 1, 1995). http://www.usajobs.opm.gov/b4d.htm (April 21, 1999).

U.S. Office of Personnel Management, Employment Service. "Presidential Management Intern Program" (Sept. 17, 1998). http://www.usajobs.opm.gov/b3.htm (April 21, 1999).

U.S. Office of Personnel Management, Employment Service. "Qualification Requirements for Federal Jobs" (Nov. 1, 1995). http://www.usajobs.opm.gov/b1n.htm (April 21, 1999).

U.S. Office of Personnel Management, Employment Service. "Student Educational Employment" (Aug. 14, 1998). http://www.usajobs.opm.gov/students.htm (April 21, 1999).

U.S. Office of Personnel Management, Employment Service. "Student Internship Programs with the Federal Government" (June 1998). http://www.usajobs.opm.gov/ei13.htm (April 21, 1999).

U.S. Office of Personnel Management, Employment Service. "Summer Employment" (Aug. 27, 1998). http://www.usajobs.opm.gov/b4b.htm (April 21, 1999).

USA TODAY Career Center. "Cover Letter Handbook." http://www.usatoday.com/careers/resource/cover1.htm (Feb. 15, 1999).

USA TODAY Career Center. "Interview Handbook." http://www.usatoday.com/careers/resource/intview1.htm (Feb. 15, 1999).

Will, Gary. "Tips on Writing a Persuasive Cover Letter." http://home.golden.net/~archeus/covlet1.htm (Jan. 9, 1999).

Subject Index

Two indexes are provided for your use: a subject index and a contacts index. The subject index is a guide to all the topics in the book. The contacts index lists internships; federal agencies and executive departments; congressional committees; associations, think tanks, and trade groups; labor unions; media; and other organizations and resources that are described in the book.

Contacts Index

Two indexes are provided for your use: a subject index and a contacts index. The subject index is a guide to all the topics in the book. The contacts index lists internships; federal agencies and executive departments; congressional committees; associations, think tanks, and trade groups; labor unions; media; and other organizations and resources that are described in the book.